Sterling in Decline

STERLING IN DECLINE

The Devaluations of 1931, 1949 and 1967

Alec Cairncross
and
Barry Eichengreen

Basil Blackwell

First published 1983
Basil Blackwell Publisher Limited
108 Cowley Road, Oxford OX4 1JF, England

British Library Cataloguing in Publication Data

Cairncross, Sir Alec
Sterling in decline.
1. Pound, British—Devaluation 2. Prices—Great Britain
I. Title II. Eichengreen, Barry
338.5′2 HF3506.5

ISBN 0–631–13368–2

Typeset by Oxford Publishing Services, Oxford
Printed in Great Britain by TJ Press Ltd., Padstow

Contents

Foreword	vii
1 Introduction	1
2 Britain's Exchange and Trade Relations	10
International Trade and Payments	12
British Trade Policy	17
Control of Overseas Lending	21
The Sterling Area and Clearing Arrangements	23
3 The 1931 Devaluation of Sterling	27
Reconstructing the Gold Standard System	27
Initial Difficulties	44
The Anatomy of Crisis	52
Banking Crisis or Balance of Payments Crisis?	72
Macroeconomic Effects of Devaluation	83
Conclusion	102
Appendix	104
4 The 1949 Devaluation of Sterling	111
A Narrative of Events	112
Lessons of the 1949 Episode	139
The Economic Background	142
The Impact of Devaluation	151
5 The 1967 Devaluation of Sterling	156
First Difficulties	160
The Initial Position of the Labour Government	166
The Formulation of Balance of Payments Policy	173
The Exchange Crises of 1965 and 1966	176
The Impact of Deflationary Measures	181
The Failure of Deflationary Measures	191
The Aftermath of Devaluation	193
The Impact of Devaluation	197
Conclusion	213
6 Concluding Reflections	218
The International Economic Situation	218

The Domestic Economic Situation 221
Common Elements in the Three Devaluations 223
The Development of Thought on Devaluation 226
The Effectiveness of Devaluation 228
References 232
Dramatis Personae 245
Index 253

Foreword

This book brings together a study of the devaluation of 1931 prepared by Eichengreen with studies of the devaluations of 1949 and 1967 prepared by Cairncross. The decision to join forces had led to revision and expansion of these studies, to a consideration of the common features of the three devaluations, and to an effort to view these three episodes in the light of subsequent developments. We have aimed to provide a comparative analysis of the three devaluations. We have not sought to write an economic history of the past half-century in terms of successive exchange crises occurring at 18–year intervals. Nor have we attempted to review exhaustively theories of exchange rates and their relation to the balance of payments or to advance theories of our own. Nevertheless, we hope that our analysis of these three devaluations of sterling will be of value in a world where exchange rate changes are so frequently the subject of attention.

We wish to thank the late G.C. Allen, David Higham, Peter Kenen, Charles Kindleberger, Donald Moggridge, William Parker, Leslie Pressnell, Lord Roberthall and Philip Williamson for providing comments on portions of the manuscript. We acknowledge the permission of the Controller of Her Majesty's Stationery Office to include in chapters 3 and 4 references to materials in the Public Record Office. We are grateful also to the Treasury for facilitating study of some of the papers relating to the devaluation of 1949 which are drawn upon in chapter 4, and to David Higham for providing some materials used in chapter 5.

AKC
BJE

1

Introduction

Few events in the economic life of a nation and its policymakers are so profoundly affecting as currency devaluation. With the advent of managed floating in the 1970s, exchange rate fluctuations were rendered commonplace and robbed of much of their drama. Things were far different under the classical gold standard and the Bretton Woods system. In those days, if a nation was forced to devalue the competence of its policy-makers was called into question. Devaluation was a symbol of defeat: it reflected the authorities' failure to contain market forces and to provide a stable basis for economic growth. On the few occasions that governments elected to devalue of their own accord, the event provided an opportunity for them to reassess their approach to managing the economy and marked a turning point in the formulation of economic policy. But regardless of the circumstances, devaluation was an event of great moment, which occurred amidst controversy, publicity and impassioned debate.

Devaluation of the pound sterling had far-reaching implications not merely for Britain but for the international monetary system as a whole. From the heyday of the classical gold standard through the middle of the twentieth century, Great Britain occupied a pivotal position in the world economy. Sterling was one of the few key currencies around which the international monetary system was organized, and changes in sterling's external value provided the occasion for new departures in international monetary relations. Britain's abandonment of the gold standard in 1931, an event with all the earmarks of devaluation though it is not often referred to as such, reflected the failure of attempts to reconstruct an international monetary system based upon the free convertibility of national currencies into gold at a fixed rate of exchange. Sterling's devaluation in 1931 plunged the world into a period of renewed exchange rate fluctuations marked by exchange control, commercial restrictions and continuous official intervention in the foreign exchange market. The 1949 devaluation of sterling set in motion the realignment of relations between the dollar and non-dollar worlds and laid the basis for two decades of pegged but adjustable exchange rates. Britain's devaluation in 1967 marked the beginning of the end for the Bretton Woods system. It cast doubt on the stability of other major currencies and shifted speculative pressures from the pound to the dollar. Thus, these three devaluations of sterling each occurred at critical junctures in the history of international monetary relations.

This volume examines the circumstances in which sterling was devalued in 1931, 1949 and 1967 and analyses the consequences of these three devaluations. Each devaluation is presented as a play in two acts. In the first act, the factors making for devaluation are introduced. The plot describes the development of exchange market pressures, culminating at the curtain's fall with the decisive event itself. After the interval, the macroeconomic sequel to devaluation is discussed, and the implications of the episode for economic policy and performance are assessed. Each of the central chapters proceeds chronologically from devaluation's early preconditions to its final, distant echoes. The concluding chapter weaves together these three tales by highlighting their important similarities and differences.

Studies of devaluation typically focus on particular aspects of a complex and multi-faceted event: the underlying causes, the role of policy-makers or the macroeconomic effects. Yet there may be much to be gained from considering these three aspects of devaluation together in a unified analytical framework. The same set of impulses tends to undermine the stability of the exchange rate, limit the range of feasible options available for its defence, and transmit the devaluation's effects. Moreover, similar aspects of the policy-making process tend to intensify the pressure on the currency, influence the authorities' response to the mounting crisis, and mediate the devaluation's impact. For these reasons, it may be illuminating to analyse the causes and effects of a number of separate devaluations in an explicitly comparative framework.[1]

Owing to the climate of crisis in which it occurs, currency devaluation is a particularly revealing event around which to organize an analysis of economic policy. The desperate battle to defend the exchange rate compresses into a period of days the protracted process of give-and-take by which economic policy is formulated. It strips away all but the most critical of considerations and lays bare attitudes towards the role of the exchange rate and of government itself in the management of the economy. Moreover, the economic effects of such a dramatic change in policy should be clearly reflected in the subsequent performance of the economy. The period following devaluation provides a valuable opportunity to identify the channels through which the exchange rate operates

[1] One study that considers both the causes and consequences of devaluation in a comparative framework is Cooper (1971).

on the economy, and to analyse the response in various markets to changes in its value. Unfortunately, governments forced to devalue despite intentions to the contrary often attempt to capitalize on their failure by altering other instruments of policy at the time of devaluation. In the three episodes considered here, devaluation was accompanied by changes in monetary, fiscal and incomes policy. As a result, it is necessary to distinguish carefully between the effects of devaluation and those of coincident changes in economic policy.

The three devaluations considered in this volume are separated from one another by 18 years and by significant differences in economic circumstance. In 1931, for example, the world was in the midst of an unprecedented slump, although conditions in Britain were mitigated to some extent by a steady improvement in her international terms of trade. In 1949, demand conditions in international markets were buoyant, but any advantage resulting from this was largely offset in the North American market, which had a disproportionate influence on the balance of payments and did not share in the general buoyancy. In 1967, a decade of rapidly expanding world production and trade was interrupted by an entire year of virtual stagnation.

Conditions in domestic markets also differed markedly at the time of the three devaluations. The 1931 crisis occurred in a month when unemployment reached a temporary peak at a level in excess of 22 per cent of the insured labour force. It could scarcely be maintained in 1931 that excess demand was contributing to balance of payments pressure. In contrast, many observers argued that excess demand was a central factor in 1949, when unemployment averaged only 1.6 per cent over the entire calendar year, and again in 1964–67, when it fell as low as 1.2 per cent in the first quarter of 1966 and averaged 2.2. per cent in 1967.

Even these differences in the level of activity pale in comparison with differences in the structure of the British economy. In 1931 the exchange rate was the only relative price of great significance that was subject to official control. Rather than attempt to suppress the market mechanism, the authorities used it to peg the price of gold, employing open market operations and using the Bank of England's discount rate to influence conditions in allied markets. The 1931 devaluation of sterling occasioned a reduction in the extent of the authorities' reliance on the market mechanism. Devaluation was followed in a matter of months by a general tariff, a prohibition of public loans to foreign borrowers, and active management of the exchange rate. By 1949 the structure of the British economy had been fundamentally transformed. International trade and payments now were tightly regulated by a system of quantitative restrictions and prohibitions; foreign loans were subject to the approval of the authorities; and the prices of many important commodities were strictly controlled. The 1967 devaluation was an intermediate case. Controls over the economy were more widespread than in 1931, but apart from capital controls less prevalent than in 1949. The existence of such dramatic differences in the scope of the market suggests that, on each of the three occasions considered here, balance of payments pressures should have manifested themselves in different markets and different ways, while the impact of exchange rate changes should have been transmitted through different channels.

All this should not lead us to lose sight of striking similarities among these three devaluations. On each occasion Cabinet ministers exhibited remarkably similar attitudes towards currency devaluation. In the last instance, each devaluation was forced upon a reluctant government. Those involved in the decision had a variety of reasons for opposing devaluation. Some judged its political costs to be prohibitive: devaluation had symbolic importance as an expression of failure and political ineptitude and brought back memories of depreciation of a different kind in the age of commodity money. In 1931 the Labour Government feared that devaluation would destroy the good faith it had cultivated among members of the financial and business communities. On all three occasions, the Labour Party was sensitive to the accusation of giving way too readily in the face of market pressures. Then there were moral objections. Philip Snowden, Stafford Cripps and James Callaghan all argued that to devalue was to write off unilaterally part of the United Kingdom's sterling debts to other countries and to the Commonwealth in particular. Since these debts were essentially the obligations of a banker to depositors, anything reminiscent of unilateral repudiation required powerful justification. On all three occasions (but especially in 1949 and 1967), devaluation created grave difficulties for the rest of the sterling area and was greatly resented by some of its members, particularly as they were not consulted and it was not in keeping with their interests.

Other individuals nourished a deep-seated aversion to any change in exchange rates on the grounds that government reaped the benefits while the private sector bore the costs. Bankers in particular reacted almost instinctively against devaluation and still more strongly against floating exchange rates. They voiced concern for the uncertainties that exchange rate fluctuations might create, while arguing that devaluation was something to be avoided by any nation aspiring to continue as an international banker of the first rank. An increase in exchange risk would encourage other countries to diversify their reserve portfolios away from sterling and might induce foreign borrowers to direct more of their business to third markets. These were certainly not developments the banking community wished to encourage.

Some deplored devaluation because it exemplified the triumph of discretion over automaticity. It reflected the decline of a system under which balance of payments equilibrium was restored automatically, albeit with the help of the Bank of England, and the rise of a regime in which government was actively engaged in managing the economy.

Others registered the opposite objection: devaluation illustrated the supremacy of market forces over planning which embodied the nation's social and economic priorities.

In reviewing the discussions in which these objections were voiced, one is constantly reminded of the haphazard manner in which economic policy is formulated. The popular image of the policy-making process is one of measured discussion based upon carefully prepared position papers. In fact, there was rarely if ever an explicit decision to devalue by a certain amount based upon carefully calculated costs and benefits and with appropriate accompanying measures. Policy-makers typically proceeded incrementally, with little willingness to contemplate either the consequences of devaluation or the steps necessary in order to avoid it. In 1931 a prevalent reaction was summed up after the fact in the famous remark, 'Nobody told us we could do that.'[2] In 1949 the Chancellor of the Exchequer would not hear of devaluation and was at pains to say so in public. In 1967 officials were instructed not to mention the subject, and from the day the Labour government took office on 16 October 1964, no official document was prepared setting out the case for and against.

Similarities are evident not merely in the attitudes of policy-makers. In all three episodes there was an element of chance associated with unfavourable movements in the world economy. In 1931 British financial markets already had come under strain as a result of worldwide deflation, and the collapse of the Austrian and German banking systems added greatly to that pressure. In 1949 an economic pause in America coincided with a growing conviction in financial circles that the current exchange rate would eventually have to be devalued. In 1967 developments in domestic markets began to undermine the strength of the external accounts at precisely the time when a temporary check to economic activity abroad reduced foreign demands for Britain's exports.

On each occasion, the authorities' options were limited by the low level of reserves. Although the actual loss of reserves incurred in any one convertibility crisis was quite modest, in each instance it was more than sufficient to force the government's hand. In 1931 sterling was suppported by loans from foreign banks, while in 1967 there was support from other central banks and from the International Monetary Fund on an unprecedented scale. Even so, the funds at the authorities' command were no match for the resources that could be mobilized by the market. This predicament rendered the restoration of confidence an essential ingredient in the battle to defend the exchange rate. The

[2] This statement is attributed to Sidney Webb by Taylor (1965), while Skidelsky (1967) and Moggridge (1969) attribute it to Tom Johnston, former parliamentary secretary for Scotland and Lord Privy Seal.

crucial signal demanded by the market was elimination of the government budget deficit, but on none of the occasions considered here were the authorities willing to modify social programmes or increase taxes sufficiently to reassure speculators of their overriding commitment to the exchange rate's defence. Although the authorities opposed devaluation, they were equally adamant in their opposition to the measures necessary to avoid it.

In assessing the effects of these three devaluations, our perceptions of historical experience inevitably are coloured by the theoretical models used by economists to analyse exchange rates and the balance of payments. In the 1920s, discussions of exchange rates typically revolved around the concept of purchasing power parity, which relates changes in exchange rates to changes in the levels of domestic and foreign prices. This had been the basis for Cassel's analysis, when in 1916, basing his work on the writings of Wheatley and Ricardo, he calculated the extent of the deflation that would be required to restore prewar parities.[3] It was Keynes's test in 1925, when he criticized the decision to return to gold at the prewar parity of $4.86. It was the approach to which Keynes again turned in 1945 when attempting to calculate the appropriate exchange rate to accompany postwar decontrol. When attempting to assess the implications of fixing the exchange rate at a level that deviated from purchasing power parity, many economists turned to what subsequently came to be known as the 'elasticities approach', which focuses on relative prices as a way to gauge the expenditure-switching potential of exchange rate changes.[4] In contemplating the probable effects of the 1931 devaluation, they estimated the size of the relevant demand elasticities, emphasizing the tendency of a lower exchange rate to raise the relative price of Britain's imports and reduce the relative price of her exports to potential foreign customers. Purchasing power parity and elasticity calculations were supplemented with dynamic analyses of the relationship of exchange rates to wages and prices. Economists drawing evidence from continental experiences with floating exchange rates in the 1920s stressed the danger that a lower exchange rate that led to a rapid run-up in import prices would feed through directly into money wage rates, setting off a vicious inflationary spiral and quickly neutralizing devaluation's potential real effects.

In 1949 the elasticities approach remained the dominant mode of analysis. But at the same time, there was a growing awareness of the importance of income effects. Foreign trade multiplier analysis was increasingly used to explain shifts in countries' payments positions.[5] In

[3] See Cassel (1920). On the origins of the purchasing power parity doctrine, see also Frenkel (1978).

[4] Notable contributions to this literature include Robinson (1937), Machlup (1939), Haberler (1949), and Harberger (1950).

[5] See for example Metzler (1948).

Britain, with the level of economic activity running so high, it was natural for some observers to consider also whether devaluation would succeed by itself in reducing the demand for traded goods, or whether additional measures to lower demand would be needed to restore external balance. In 1949 the Chancellor of the Exchequer made an explicit estimate of the amount of demand pressure that would have to be withdrawn from the economy for devaluation to have the desired effect. Within two years these ideas had surfaced in the academic literature as the 'absorption approach'.[6]

By 1967, economists had been reflecting for more than a decade on reasons why absorption might exceed income. Many of them came increasingly to emphasize an apparent tendency in chronic deficit countries for money supply to grow more rapidly than money demand. On this view, the roots of balance of payments problems were largely monetary, as were the solutions.[7] Popular monetary theories bore a striking resemblance to the price–specie–flow mechanism developed by David Hume to analyse the classical gold standard, but often with a strict purchasing power parity assumption and elements drawn from the absorption approach in place of relative price adjustments.[8] Yet attempts to generalize on the basis of such theories often encountered difficulties. Apparently stable money demand functions seemed to shift suddenly precisely at the moment when the spectre of devaluation first was raised, as speculators substituted foreign for domestic assets in order to reap the capital gains offered by the prospective change in parities. Financial innovation undermined the coherence of monetary statistics and rendered difficult the attempt to manage the balance of payments with monetary instruments. In any case, such a view was far removed from the ideas in vogue in official circles in Britain. There is little indication that in 1967 ministers were in the least concerned with the impact of monetary policy on the balance of payments or with the implications of balance of payments pressures for money demand.

In recent years, discussion of devaluation has ranged far and wide, and there has been no generally accepted approach to analysing its effects.[9] Many economists have assumed that devaluation will have no long-run impact on output, employment or the balance of payments. This belief is founded on the presumption that domestic prices and costs

[6] See Meade (1951) and Alexander (1952).

[7] For precursors to the monetary approach, see Polak (1957) and Johnson (1958). Also noteworthy are Meade (1951), Machlup (1955), Michaely (1960), Kemp (1970) and the essays collected in Mundell (1968) and in International Monetary Fund (1977). For an early survey, see Krueger (1969, section 2.3). Harry Johnson (1972, p. 229) argues that the stimulus for subsequent work on the monetary approach was provided by the failure of the 1967 devaluation to 'have the desired results'.

[8] See Frenkel and Johnson (1976) and Johnson (1977).

[9] The diversity of competing models is illustrated by McKinnon's recent survey article; see McKinnon (1981).

will eventually adjust sufficiently to offset the initial effects of devaluation on a country's competitive position. Hence the emphasis of many recent analyses has shifted from the short-run impact of a change in the exchange rate to the dynamics of the adjustment towards the long-run equilibrium.[10] The speed and pattern of adjustment typically are shown to depend on the responsiveness of wages and domestic currency prices to the change in import prices and on the implications for spending and the trade balance of the reduction in real balances attendant upon devaluation. Considerable effort has been devoted to refining these conclusions by showing how, for example, the dynamics of adjustment depend on portfolio considerations such as the substitutability of money, bonds and equities, and on the substitutability in consumption of traded and non-traded goods.[11]

Subsequent research has led to the development of models in which the adjustment to devaluation is instantaneous, thus throwing doubt on the ability of exchange rate changes to alter output and employment and to affect the balance of payments even in the short run. Output and employment changes are weakened by introducing into familiar models the concept of real–wage resistance. In extreme versions real wages are taken as rigid while prices are taken as flexible, so that a devaluation that raises import prices leads immediately to a proportional rise in nominal wages and domestic product prices, providing producers no incentive to hire labour and expand output.[12] In these models, devaluation can still move the balance of payments into surplus in so far as it reduces the real value of marketable assets and induces residents to cut back their absorption and acquire assets from foreigners until their wealth is restored to desired levels.

Even this result has been called into question. Currently fashionable models of optimizing agents with rational expectations have shown that, under certain assumptions, devaluation need be accompanied by no balance of payments effect. In the previous generation of models, a devaluation is thought, by raising the price level, to reduce the real value of privately held, marketable assets, moving the balance of payments into surplus as residents reduce their absorption in order to rebuild the real value of their asset stocks to desired levels.[13] However, in the presence of a public with rational expectations that optimizes over

[10] Examples of this approach include Bilson (1978), Dornbusch (1974), Ethier (1976), and Salop (1974).

[11] Portfolio considerations are emphasized by Frenkel and Rodriguez (1975) and Boyer (1977), while the implications of the distinction between traded and non-traded goods is the concern of Dornbusch (1973).

[12] See for example Casas (1975), Argy and Salop (1979), Eichengreen (1983b), Sachs (1980), and Calmfors (1982). The applicability of such models to recent British experience has been argued by the Cambridge Economic Policy Group.

[13] This is the mechanism featured, for example, in Frenkel and Rodriguez (1975).

time, no such wealth effects on spending arise. In Obstfeld's model, for example, a devaluation brings about a sharp rise in the price level and a fall in real balances. Residents wish to restore real balances to previous levels, and their incipient excess demands for money will tend to strengthen the exchange rate, forcing the central bank to intervene immediately in financial markets, purchasing bonds and issuing money until the public's real balances have been restored to their initial level. What is crucial is that there is no change in private absorption associated with this transfer of bonds from the public to the central bank. The public is aware that the bonds acquired by the government continue to earn interest that will subsequently reduce the authorities' need to raise taxes. Since residents anticipate and capitalize this change in their stream of disposable income, they perceive no change in their level of wealth.

Theorists responsible for these models realize, of course, that their conclusions hinge upon a battery of restrictive assumptions.[14] Typically, it is assumed that individuals use a life-cycle model and form expectations about the distant future when making current consumption decisions, that capital is perfectly mobile internationally, and that no one is liquidity–constrained. Few of the models' strong conclusions continue to hold when these assumptions are relaxed. As yet, little empirical work has emerged designed to test the predictive power of these formulations.

Attempts to apply theoretical models to actual historical experience must surmount a number of methodological problems. This is certainly true in studies of devaluation, where a multitude of factors comes into play. What such models do, however, is focus attention on the critical economic relationships that determine the effects of devaluation: the response of prices to exchange rates, the response of wages to prices, and the impact of depreciation on individuals' financial positions. Different simplifications, and hence different theoretical models, are appropriate for analysing events that occurred under different historical circumstances.

Nowhere is it so evident that circumstances have changed as in the attitudes of economists and politicians towards the role of the exchange rate in the management of the economy.[15] Some of the most ardent supporters of active exchange rate management now shun this approach and look to other remedies for balance of payments problems. Other long-time proponents of exchange rate flexibility have become alarmed by the volatility of freely floating rates and now advocate more frequent exchange market operations. Perhaps when opinion about exchange rates has reached such a state of disarray, there are lessons to be learned from reviewing the record of the past.

[14] See for example Obstfeld (1981, p. 220), and Lucas (1982, p. 336).
[15] See the discussion in Cairncross (1982).

2

Britain's Exchange and Trade Relations

The pound sterling occupies a unique position in the history of the world economy. From the middle of the nineteenth century to the first quarter of the twentieth, no national currency rivalled sterling's role in international transactions – as a unit of exchange, a means of payment or a temporary store of value. For almost a century, sterling remained the dominant vehicle currency in international trade. Considerable quantities of trade that neither touched British shores nor passed through the hands of British merchants were invoiced in British currency. Transactions the world over were settled with the transfer of sterling balances between accounts maintained in London. The 'imperial banks' that provided commercial credit throughout the British Empire, and many European and American banks as well, habitually held sterling balances for transactions purposes. When Dominion central banks were established in the 1920s they adopted similar practices. Commercial traders found it convenient to maintain working balances in London not just to facilitate transactions, but because their funds could be lent when idle with minimal risk and at competitive interest rates through the facilities of the British money market. With the possible exception of the dollar in the three decades immediately after the Second World War, no other national currency has achieved a comparable position in the international economy.

Accounting for sterling's prominence is no simple task. The sheer volume of Britain's external trade undoubtedly contributed to the currency's popularity. British exports more than quadrupled between 1800 and 1850, but even this expansion was dwarfed by the eightfold increase in export value that occurred between 1850 and 1913.[1] To acquire the attractive manufactured goods produced by British industry, foreign purchasers were forced to develop ready access to sources of British currency.

The magnitude of British capital exports provides another part of the

[1] See Imlah (1958).

explanation for sterling's exceptional status. Within half a century of industrialization, Britain had emerged as the world's premier lending nation. In the 50 years prior to 1914, Britain's foreign assets matched in value her entire industrial and commercial capital stock.[2] Borrowers often took for granted that international loans would be denominated in sterling and soon grew accustomed to making their quarterly debt service payments in British currency. Moreover, Britain's central position in the international monetary system was attributable in part to the absence of restrictions on convertibility. Restrictions on the export of gold coin and bullion had been abolished in 1819, and full redeemability of Bank of England notes in gold bars and coin was achieved in 1821. Convertibility contributed to sterling's attractions as a currency in which to quote prices, complete transactions and accumulate export receipts.

Of course, this stylized account of nineteenth-century British institutions, emphasizing the role played by largely self-regulating financial and commercial markets, is a highly selective view. Import duties were never entirely absent, although they were used to raise revenues for the Exchequer rather than to protect domestic producers. Throughout the late Victorian period, the Bank of England and government officials used moral suasion to discourage foreign lending that would have rendered management of Bank of England reserves or achievement of other goals of policy increasingly difficult. In reality, the international gold standard was actively managed by the Bank of England.[3] But if the Victorian and Edwardian periods were not entirely free of government intervention in the economy, the scale of intervention in international trade and finance increased dramatically in subsequent decades. New trade restrictions were imposed during the First World War and retained in modified form at its conclusion. Restraints on the export of capital, also adopted in wartime, were maintained until the end of 1923 and replaced thereafter with moral suasion by the Bank of England. Following the 1931 devaluation of sterling, many of Britain's principal trading partners and political dependencies pegged their currencies to the pound rather than gold, giving birth to the 'sterling area'. An Exchange Equalisation Account was established to control the movement of the exchange rate, and a wide range of imported goods was taxed under the Import Duties Act of 1932. Public loans to overseas borrowers were prohibited at first and later were subjected to rigorous control. Thus, by 1932 Britain's links with the world economy had been fundamentally and permanently transformed.

These links with overseas markets continued to evolve rapidly over the next quarter of a century. Britain's foreign trade and lending were

[2] Cairncross (1953, p.3); Cottrell (1975, pp. 35–41). See also Feis (1930).

[3] See Bloomfield (1959), Ford (1962) and Triffin (1964).

placed under strict official control during the Second World War. A growing belief that government should be actively engaged in economic management designed to stabilize the economy lent further impetus to the trend towards stricter exchange and trade control. However, these tendencies to tighten exchange and trade restrictions were restrained by several countervailing forces, notably the desire for political reasons to emulate the multilateralism of the 1920s rather than the bilateralism of the 1930s, and the need to obey codes of conduct laid down for members of international institutions such as the General Agreement on Tariffs and Trade and the International Monetary Fund. None the less, quantitative restrictions continued to play a major part throughout the first postwar decade and lingered for another five years. In the 1960s, efforts to continue the process of liberalization met with only sporadic success.

The structural transformation of foreign economic relations that took place in the half-century between 1920 and 1970 was by no means confined to Britain. Many developments evident there also were manifest abroad. For Britain, this implied continuous change in the structure of the external accounts, in the commodity composition and in both the origin and the destination of foreign trade, and in the magnitude, direction and maturity of foreign lending. The evolution of economic structure and institutional arrangements had profound implications for the stability of exchange rate and for the consequences of exchange rate adjustments.

International trade and payments

The nature of Britain's links with overseas markets is reflected in the consistent patterns evident in the structure of her external accounts. For much of the twentieth century and for a considerable period before it, Britain was a net importer of services. Her trade balance deficits were more than offset by surpluses in invisible transactions, including such items as shipping, tourism, insurance, banking and brokerage services, and earnings on outstanding foreign investments.

Figure 2.1 depicts the share of merchandise imports and exports in Britain's gross domestic product since 1920. It illustrates the irregular decline in the share of trade in domestic production experienced between the beginning of the 1920s and the end of the Second World War, and the rise in the export ratio that took place thereafter. It also indicates how, in the 50 years from 1920 to 1970, Britain's trade balance regularly remained in deficit. There were but two surplus years in the entire period spanned by the devaluations of 1931 and 1967. However, the size of the deficits in comparison with the economy as a whole declined somewhat between the interwar and postwar periods.

Until the 1970s, when entry into the European Community trans-

TABLE 2.1 United Kingdom regional trade pattern, 1928–78[a]

Regions	*Exports*						*Imports*					
	1928	*1938*	*1952*	*1956*	*1968*	*1978*	*1928*	*1938*	*1952*	*1956*	*1968*	*1978*
	%	%	%	%	%	%	%	%	%	%	%	%
USA	6.5	5.4	6.7	7.8	14.2	9.3	16.6	12.9	9.2	10.5	13.5	10.3
Canada	4.8	4.4	4.9	5.5	4.2	2.0	5.1	8.6	9.2	8.9	6.5	2.7
Latin America	11.1	8.7	7.8	7.0	3.6	2.5	12.8	11.4	7.7	9.8	4.0	1.9
Icel. and Eire[b]	5.0	5.0	3.5	3.4	5.3	5.5	4.2	2.5	2.6	2.4	3.5	3.9
Cont. Europe	25.6	29.4	27.7	29.6	37.3	47.5	33.6	25.1	25.5	26.6	36.4	53.6
Japan	2.0	0.4	0.3	0.7	1.5	1.5	0.6	1.0	0.8	0.6	1.5	3.1
Soviet bloc	4.6	7.4	2.1	2.7	3.6	2.7	4.8	6.4	2.5	2.9	3.8	3.2
Other	40.4	39.3	47.1	43.4	30.1	29.0	22.3	32.2	42.6	38.4	30.8	21.3
Total	100	100	100	100	100	100	100	100	100	100	100	100
(Sterling area)	(–)	(41.8)	(46.7)	(44.1)	(27.5)	(–)	(–)	(31.5)	(41.2)	(39.0)	(26.6)	(–)

[a] Columns may not sum to totals because of rounding [b] Ireland only for 1978

Source: International Monetary Fund, *Direction of Trade Yearbook*, 1979, Washington, DC; Central Statistical Office, *Annual Abstract of Statistics*, various issues; Thorbecke (1960)

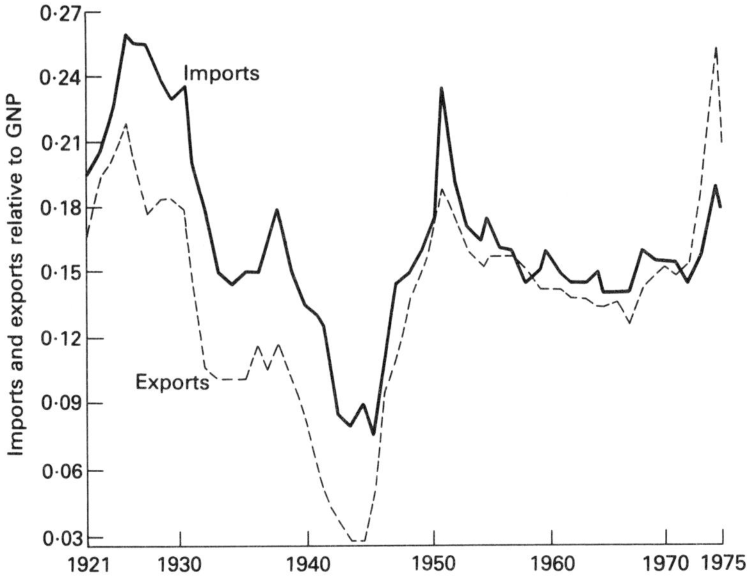

Figure 2.1 Share of merchandise imports and exports in GNP, 1921–75

Source: Feinstein (1972) and *International Financial Statistics*, various issues

formed the character of her foreign trade, Britain's regional trade pattern remained remarkably stable. As shown by table 2.1, between 1920 and 1960 continental Europe typically accounted for 25 to 30 per cent of Britain's exports and 25 to 35 per cent of her imports. North American markets absorbed 10 to 15 per cent of her exports and provided 18 to 22 per cent of her imports. Over time, Latin America and Eastern Europe became less important as trading partners, in contrast to Africa and Asia, upon whose markets the UK grew increasingly dependent. Until the 1950s, the sterling area became increasingly important to Britain as a market for exports and a supplier of imports, but thereafter sterling area trade grew less rapidly than the total.

Over the course of the twentieth century, trade in manufactures increasingly came to dominate Britain's visible balance. Table 2.2 presents basic facts about the commodity composition of British trade. On the import side, manufactures account for less than 20 per cent of total outlays in 1938 and the mid-1950s, reflecting in the first instance the effects of import duties on manfactures imposed after 1931 and in the second the incomplete recovery of the continental European economies. After the mid-1950s manufactured goods become an increasingly important component of Britain's import trade, with the rate of increase of finished imports outstripping the rate of growth of both industrial raw materials and agricultural imports. On the export side, the shares of

TABLE 2.2 Commodity composition of United Kingdom's external trade, 1928–78

Commodities	*Exports*					*Imports*				
	1928	*1938*	*1954*	*1968*	*1978*	*1928*	*1938*	*1954*	*1968*	*1978*
	%	%	%	%	%	%	%	%	%	%
Food, drink and tobacco	8	8	6	7	8	47	49	40	24	15
Raw materials[a]	11	14	11	6	9	29	31	41	27	20
Manufactures	79	76	80	84	80	23	19	19	48	64
Unspecified	2	2	3	3	3	1	1	0	1	1
Total	100	100	100	100	100	100	100	100	100	100

[a] For 1968 and 1978 includes mineral fuels and lubricants

Source: Baldwin (1958); Central Statistical Office, *Annual Abstract of Statistics*, various issues

foodstuffs, materials and manufactures in British receipts remain strikingly stable for half a century. Table 2.3 indicates how the shares of different products in British exports of manufactures evolved over the period: most evident are a fall in the share of textiles in manufactured exports from 35 to 3 per cent over the half-century from 1928 and the rise in the share of vehicles and machinery from 15 to 37 per cent over the same years.

TABLE 2.3 Commodity composition of British exports of manufactures, 1928–78 (percentages of total export value)

	1928	*1938*	*1952*	*1954*	*1968*	*1978*
	%	%	%	%	%	%
Metals	12	12	11	12	12	8
Machinery	9	15	21	22	27	25
Vehicles	6	9	18	15	14	12
Textiles	35	22	15	13	5	3
Chemicals	4	5	5	5	9	11
Misc. manufact.	13	14	14	14	17	21
Total	79	76	84	80	84	80

Source: Baldwin (1958); Central Statistical Office, *Annual Abstract of Statistics*, various issues. Columns may not sum to totals because of rounding.

The relative stability of the share of trade in gross domestic product conceals substantial variation in the UK's barter terms of trade. The relative price of Britain's commodity exports and imports from 1920 to 1975 is depicted in figure 2.2. Fluctuations in the barter terms of trade during the interwar period are largely explicable in terms of supply and demand conditions in Britain's staple export industries and in the world's primary producing regions. The deterioration in the terms of trade over the course of the 1920s reflects persistent over-capacity in Europe's coal, iron and steel, textile and shipbuilding industries; and their recovery thereafter is due primarily to the worldwide slump in the prices of foodstuffs and raw materials. With her emergence from the Great Depression and the impact of the Second World War on the demand for primary products, Britain's barter terms of trade continue to deteriorate until 1951. A period of secularly improving terms of trade begins following the end of the commodity boom associated with the Korean War. For the next decade, the terms of trade continue to improve at a speed comparable to their rate of deterioration in the 1930s. For much of the 1960s they remain relatively stable at the level experienced in the 1930s.

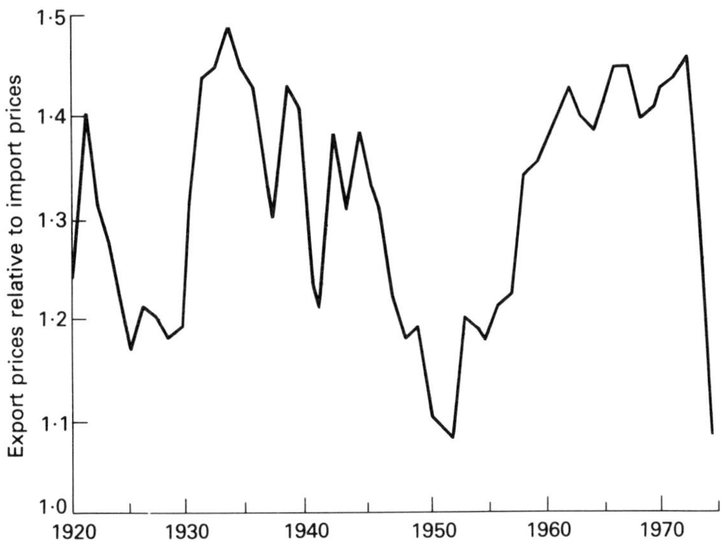

Figure 2.2 UK barter terms of trade, 1920–75

Source: Feinstein (1972) and *International Financial Statistics,* various issues

Table 2.4 presents the principal categories of invisible transactions in Britain's current account. Receipts from trade in invisibles account for 9 to 13 per cent of gross domestic product over the entire period. The share of services in invisible receipts rises slowly over the half-century, reflecting the expansion of Britain's shipping industry and the continued importance of London as a financial centre. In contrast, the share of property income from abroad declines steadily as a result of wartime divestiture and the retention of controls on investment abroad.

British trade policy

The commercial restrictions imposed by Britain during the First World War represented 'the first serious breach with free trade at home' and 'the first step towards . . . protectionism'.[4] The McKenna duties, imposed in the autumn of 1915 in order to save scarce shipping space and economize on foreign exchange, applied a 33 ⅓ per cent *ad valorem* tariff to imports of selected luxury items. These were Britain's first import duties in 55 years imposed for purposes other than raising revenue. Additional commercial restrictions were adopted following the war. The dyestuffs shortage that arose in 1914 demonstrated how criti-

[4] Skidelsky (1967, p. 5).

TABLE 2.4 Invisible items in the current account, 1928–78 (percentages of GDP)

	Exports of services	*Imports of services*	*Property income from abroad*[a]	*Property income paid abroad*[a]
1928	6.5	3.5	7.8	1.8
1938	3.9	3.2	4.9	0.9
1948	5.4	6.5	4.4	1.8
1958	6.5	6.1	5.2	2.4
1968	6.7	6.0	3.4	3.2
1978	8.6	6.2	4.3	5.2

[a] Includes transfers

Sources: Feinstein (1972); Central Statistical Office, *Annual Abstract of Statistics*, various issues

cally dependent Britain had become on the German chemical industry. In response, in January 1921 a Dyestuffs Importation Act was voted, protecting the domestic industry that had grown up during the war by allowing imports of organic dyestuffs only under Board of Trade license.[5] Five months later the Conservatives introduced a proposal for a selective system of *ad valorem* tariffs. The intent of this bill was to protect other infant industries besides dyestuffs and to promote the production of commodities deemed strategically important. Part I of the Act, which gave the Board of Trade power to enumerate goods that were produced by key industries meriting protection on national security grounds, was applied initially to some 6,000 articles.

Although the Safeguarding of Industries Act has been called the 'thin end of the wedge for future instalments of protection', there were few notable changes in British commercial policy for the remainder of the decade.[6] The next stage in the evolution of British commercial policy was marked by the introduction of general protection following the 1931 devaluation of sterling.[7] Protection was introduced in the form of the Abnormal Importations Act of November 1931 and the Import Duties Act of April 1932. The former, which was designed to deter anticipatory purchases by importers while the provisions of permanent measures were debated, conferred on the Board of Trade temporary power to impose duties of up to 100 per cent *ad valorem* on imports judged to be

[5] Plummer (1937, pp. 257–8); Snyder (1944, pp. 75–91).

[6] Francis (1939, p. 42). For accounts of developments in British commercial policy during the 1920s, see Eichengreen (1979, ch. 2), and Capie (1980, pp. 431–48).

[7] Events leading up to the introduction of this tariff are analysed in Eichengreen (1981a).

entering the country in abnormal quantities.[8] Those permanent measures included three types of duties: a general 10 per cent import levy, special taxes and exemptions for selected commodities, and retaliatory duties. Imports from the Empire were exempted pending negotiations at the Ottawa Conference, and an Import Duties Advisory Council (IDAC) was created to receive applications for changes in tariff rates and to make recommendations to the Treasury in response to requests or on its own initiative. The Treasury was required to evaluate the IDAC's recommendations, which became law if approved within 28 days by the House of Commons. The IDAC's first set of recommendations, issued in April 1932 and quickly approved, proposed a 20 per cent *ad valorem* tariff on imports of all manufactures not specifically exempted and recommended preferential treatment for the iron and steel industry, which was said to be experiencing exceptional difficulties justifying a 33 ⅓ per cent duty.

Although there was some tendency for tariff rates to rise over the course of the 1930s, the IDAC generally adhered to a policy of recommending low rates on food, drink and materials, rates of about 20 per cent *ad valorem* on manufactured goods, and rates of 33⅓ per cent for industries that merited protection on national security grounds. Between 1933 and 1938 no new duties were levied, although by 1935 the IDAC had issued some 150 recommendations for modifications to existing duties.

Besides the imposition of the General Tariff, several other important developments in British commercial policy took place in the 1930s. Under the Ottawa Agreements Act of 1932, the principle of trade discrimination in favour of the Empire was established. Free entry of all Empire products was guaranteed, and extra duties were imposed on foreign products viewed as competitive with imperial exports.[9] In the name of Imperial Preference, a levy was placed on non-imperial wheat imports, with the proceeds earmarked to subsidize domestic wheat production, and quotas were placed on foreign imports of bacon and other meat and dairy products.[10] In addition, the government attempted to exploit the nation's market power by negotiating a series of bilateral trade agreements with Empire and foreign countries. A long series of treaties began at the Ottawa Conference in 1932 and ended with the Anglo American Agreement in 1938; by the end of the period, trade agreements had been concluded with most of the world's principal trading countries.[11]

[8] Three orders were issued almost immediately, imposing duties of 50 per cent *ad valorem* on imports of a variety of products. For a list of commodities affected, see National Institute of Economic and Social Research (1943).

[9] See Drummond (1974).

[10] See National Institute of Economic and Social Research (1943).

[11] These developments are described in detail by Condliffe (1940).

At the beginning of the Second World War, tariff and non-tariff barriers to trade gave way to comprehensive system of import control designed to conserve hard currency. The government assumed complete control of trade in Britain's principal producer and consumer goods, obtaining those items on government account. Commodities left in the hands of private traders were made subject to licence.[12] The process of decontrol that began at war's end took more than a decade to complete. In the first year following the war, approximately two-thirds of Britain's imports were purchased by the government. While the import of raw materials reverted to private hands soon after the conclusion of hostilities, beginning with wool and iron ore in 1946, most semi-manufactured imports and all subsidized or rationed foodstuffs (the so-called 'basic foodstuffs', which amounted to some 80 per cent of total food) continued to be purchased by the government until 1950.[13]

The fortunes of liberalization rose and fell with Britain's balance of payments position. The 1947 balance of payments crisis retarded the process of decontrol, particularly of imports from the dollar area, as did the 1949 exchange crisis, which resulted in cuts of imports of sugar, tobacco, timber, paper and pulp, non-ferrous metals, steel and machinery from the dollar area. Following the 1949 devaluation, the establishment of the European Payments Union accelerated the liberalization process. With the removal of most of the restrictions on trade with Western Europe and the absence of controls on sterling area trade, more than half of total private imports were free of control at the end of 1950. However, the 1951 balance of payments crisis led to the reimposition of controls on non-sterling area imports. Among the principal items affected were imports of foodstuffs from non-sterling countries, tobacco and strategic materials.

By 1953 the process of decontrol was underway once more. Raw materials and semi-manufactured industrial materials reverted to private trade by 1954 and government purchase of food finally was eliminated in 1957. Between 1955 and 1958 British negotiators were largely

[12] See Hancock and Gowing (1949).

[13] Import control was supplemented by elaborate rationing schemes and price controls. Foodstuffs were the most important category of goods subject to rationing; rationed foodstuffs matched in value all other categories of rationed goods even in the immediate postwar years. 1948 saw the most dramatic reduction in rationing of manufactured goods, but rationing schemes still extended to perhaps 30 per cent of consumer spending in 1948, before falling to 12 per cent in 1949 and a mere 2 per cent in 1955 (see Dow, 1964, p. 173). Rationing of foodstuffs, a particularly sensitive issue politically, remained in force at the time of the 1949 devaluation. Moreover, regulations governing the allocation of intermediate goods other than steel sheet, steel plate and timber were retained until 1950. At the time of the 1949 devaluation, these rationing and allocation schemes were supported by a price freeze imposed under the provisions of the Price Control Orders of 1948. However, this freeze tended to be enforced half-heartedly and was far from fully effective. See Hemming, Miles and Ray (1959, p. 83).

preoccupied by unsuccessful attempts to establish a limited free trade area comprised of OEEC members. With the collapse of OEEC negotiations for a free trade area encompassing all of industrialized Europe, Britain turned in 1959 to countries on the periphery of the European Community, namely Austria, Switzerland, Portugal and Scandinavia, to form the European Free Trade Association. The EFTA agreement entailed the eventual abolition of tariffs and quotas on internal trade in industrial products and the replacement of Britain's import licensing scheme for dyestuffs with a 33⅓ per cent *ad valorem* tariff. The EFTA agreement reflected much of what Britain had proposed in the unsuccessful OEEC negotiations.

The shadow of the EEC hung over Britain's commercial negotiations throughout the 1960s. The danger of failing to reach an agreement with the European Community, after the veto by de Gaulle in January 1963 of Britain's first attempt to gain admission, rendered the authorities receptive to other avenues for gaining freer access to foreign markets. Britain had been an enthusiastic participant in the Dillon Round of multilateral negotiations ending in 1962; in return for foreign concessions on the treatment of her exports, she agreed to reduce duties on industrial imports by up to 20 per cent. The Kennedy Round of GATT negotiations, which opened in May 1963, shortly after de Gaulle's first veto, and concluded a bare five months before the 1967 devaluation, was the occasion for further reductions in duties on manufactures by more than one-half. The first of the Kennedy Round cuts was implemented on 1 July 1968 and the remainder took place between 1970 and 1972. Thereafter, ministers' efforts were directed primarily at obtaining EEC membership on acceptable terms. The final round of negotiations with the EEC, which formally began in the summer of 1970, opened a new era in British commercial policy.[14]

Control of overseas lending

Control of overseas lending in the United Kingdom goes back to the First World War. From the end of 1914, dealings in securities in foreign stock markets were prohibited and new issues for foreign borrowers were made subject to official approval. The controls then introduced were maintained after the war but were gradually relaxed until their final disappearance at the end of 1923 when the ban on foreign lending was removed. (The embargo against loans to Empire countries had been withdrawn two years previously.) Thereafter, the only restrictions on foreign investment governed loans to countries in default and to

[14] For details, see Morgan (1978).

countries with unfunded war debts.[15] But the Bank of England continued to use moral suasion to limit new issues by foreign borrowers, while the Treasury exerted pressure on the Empire to limit its demand for funds. This informal embargo was lifted in November 1925, five months after Britain's return to the gold standard, and foreign lending remained largely unrestricted for the remainder of the decade.[16]

Following the 1931 devaluation, a complete prohibition of public loans to overseas borrowers was imposed. In 1933 this restriction was extended to encompass purchases of existing securities in foreign markets. This embargo, like that of the early 1920s, while without legal foundation was effectively enforced. Restrictions on loans to Commonwealth borrowers were relaxed at the beginning of 1933, but foreign issues were permitted only if there was a compelling case that they would benefit British industry.[17] While official control extended to direct investment abroad, that source of capital outflows was treated with greater leniency by the authorities.

Stringent capital controls were imposed once more at the beginning of the Second World War. Official permission was made mandatory for any purchase of foreign exchange, whether for current or capital transactions. At the time of the 1949 devaluation of sterling, external lending was still restricted under the provisions of the Exchange Control Act of 1947.

During the 1960s, the stringency of UK capital controls varied with the state of the balance of payments. Throughout the decade foreign exchange continued to be supplied at the official rate for all direct investment projects in the sterling area; but when the balance of payments deteriorated in 1964–66, companies planning direct investment with United Kingdom finance in the four main developed countries of the sterling area – Australia, New Zealand, South Africa and the Irish Republic – were urged, in the so-called 'Voluntary Programme' of May 1966, to postpone or cancel projects already under way and to seek the Bank of England's approval for new projects. As for direct investment outside the sterling area, beginning in 1961 this was required to meet the test of promising 'clear and commensurate benefits' to Britain's export earnings and balance of payments. The following year, in less critical conditions, other projects were allowed to seek finance through the

[15] See Cairncross (1973 , pp. 57–61), and the references cited therein.

[16] For 1926 and 1927 there are only scattered indications that the Bank of England attempted to exert influence over foreign lending. When the first effects of the New York stock market boom were felt in 1928, the Bank intensified its informal surveillance of overseas loans, but there is little evidence that the Bank of England's moral suasion served as a binding constraint on the rate of overseas investment. See Moggridge (1971, pp. 123–4).

[17] Over the four years 1932–35, less than 3 per cent of new issues were by foreign borrowers, and that 3 per cent went largely to sterling area countries.

investment currency market in which British residents could dispose (at a premium) of foreign currency acquired through the sale of foreign securities and other assets. When, however, the balance of payments weakened again and the restrictions were further tightened in 1965–66, this concession was withdrawn. Projects meeting the official criteria were no longer provided with currency at the official rate and had to make use of the investment currency market or seek finance through loans in foreign currency.

No official exchange was made available for portfolio investment outside the sterling area. Sales and purchases were confined to the investment currency market, where the effectiveness of the control was reflected in the premium paid. This fluctuated around 10 per cent in 1963–65 and reached a peak of nearly 50 per cent at the end of 1968. The volatility of the premium was a considerable discouragement to foreign investors, and a further discouragement was introduced in April 1965 when investors were required to surrender 25 per cent of the sales proceeds of foreign currency securities at the official rate of exchange instead of enjoying the premium rate. Portfolio investment outside the sterling area thus became subject to a stiff tax that fluctuated with the size of the premium. Investment trusts and other institutions with a large turnover in foreign securities were, however, allowed to borrow foreign currency for the purposes of portfolio investment and to use the proceeds for transactions in foreign securities without the application of the 25 per cent rule.

The sterling area and clearing arrangements

By definition, the sterling area has been made up of countries that endeavour to keep their currencies pegged to the pound, invoice the bulk of their trade in sterling, and maintain the largest portion of their foreign exchange reserves in the form of sterling balances held in London.[18] As J.R. Sargent has pointed out, currency areas are an outgrowth of currency inconvertibility.[19] Thus, it is not surprising that the ban on overseas loans that accompanied the 1931 devaluation was the occasion for the birth of the 'sterling area' as we now know it.[20] The entire British Commonwealth, with the exception of Canada, whose economy is linked geographically to the United States, and with some delay by South Africa, which had a special interest in the established gold price, continued to base their currencies on sterling. Many mem-

[18] Harrod (1952, p. 9); Robertson (1954, pp. 34–5); Nurkse (1944, p. 47).
[19] Sargent (1952, p. 531). See also Bell (1956).
[20] The term 'sterling area' was actually coined during the Second World War. For previous years we refer here to the 'sterling bloc'.

bers of the Commonwealth undoubtedly were influenced in their decision by the fact that the dominant share of their exports was destined for the UK: British market shares ranged from 95 per cent for Ireland and 80 per cent for New Zealand to 45 per cent for Australia, 40 per cent for South Africa and 30 per cent for India. The Commonwealth was joined by independent nations with close political or economic ties to Britain, including Ireland, Iceland, Egypt, the Sudan, Portugal and Iraq. Estonia and Siam joined the sterling bloc in 1933, while Iran and Latvia joined in 1936. The Scandinavian countries initially allowed their exchange rates against the dollar to move by half of the change in the sterling–dollar rate, but once the dollar began to fluctuate in 1933 they effectively joined the sterling bloc. Still other countries, such as Japan, Bolivia, Argentina, Greece and Yugoslavia, pegged their exchange rates to sterling for extended periods of time, but since they maintained exchange control or multiple exchange rates, they were not considered members of the sterling bloc.

The Second World War provided the occasion to transform this informal arrangement among countries into a coherent, formal organization. The outbreak of the war caused the European members of the sterling bloc to drop out and the United Kingdom to impose exchange control on payments outside the bloc while maintaining relative freedom of payments within it. The remaining participants (members of the Commonwealth and Empire along with Egypt, Iraq, Sudan and Iceland) took advantage of increased spending by Britain to accumulate large sterling balances, which they generally held in the form of British Treasury bills and soon-to-mature government securities. By the war's conclusion, at the end of 1946, more than 65 per cent of all externally held sterling balances, which came to £3,700 million in total, were in the hands of the sterling area. In part, sterling area countries were encouraged to accumulate sterling balances by the expectation that sterling would be made convertible immediately after the war. Instead, exchange control was maintained, and bilateral agreements governing the gradual release of these balances were negotiated by the UK and various sterling area countries.[21]

A new monetary area was created in 1945 when a number of Central American countries, previously grouped and treated on a bilateral basis, were combined with the United States in a composite group known as the 'American accounts'. Payments for current account debits by ster-

[21] These agreements allowed the unlimited use of sterling balances to settle accounts with sterling area countries, permitted (subject to Bank of England approval) limited transfer of sterling to non-sterling countries, and provided for settlement in gold when indebtedness exceeded an agreed amount. By 1949 these individually negotiated agreements had been replaced by a multilateral understanding designed to limit dollar expenditure through the application of an accepted formula. See Economic Cooperation Administration (1951, p. 181); Bank for International Settlements (1953, p. 17).

ling area countries credited to this account were made freely convertible into dollars on demand. Thus, American sterling balances could be used for purchases from any country. Two years later, 'transferable account' status was introduced. Transferable account countries, initially including Argentina, Brazil, Ethiopia, Canada, Egypt, the Sudan, Newfoundland and a number of European nations, agreed to accept sterling from all countries in payment for goods and services, to hold it as international reserves, and to block sterling balances accumulated prior to 15 July 1945. Subject to this restriction, the sterling balances of these countries could be used for current account transactions within the sterling area and with other transferable account countries.

At the end of the war, two types of sterling area countries could be distinguished: those with rigidly dependent currencies (i.e., those that backed local currency fully in sterling and intervened automatically in the foreign exchange market to peg the sterling parity), including most of Britain's colonies, protectorates and mandates; and countries with independent currencies (i.e., those with some discretion over the parity and the composition of reserves), such as Australia, New Zealand, India, South Africa and Iceland.[22] The members of both groups participated in the dollar pool (except for South Africa, which withdrew at the end of 1947). This arrangement had been established during the war to co-ordinate the management of dollar reserves, and it was kept in place thereafter in the interest of limiting the dollar losses of the sterling area. Under the dollar pooling arrangement, residents of member countries were required to surrender dollars and gold to their central authorities, who agreed in turn to deposit any increase in their holdings of dollars and gold at the Bank of England. Furthermore, members of the pool agreed to control the potential loss of dollar reserves by imposing licensing systems on dollar imports.[23] Subject to those restrictions, the dollar reserves of members of the pool could be freely drawn down.

An abortive effort to restore convertibility was attempted in 1947. In return for an American loan, the British authorities agreed to remove all impediments to payments for current transactions and to eliminate the discriminatory provisions of the dollar pooling arrangement. In February 1947, sterling balances in transferable accounts were rendered fully convertible into dollars, and over the next four months successive additions were made to the list of transferable account countries. When this process culminated in free convertibility in July 1947, the UK experienced an alarming drain of gold and hard currency reserves; gold and dollar losses in the first month of convertibility exceeded the total for the first half of 1947. The British authorities viewed the position as

[22] On this distinction see Clauson (1939).

[23] Wright (1954, pp. 554–76).

unsustainable and suspended convertibility after five weeks by halting all transfers between transferable and American accounts.

The 1950s were a decade of relatively minor change in British clearing arrangements. Sterling balances overseas continued to preoccupy the authorities, although by 1950 they had fallen to one-half their immediate postwar level. At the beginning of the decade, the sterling area included some 20 colonies and other dependent territories, members of the Commonwealth (Australia, Ceylon, India, New Zealand, Pakistan and South Africa), plus Burma, Iceland, Iraq, Ireland and Jordan.[24] The treatment of the sterling area, the American and transferable accounts, and countries under bilateral agreements remained basically unchanged until 1954, despite the development of a sophisticated sterling market in New York and Zurich which undermined the authorities' attempts to segregate transactions. Negotiations to restore convertibility began in earnest only at the Commonwealth Conference in 1952. In March 1954 bilateral status countries were converted to the transferable account, and restrictions on capital transactions in transferable sterling were abolished. To discourage commodity shunting, from February 1955 transferable sterling in New York and Zurich was supported within 1 per cent of the official rate by the Exchange Equalisation Account.[25] With the restoration of non-resident convertibility in 1958, the transferable account and American account were combined into a unified 'external account'.

The membership of the sterling area continued to change with the establishment of full current account convertibility in 1961, with the independent status gained by former British colonies in the 1960s, and with the 1967 devaluation. Prior to devaluation, the overseas sterling area included five countries classified as developed (Australia, Iceland, Ireland, New Zealand and South Africa), the dependent territories of the UK and the overseas sterling area, and the following developing countries: Bahrain, Barbados, Brunei, Ceylon, Cyprus, Fiji, the Gambia, Ghana, Guyana, India, Jamaica, Jordan, Kenya, Kuwait, the Libyan Arab Republic, Malawi, Malaysia, Malta, Mauritius, Nigeria, Oman, Pakistan, Qatar, Sierra Leone, Singapore, South-west Africa, Tanzania, Tonga, Trinidad and Tobago, the Trucial States, Uganda, Yemen and Zambia.[26] Britain had come a long way since 1931, when it could be said that 'the whole world was in the Sterling Area. . . .'[27]

[24] See Bank for International Settlements (1953).
[25] Dow (1964, pp. 85–6).
[26] International Monetary Fund (1972, p. 13).
[27] Mallalieu (1956, p. 184).

3

The 1931 Devaluation of Sterling

The 1931 devaluation of sterling ended a decade of financial struggle. It marked the collapse of an international financial order that had served the world for generations and had been reconstructed at considerable expense following the First World War. The gold standard parity of sterling, officially re-established in 1925, was a reference point for exchange rate stabilization by a number of countries: France in 1926, Italy in 1927, Norway in 1928, and Portugal in 1929, to name but a few. Thus the pound's devaluation in 1931 symbolized a radical change in the structure of international economic relations.

Devaluation in 1931 was not a planned act of policy. The British authorities had gone to great lengths to ignore the possibility of devaluation, and when events rendered further disregard impossible, they went to similar lengths to minimize the likelihood of its occurrence. But once it was forced upon them, devaluation cleared the way for a fundamental re-orientation of economic policy, and it radically altered the role of the exchange rate in the regulation of the economy.

Reconstructing the gold standard system

The story of the 1931 devaluation of sterling begins with the Interim Report of the Cunliffe Committee in August 1918. This document, entitled the *First Interim Report* of the Committee on Currency and Foreign Exchanges after the War (1918), addressed the questions of how and when to return sterling to the gold standard at its prewar parity. Other options were not considered. The Committee recommended restoring the prewar parity at the earliest possible opportunity, thus elevating this objective to the point where it dominated all other goals of economic policy. In so doing, the Committee's Report reflected the consensus in academic, business and financial circles alike that restoring convertibility at the traditional rate of $4.86 was an indispensable component of any economic recovery programme.[1]

For the next six years the nation had the opportunity to ponder the desirability of returning to the gold standard. During the war, foreign moratoria and gold embargoes, the difficulty of obtaining insurance for gold shipments and the demands of war finance had forced the British authorities to tolerate a weakening of the pound. Considerable intervention had been required to support the currency at $4.76. This reality was acknowledged in March 1919, when the official sale of dollars was halted, and in April, when the export of gold without official permission was prohibited.[2] For a time, the Governor of the Bank of England believed that an early rise in interest rates would be sufficient to return sterling to parity.[3] Indeed, had the government turned immediately to a policy of severe credit restriction, it is conceivable that the prewar parity could have been restored upon the conclusion of hostilities. However, such austerity measures were judged to be politically inexpedient at a time when demobilization and reconstruction required monetary accommodation. Instead, the war-time expansion of credit was allowed to continue into 1920.[4]

In Western Europe and the United States, the Armistice was followed by a sudden and dramatic boom. Consumers finally were permitted to vent demands that had been pent up during the war, and producers took the opportunity to replenish their stocks. In Britain this demand pressure, along with the relaxation of price controls, led to a run-up of prices unprecedented in peacetime. Employment expanded rapidly, and wages rose in response. As early as 1918, the Bank of England had become alarmed by the prospect of inflation, and by the spring of 1919 this concern had spread to the Treasury. By the end of the year such fears were common throughout the government. The response took the form of a more restrictive fiscal stance, accompanied by two increases in the Bank of England's discount rate, in November 1919 and April 1920. A precipitous decline in industrial production ensued, with the percentage of trade union members registered as unemployed climbing from 1.4 to 16.7 per cent within a year.[5] Unemployment suddenly became the dominant social issue of the day, and so it remained: over the next decade, the unemployment rate among insured persons never fell below 9 per cent, and more parliamentary time was devoted to unemployment than to any other single question.

1 See Committee on Currency and Foreign Exchanges After the War (1918). There were a very few who questioned the desirability of restoring sterling's prewar parity at this time. Keynes's views on the subject appear in Keynes (1971), and Keynes (1977, pp. 355–7).

2 See Brown (1940, pp. 7–26); Morgan (1952, pp. 344–60).

3 Sayers (1976, volume 1, p. 115).

4 See Johnson (1968, *passim*); Howson (1974, pp. 88–96); and Dowie (1975).

5 The impact of the downswing on the percentage unemployed was greatly exacerbated by the effects of the general coal mining stoppage of the spring and summer of 1921.

It is often remarked that the decision to return to the gold standard was based upon instinct rather than careful calculation of potential costs and benefits. Yet such analysis of costs and benefits was never totally absent. Some observers believed that inflation in the United States would be sufficient to relieve Britain of the burden of adjustment. Others remained convinced that restoration of the prewar parity required deflation and, in light of Britain's limited wage flexibility, that this would be costly in terms of output and employment forgone. The Bank of England recognized that adjustment would be painful, and Treasury memoranda alluded to the transition costs associated with the adjustment. Keynes was not alone in suggesting that the export industries would be forced to shoulder a disproportionate share of the burden, but his analysis was influential precisely because of his willingness to hazard an estimate of the magnitude of the problem. Nevertheless, apart from Reginald McKenna (chairman of the Midland Bank), Hubert Henderson (editor of the *Nation and Athenaeum*), Lord Beaverbrook and some members of the House of Commons, Keynes had little company when he argued that unemployment and excess capacity in the export trades were unacceptable prices to pay for restoration of the prewar parity.[6]

It is undoubtedly true that, to some extent, the decision to resurrect the prewar parity was an instinctive reaction. The gold standard was a symbol of past economic glories, and there was a desire to turn the clock back to a time when Britain played a dominant role in international trade and finance. This desire to restore prewar financial arrangements did not reflect any peculiar British failing; the belief that exchange rates should be restored to 'normal' was shared worldwide.[7] Yet there also existed distinctly British arguments for returning to the old parity. That parity represented financial strength and security, and its restoration would help to win back the trade in financial services that was so important to the City of London. Invisible earnings, acquired through the export of shipping, insurance and financial services, were a critical component of the balance of payments, and a surplus on current account might loosen the restraints that limited the scope for reducing interest rates. A return to the prewar parity was seen as good for business confidence, symbolizing the government's commitment to cur-

[6] Keynes's articles on these questions, which appeared in the *Evening Standard* on 22, 23 and 24 July 1925, are collected in Keynes (1931). The debate is reviewed by Sayers (1960), Hume (1963), Moggridge (1969), Wright (1981) and Dimsdale (1981).

[7] Yeager (1966, pp. 267–8); Einzig (1935, pp. 96–7). Other countries that ultimately succeeded in restoring their prewar parities included Switzerland, the Netherlands, Denmark, Sweden, Norway and Japan. Even in France, where in 1928 a conscious decision was made to restore convertibility at a lower gold price, there was considerable sentiment among ministers and Regents of the Bank of France favouring an eventual return to the prewar parity. See Brown (1940, pp. 458–9); Jack (1927, p. 134); Sauvy (1965, volume 1, pp. 89–90). See also below, pp. 45–6.

tail its intervention in the economy. Most important was the belief that the health of the export industries could be insured only by measures that established a stable basis for world trade.

The distinction between stable exchange rates and a particular set of rates, namely those that had been maintained under the late Victorian gold standard, was not always carefully drawn. Among those who made this distinction, the gold standard's advocates argued that restoration of the prewar parity would provide not just immediate stability but, in addition, a measure of credibility for the authorities' assurances that current exchange rates would be maintained. Treasury officials saw reconstruction of the gold standard system as the single most effective step they could take to increase the volume of world trade. While the exchange rate appreciation required by restoration might cause the export trades to suffer a temporary loss of competitiveness, in the long run they could be returned to a firm footing only by the stability and certainty created by a return to gold. It was from this perspective that Cassel remarked in 1936 that

> the relatively small sacrifices involved in [returning to gold] were much more than counterbalanced by the restoration of international confidence and by the stimulus given to international trade through the replacement of the pound sterling in its old position as the principal currency of the world's trade.[8]

The struggle that culminated in 1925 with Britain's return to gold was long and arduous. Speculation that an early return was in the offing caused the exchange rate to rise at first, from a low (on a monthly average basis) of $3.63 in July 1921 to a high of $4.70 in March 1923. Despite indications that the Bank of England was contemplating the restoration of convertibility, sterling sank gradually thereafter to a trough of $4.26 in January 1924, before rising steadily towards the prewar parity.[9] The speed and accuracy with which the exchange rate approached its gold standard parity depended in part on current economic conditions but also upon expectations of future government policy. From the end of 1920 to the end of 1922, as wholesale prices, the cost of living and average weekly wages all declined steadily, the exchange rate tended to appreciate. These trends reflected money market conditions: the sum of currency plus deposits of the ten principal London clearing banks declined by 8 per cent over this period, and interest rates tended to fall.[10] After 1922 British price indices levelled off, and, despite the continued decline of nominal wages and the broadly defined money

[8] Cassel (1936, p. 40).
[9] Aliber (1962, pp. 188–90).
[10] For its monetary statistics, this chapter relies heavily on returns of the ten banks that comprised the London Clearing Banks Association, whose assets amounted to roughly three-quarters of the total for all UK commercial banks. Figures for 1920–31 are drawn from Committee on Finance and Industry (1931).

stock (currency plus deposits), the appreciation of the exchange rate was temporarily interrupted. A much-hoped-for rise in the American price level failed to materialize. But the exchange rate's weakness in 1923 was not due exclusively to current conditions; sterling also may have been undermined by suspicions that the new Labour government might adopt expansionary measures designed to reduce unemployment. Similarly, sterling's recovery in 1924 can be attributed in part to the Labour government's acceptance of the dictates of the Cunliffe Committee.

By 1924, when manufacturing output finally surpassed its 1920 level, many of the strengths and weaknesses of the interwar economy had become apparent. Employment in Britain's new industries (chemicals, electricity and electrical engineering, hosiery, silk and rayon, and vehicles) had risen by more than 2 per cent since 1920, foreshadowing the subsequent expansion of those sectors. These new industries were distinguished from the old by their reliance on new technologies, the small scale of many firms, and relative independence from the export market. Except for motor vehicles, the share of exports in the output of the new industries rarely exceeded 25 per cent.[11] By 1924 a further contrast between Britain's new industries and her export trades was evident: while unemployment had fallen below 9 per cent in each of the new industries, it continued to exceed 15 per cent in cotton, shipbuilding and iron and steel. Depression in the staple trades was reflected in British export performance: by 1924 consumption and import volume had been restored to their 1913 levels, but exports had risen to less than three-quarters of their prewar volume.

There can be little doubt that the depression in Britain's export industries and the magnitude of her trade balance deficit were due in part to policies designed to induce exchange rate appreciation. The picture of healthy expansion in relatively sheltered industries and persistent difficulties in the unsheltered sector is consistent with the view that the old industries' problems were attributable partly to the impact on international competitiveness of overvaluation. With home currency prices lagging behind exchange rates, British producers of traded goods found it increasingly difficult to defend their market shares at home and abroad. Moreover, domestic money wages lagged behind falling prices and thereby created a squeeze on profits.[12] Money wages rates in Britain responded less rapidly to cost of living reductions after 1922 than in the years immediately succeeding the war. However, the postwar experience clearly was unique: 55 to 60 per cent of all wage reductions that took place in 1921 and 40 per cent of those occurring in 1922 resulted from sliding scale agreements of the sort widely adopted during

[11] Richardson (1961, p. 363).

[12] Kindleberger (1973, pp. 32–3); Keleher (1975, *passim*).

hostilities.[13] Thereafter, indexation fell out of favour, and money wage rates exhibited the limited downward flexibility characteristic of both the late Victorian and interwar periods.[14] Although limited wage flexibility was an economic fact of life, it was not a new one.

With time, British exporters began to complain publicly that the appreciation of sterling and the rigidity of wages were permitting foreign producers to undersell them in both home and overseas markets. Symptomatic of this agitation was the Conservative government's decision in 1923 to go to the electorate for a mandate to impose a general tariff on imports from foreign countries.[15] Yet calculations of purchasing power parity based on the assumption that 1913 prices and exchange rates were consistent with international equilibrium do not uniformly support the hypothesis of over-valuation in 1925.[16] How can we reconcile the fact of depression in the staple trades and the complaints of British exporters with these calculations?

The answer appears to lie in changes in the structure of supply and demand that had taken place during the war. In light of these changes, a deterioration in Britain's net barter terms of trade, accomplished through some combination of depreciation and a decline in the sterling prices of British goods relative to the foreign currency prices of substitutes produced abroad, was needed to restore the export volume of the staple trades to traditional levels. During the war, Britain's continental competitors had expanded the capacity of their iron and steel industries. The introduction of the Thomas process, suitable to continental but not to British ore deposits, had further eroded the competitive position of domestic steelmakers. Lancashire suffered the effects of new competition from India and Japan and found it difficult to absorb the impact of protective tariffs imposed in the United States, Brazil and elsewhere. Coal producers felt the effects of conversion to oil and petrol, and the shipbuilding industry was depressed by the combination of Scandinavian competition and worldwide over-capacity. Meanwhile, the growth of demand for other traditional exports seemed to lag. Cotton and wool gave way to silk and rayon as consumption shifted towards lighter and finer types of cloth, and the market for new consumer goods such as

[13] Aldcroft (1970, p. 356). Figures on the value of wage adjustments concluded under the provisions of sliding scale agreements can be found in the *Ministry of Labour Gazette* (various issues).

[14] Although standard statistical series for the period 1870–1913 show several instances of declining average weekly wage rates, they show fewer examples of falling average weekly earnings. See Triffin (1964, p. 5); Feinstein (1972, p. T140); Lewis (1980). It should be noted that sliding scales were also used in certain sectors before the war, and that they remained in limited use into the 1930s. See for example Kirby (1977).

[15] These protectionist pressures were more than just a response to industry's current difficulties. Indeed, the roots of the 1923 tariff proposals can be traced to the Tariff Reform Movement at the turn of the century. See Snyder (1944, chapter 8).

[16] Moggridge (1969, pp. 72–5).

gramophones and electrical appliances expanded rapidly. Social commentators noted 'a veritable revolution in the taste and requirements of the consumer'. In the words of a League of Nations report published in 1931, 'Slow changes in tastes and habits are no new phenomena. . . . But the intensity of certain of the recent changes has been peculiar.'[17] As Svennilson put it, British producers faced a 'transformation problem'.[18] In the meantime, these changes in the composition of supply and demand meant that, even if purchasing power parity calculations revealed no obvious deterioration in the export industries' competitive position, some decline in the relative price of their products was needed to reverse the loss of sales.

The return to gold in 1925 was not followed by a strong cyclical upswing.[19] None the less, real gross domestic product rose at a respectable rate, slightly in excess of 2 per cent annually, from 1925 to 1929, with the General Strike year of 1926 providing the only interruption to the upward trend. The impulses driving this growth included persistent expansion in the new industries, resilient demands for housing and social overhead capital, and rising public authority and public utility expenditures. But despite these advances, the economy's performance was perceived as disappointing. There were at least three reasons for this impression. First, output growth was unevenly distributed across sectors. Industry in general and the staple trades in particular remained depressed relative to other sectors of the economy. Furthermore, the persistence of high levels of unemployment incessantly reminded observers of the uneven incidence of Britain's economic difficulties. On an annual average basis, unemployment among the insured reached its lowest level in 1927, when the rate was 9.7 per cent; for the entire civilian working population unemployment that year was 6.8 per cent.[20] Finally, the growth of British industrial production was perceived as disappointing in comparison with other countries. Table 3.1, which presents the figures available at the time, indicates the extent to which foreign industrial growth appeared to surpass growth in Britain.[21]

While the development of Great Britain's international trade and payments position in the 1920s gave little cause for alarm, the external accounts evinced a number of disturbing tendencies. For more than half a century, Britain's balance of payments had exhibited remarkable

[17] League of Nations (1931a, p. 19). See also Siegfried (1931, p. 94).

[18] See Svennilson (1954, p. 46) and, for a similar analysis at an earlier date, Metzler (1947, p. 19). For a contrasting view, see Lundberg (1968), and for an historical perspective, see Jenks (1927).

[19] Burns and Mitchell (1946, p. 79).

[20] Tinbergen (1934, p. 101); Feinstein (1972, p. T126).

[21] Subsequent research suggests that British growth in this period compares more favourably with the growth of other economies. See Aldcroft (1967) and Dowie (1968). The index for Britain in 1926 seems implausibly low; that figure may have been biased downwards by the way the effects of the General Strike were calculated.

TABLE 3.1 National indices of industrial production, 1926–29

	(1925 = 100)			
	1926	*1927*	*1928*	*1929*
France	116	102	119	130
Germany	95	120	120	122
Poland	98	123	138	138
Sweden	103	108	104	127
United Kingdom	77	111	105	113
USSR	139	164	198	223
Canada	117	125	138	154
United States	104	102	107	114

Source: League of Nations (1931a, p. 17)

stability, and its various components followed a highly predictable pattern. Britain regularly ran trade balance deficits that were more than offset by surpluses on invisible account: in the century ending in 1913, she experienced only two current account deficits. These surpluses on current account enabled Britain habitually to run capital account deficits, investing abroad and acquiring a huge stock of claims on foreigners.

It is sometimes argued that the components of the capital account followed an equally stable and predictable pattern: that, befitting one of the world's leading financial intermediaries, Britain borrowed short and lent long. There are records of substantial long-term lending in the 1920s; according to the Midland Bank's figures, new overseas issues in the London market exceeded £80 million in every year from 1920 to 1929.[22] At the same time, the evidence on short-term capital flows, presented in table 3.2, is mixed. It should not be forgotten that, in addition to bonds and direct foreign investments, Britain held valuable stocks of short-term assets. Prior to 1914, Morgan argues, these assets were sufficient to render Britain a net short-term creditor.[23] In fact, little is known about her short-term position before the war, and attempts to work backwards from interwar estimates on the basis of balance of payments statistics are hampered by limited knowledge of the magnitude of asset sales during wartime.[24] To have rendered London a short-term creditor before the war, such sales had to amount to almost £100 million, using the Macmillan Committee's 1931 estimates as a

[22] Sayers (1976, volume 3, pp. 310–13).
[23] See Morgan (1952, p. 332). For sceptical views, see Bloomfield (1963, p. 76), Oppenheimer (1966, p. 92), and Wright (1981, p. 287).
[24] However, see Lindert (1969) for a notable attempt.

TABLE 3.2 UK balance of payments, 1925–38

	(£ million)													
	1925	*1926*	*1927*	*1928*	*1929*	*1930*	*1931*	*1932*	*1933*	*1934*	*1935*	*1936*	*1937*	*1938*
Imports (f.o.b.)	1208	1140	1115	1095	1117	953	786	641	619	683	724	786	950	849
Exports (f.o.b.)	943	794	845	858	854	670	464	425	427	463	541	523	614	564
Visible balance	−265	−346	−270	−237	−263	−283	−322	−216	−192	−220	−183	−263	−336	−285
Private services, transfers and earnings	307	311	342	333	328	280	200	179	184	194	205	232	288	237
Public services, transfers and earnings	−11	−4	6	8	11	18	8	−25	−10	−6	−9	−9	−9	−17
Invisible balance	296	307	348	341	339	298	208	154	174	188	196	223	279	220
Current account	31	−39	78	104	76	15	−114	−62	−18	−32	13	−40	−57	−65
Net long-term capital[a]	−78	−89	−138	−111	−52	−61	−5	9	−12	−36	−18	−2	−3	20
Net short-term capital[b]	45	151	78	−11	−32	53	3	196	152	78	84	253	189	−223
Foreign assistance							82	−114						
Capital account	−33	62	−60	−122	−84	−8	80	91	140	42	66	251	186	−203
Currency flow	−2	23	18	−18	−8	7	−34	29	122	10	79	211	129	−268

[a] UK net investment overseas plus sinking funds, repayments on existing issues and official long-term capital
[b] All items (including the balancing item) not readily identifiable as current transactions, long-term capital, foreign assistance or changes in reserves
Source: Sayers (1976, volume 3, pp. 312–13), reprinted from *Bank of England Quarterly Bulletin* (September 1972 and March 1974)

benchmark, and more than four times that amount if estimates of sterling bills held by foreign banks less the Bank of England's reserves of foreign exchange are added to the Macmillan Committee series.[25] If the available estimates for long-term capital movements during the war are to be believed, then Britain had been a net short-term debtor in 1913, but not to any great extent.[26]

Prewar trends continued into the 1920s. Neither the current account nor the capital account, set out in Table 3.2, individually presents any indication of serious imbalance. The trade balance deficit exhibits impressive stability, with the exception of 1926, when the General Strike and associated supply disruptions depressed export receipts, and 1930–31, when the effects of the worldwide depression were felt. Britain's positive invisible balance exhibits similar stability. Overall, the current account was in surplus in every year except 1926 and 1931.

The figures in table 3.2 on the capital account are constructed by consolidating under 'short-term capital' all items (including the balancing item) not readily identifiable as current transactions, long-term capital, foreign assistance or changes in reserves. The propensity to lend long is evident in the debit on net long-term capital in each year of the 1925–30 period. However, the stabilizing function of short-term capital is not always evident: in every year except 1928 and 1929, short-term funds moved so as to assist in financing Britain's basic balance, but the short-term outflow in those two years reached substantial proportions. With the exception of 1928 and 1931, flows of gold and foreign exchange were much less important than private short-term capital in financing the basic balance.

Many of these regularities were reassuringly similar to Britain's experience under the prewar gold standard. What was disturbing was the relative size of the balance of payments' different components, and Britain's dependence, for external balance, on continued short-term capital inflows. Although the current account tended towards surplus, that surplus was insufficient to cover the deficit on capital account arising from long-term lending. The surpluses of the 1925–30 period rarely approached one-half the level familiar from the decade preceding the war, so for much of the interwar gold standard period Britain's basic balance remained in deficit. That deficit was not the result of any unprecedented tendency to invest abroad; rather, it was due to Britain's

25 Balance of payments estimates for the interwar period are from Sayers (1976, volume 3, pp. 312–13), and current account figures for wartime are from Feinstein (1972, p. T82). The extent to which the Macmillan Committee estimates understated Britain's sterling liabilities is discussed by Royal Institute of International Affairs (1937).

26 Morgan (1952, chapter IX); see also Moulton and Pasvolsky (1932). Oppenheimer (1966) makes similar calculations, using different data, and comes to basically the same conclusion.

inability to maintain a current account surplus large enough to finance her customary foreign lending.

Part of the explanation for this current account shortfall lies with the exchange rate. With time, payments deficits would have begun to put downward pressure on domestic prices and upward pressure on foreign prices, in the absence of sterilization and other intervening factors. In the interim, as Keynes pointed out in 1925, 'The effect of a high exchange is to diminish the sterling prices of both imports and exports. The result is both to encourage imports and to discourage exports, thus turning the balance of trade against us.'[27] It is not surprising, therefore, that the relatively small current account surpluses of the second half of the 1920s were associated with growing deficits on merchandise trade account with countries that had declined to peg to sterling at the traditional parity. A high exchange rate had relatively little effect on the invisible accounts: although some shipping income was lost, restoring the prewar parity seemed to have succeeded in promoting London's short-term interest and commission earnings, as the gold standard's advocates had predicted.[28]

Associated with this new dependence on short-term capital inflows was the chronic weakness of the exchange rate. Between 1888 and 1914, the annual average sterling–dollar rate had been below par only four times and above par 23 times. In the six years of the interwar gold standard, the sterling–dollar rate was above par on average only in 1928, owing to exceptional strength in the first half of the year, and it remained below par in 60 of 76 months.[29] The Bank of England continually was battling a gold drain, and the situation, while usually under control, was often precarious.

The exchange rate's chronic weakness, and the exchange market difficulties with which that weakness was associated – in 1927, again in 1929 and most dramatically in 1931 – were of the utmost concern to the Bank of England. The interwar period has been called the 'heyday of central banking' and the 'reign of Montagu Norman'.[30] The Bank of England had been forced into the political arena by the breakdown, during the war, of its traditional insulation from political pressures. The Bank's activities were further politicized by the incompatibility of successive governments' domestic objectives with the Bank's conception of its external obligations. The Bank's need to maintain high interest rates to buttress the sterling parity, in conjunction with the Treasury's desire

[27] Keynes (1931, pp. 215–16).

[28] Here once again it is necessary to distinguish the effects of stable exchange rates from the impact of the particular rates selected. In the case of the invisible accounts, we may speculate that the balance was little affected by the parity actually adopted, but considerably strengthened by the restoration of stability.

[29] For weekly exchange rate quotations, see Einzig (1937).

[30] Sayers (1957, p. 21); Strange (1971, p. 49).

for low rates to ease the task of debt management, created the potential for serious political conflict.[31] As evidence of this conflict surfaced, public perception of monetary policy was fundamentally transformed. In the early 1920s, 'the prevailing view of monetary policy was neither controversial nor to be considered as intimately connected with unemployment. . . .'[32] By the end of the 1920s considerable uneasiness about the internal repercussions of monetary policy had developed, and it was suggested in particular that, in the conduct of monetary policy, 'the interests of finance and industry are divergent. . . .'[33] In 1936, after the advent of 'cheap money', J. Henry Richardson wrote, 'Few economic questions have received so much attention during recent years as monetary policy.'[34]

In the nineteenth century, the classic response to a drop in the exchange towards the gold export point, the level at which it became profitable to ship gold abroad, was a rise in Bank rate. Bank rate was the lowest rate at which the Bank of England was prepared to make loans to discount houses, either by rediscounting or by lending against securities.[35] While the Bank normally stood ready to act as lender of last resort, during the 1920s, as in previous decades, actual borrowing was quite limited. Maintenance of a high Bank rate was not designed to reduce prices and thereby strengthen the long-run competitive position of British industry; rather, it was relied upon to attract capital inflows whenever the exchange rate weakened.[36] In order to achieve the desired inflow of short-term funds, the Bank kept its discount rate high relative to both prewar and foreign standards. On a quarterly average basis, Bank rate ranged from 4.3 to 5.6 per cent during the years of the interwar gold standard.[37] Over the first part of this period, from 1925 to 1927, Bank rate in London consistently exceeded the Federal Reserve's discount rate by 0.5 to 1.5 percentage points. Only in the final two quarters of 1928 did the American rate exceed the British rate, and then by a mere half a percentage point.

Since the Bank of England has been accused of ignorance of the domestic repercussions of its monetary policies, it is useful to review its operating procedures.[38] Bank of England policy was formulated by rules

[31] See below, pp. 45–6, 63–4.

[32] Hancock (1962, p. 333).

[33] *Westminister Bank Review* (November 1929), p. 3.

[34] Richardson (1936, p. 32).

[35] The Bank did not always actually lend at Bank rate. None the less, the official rate provides a useful if imperfect measure of the cost of its discounts.

[36] For the Bank's own description of its use of Bank rate prior to 1914, see National Monetary Commission (1910).

[37] Previously, Bank rate had been higher only during wartime and during financial crises at home or abroad: in 1847, 1854–57, 1861, 1866, 1907, and 1913–21.

[38] Skidelsky (1967, p. 14) asserts that the Bank of England simply was ignorant of the effects of its monetary initiatives on the economy. Similarly, Williams (1959, pp. 39,

of thumb: in setting the discount rate, as in its other operations, the Bank focused on the exchange rate, referring also to mitigating factors such as the size of the gold reserve and the time of year. Only occasionally did the Bank take note of statistical indicators beyond the foreign exchange and gold markets.[39]

Sympathetic observers of the Bank of England defended its penchant for adjusting Bank rate in response to conditions in the gold and foreign exchange markets by arguing that supply and demand could be relied upon to restore equilibrium in domestic labour and commodity markets. For those whose primary concern was exchange stability, this was partly an argument of convenience: it is difficult to identify individuals who actually believed that monetary policy had no impact on internal conditions. Promoting industrial expansion and contributing to the reduction of unemployment figured among the objectives of at least some of those within the Bank. But if there was genuine concern within the Bank for the state of the British economy, the immediate fear was that failure to respond to domestic developments would give rise to political pressures which ultimately might undermine the Bank's independence.[40] Thus, the vigour with which the Bank responded to external disturbances depended on domestic developments. On a number of occasions after 1925, internal conditions left the Bank hesitant to adjust its rate in response to external events. In the second half of 1928, for example, Bank rate was not used to stem the outflow of funds to the United States.[41] To strengthen Britain's external position while minimizing the internal repercussions, the authorities relied instead on less conspicuous measures, such as direct intervention in the gold and foreign exchange markets, impediments to short- and long-term lending abroad, and foreign borrowing. The 38 months following the one-half-point increase in Bank rate in December 1925 are remarkable for the fact that only one further change in the discount rate took place.

The view that Governor Norman was oblivious to the domestic effects of a high Bank rate usually is based upon his testimony before the Chamberlain-Bradbury Committee on the Currency and Bank of England Note Issues in 1924 and 1925 and the Macmillian Committee on Finance and Industry early in 1930.[42] On the first occasion, Norman suggested that the high Bank rate and dear money required to achieve a

---

44) suggests that 'Norman interpreted monetary policy in the short-run sense and tended to ignore the long-run implications of policies. He . . . failed to recognize explicitly that the state of trade and the use of money are both influenced by the price of money.' For a sharply contrasting view, see Scammell (1957, p. 41).

[39] A detailed analysis of the Bank's operating procedures is in Moggridge (1972, ch. 6).

[40] Sayers (1979, p. 201).

[41] Mowat (1955, p. 357); Clay (1957, p. 241); Sayers (1976, Volume 1, pp. 217–25).

[42] Moggridge (1969, chapter 2) provides a detailed analysis of the Chamberlain–Bradbury Committee's proceedings.

return to gold might lead to some contraction, but that the impact on industry would not be catastrophic.[43] On the second occasion, he maintained that the ill effects of a high Bank rate on British trade and industry were 'more psychological than real'.[44] He argued that Bank rate affected industry and trade only when a high rate was maintained for extended periods, and emphasized the view, popular within the Bank, that the impact of its initiatives was confined to the short side of British financial markets. Only when prodded by Keynes did he admit that there existed circumstances in which a high Bank rate might contribute to domestic unemployment and industrial difficulties. The Bank had developed a well articulated view of the channels through which changes in its rate affected British industry. Officials argued that only when Bank rate exceeded a certain crucial threshold did it begin to affect short-term interest rates, and only when it remained above that threshold for extended periods were long-term rates affected. They held that Bank rate had little if any effect on the cost of commercial bank loans and overdrafts until it exceeded 4 per cent.[45] Although overdrafts were extended at rates 1 per cent above Bank rate, and although exceptions sometimes were made for favoured customers and for those able to put up gilt-edged securities as collateral, these rates normally were subject to a floor of 5 per cent. (In the case of larger customers the markup was usually taken as ½ per cent with a floor of 4½ per cent.) Since Bank rate remained at or below 4 per cent for portions of 1925, 1930 and 1931, supporters of Bank policy could argue that in such instances the cost of credit obtained in this manner was unaffected by changes in the Bank of England's discount policy.[46]

Discussions of monetary policy, phrased in terms of interest rates, revolved around the question of how changes in the cost of credit affected British industry. There was also some concern that high interest rates were associated with reductions in the availability of funds: for example, the Macmillan Committee considered the effects of credit

[43] Moggridge (1969, p. 27).

[44] Norman's evidence before the Macmillan Committee is reprinted in Sayers (1976, volume 3, pp. 116–256) and criticized by Williams (1959, *passim*). See also Einzig (1932). Questions 3317–3517 from Norman's evidence of 26 March 1930 touch on Norman's views of the relationship between Bank of England policy and the state of trade and industry. See especially the interchange between Keynes and Norman in Questions 3377–3402.

[45] Thus, see Sir Ernest Harvey's evidence before the Macmillan Committee reprinted in Sayers (1976, volume 3, pp. 117–71, 218–28), especially Question 7597.

[46] This account of British banking practice draws on Balogh (1947, p. 75). See also Brown (1938, p. 57). For a sceptical view, in which it is argued that loan and overdraft rates exhibited considerably greater flexibility than this stylized account suggests, see Keynes (1930, ch. 37) and Hawtrey (1938, pp. 57–62). See also Courakis (1981, pp. 114–15).

rationing, particularly as it affected relatively small enterprises.[47] Given contemporary views of the channels through which financial policy operated on the economy, members of the Committee devoted more attention to the cost and availability of credit than to the fluctuation of the monetary base, despite the fact that the policies pursued by the authorities prior to the return to gold had important implications for the volume of currency and deposits. Indeed, in 1930 Deputy Governor Harvey pointed out that, excepting the semi-annual reports of the clearing banks, the Bank of England knew few details about the fluctuation of financial aggregates.[48] Yet between the first quarter of 1920 and the first quarter of 1925, the stock of high-powered money (currency plus reserves of the ten London clearing banks) declined by 11 per cent, while the broad measure of money (currency plus total deposits of the ten London clearing banks) fell by more than 7 per cent.[49]

Among the steadiest critics of the Bank of England's credit policies was the British Treasury. While for the Bank it was more important 'to get the debt firmly held than to get it cheaply held', the Treasury attached great weight to the cost of debt service.[50] The principal goal of Treasury policy in the 1920s was to reduce the burden of debt service charges (which rose from 11 per cent of central government spending in 1913 to 24 per cent in 1920 and more than 40 per cent by the end of the decade) through conversion of the 5 per cent government loans of 1917 at lower interest rates.[51] Hence, between 1925 and 1929 the Treasury consistently opposed Bank of England initiatives that raised the price and reduced the availability of credit.[52] Churchill, for example, objected strenuously to each rise in Bank rate that took place during his tenure as Chancellor of the Exchequer, thereby contributing greatly to the politicization of Bank rate. Given the Treasury's goal of converting the debt, great importance was attached to measures that would reduce the level of long-term interest rates. This explains the Treasury's desire to balance the budget by reducing government expenditure. By the second half of the 1920s, the Treasury's two primary concerns had become day-to-day debt management and control of the expenditure of other

47 Committee on Finance and Industry (1931). See also Brown (1940, p. 666) and Wright (1981, p. 283).

48 Sir Ernest Harvey's Macmillan Committee Evidence (Q7598), 2 July 1930.

49 Committee on Finance and Industry (1931). See also above, p. 30, and *Bank of England Statistical Summary* (various issues). Monetary fluctuations in this period are considered in detail in Howson (1975, pp. 17–19 and 43).

50 Sayers (1976, volume 1, pp. 114–15).

51 As a percentage of gross national product, debt service leapt from 1 per cent in 1913 to 7 per cent in 1930. Details on the debt are provided in Financial Secretary to the Treasury (1932) and Middleton (1981, p. 54) and are summarized in table 3.3.

52 See Howson (1975, chapter 3).

departments. In subsequent years, it was roundly criticized for permitting its outlook to be 'narrowly limited by budgetary considerations'.[53]

Trends in government expenditure and receipts are summarized in table 3.3. The budget surplus achieved in 1920 arose from a substantial increase in tax rates, while the surpluses of 1921–23 resulted from measures to hold down government spending, both to aid debt conversion and to assist the Bank in its effort to return to gold. The deficits of 1926 and 1930–31 occurred despite continued austerity measures and reflected unusual circumstances: the General Strike and the impact of the depression, respectively.[54]

Given its preoccupation with debt management and expenditure control, the Treasury had a natural sympathy for the argument that public spending and public employment were incapable of mitigating the depression in trade and industry. Historians have asserted that Treasury antipathy towards expansionary fiscal measures was based upon explicit theoretical foundations, usually attributed to R. G. Hawtrey, Treasury Director of Financial Enquiries. By 1929, it is said, 'The official Treasury [coolness] . . . on public works as a solution to unemployment . . . had hardened into the dogma known as the "Treasury view".'[55] Churchill's budget speech of that year is cited as a typical statement of that view:

> It is orthodox Treasury dogma, steadfastly held, that whatever might be the political or social advantages, very little additional employment can, in fact, and as a general rule, be created by State borrowing and expenditure.[56]

Several variants of this view can be discerned in the popular debate over economic policy. One version simply did not acknowledge the existence of involuntary unemployment. Since it was held that existing resources seeking employment were continuously fully employed, it followed that public spending merely crowded out a corresponding amount of private spending. In other variants of this view, it was argued that public spending could alter only the intertemporal distribution of employment; the implication of this position was that government policies designed to stimulate employment were warranted only to the extent that those who gained employment in the present were more deserving than those who lost it in the future.[57]

[53] Amery (1955, volume 3, p. 50). On Treasury policy, see also Howson (1975), Middleton (1982), Moggridge (1972), Skidelsky (1967) and Winch (1969).

[54] Howson (1975, p. 42). The budget is adjusted to a constant employment basis by Middleton (1981).

[55] Winch (1969, p. 109); see also Tomlinson (1981, chapter 5).

[56] House of Commons Debates, 15 April 1929, p. 54; quoted in Winch (1969, p. 109).

[57] On the development of these arguments, see Hawtrey (1925, 1933). Recently, the view that much unemployment in the 1920s was voluntary in nature has enjoyed renewed popularity; see Benjamin and Kochin (1979).

TABLE 3.3 Budget of combined public authorities, 1920–37[a]

(£ million)

	Receipts		Expenditures		Surplus (+) or Deficit (−)	Central government saving	Central govt budget balance on a constant-employment basis
	Taxes (1)	*Other* (2)	*Debt service* (3)	*Other* (4)	(5)	(6)	(7)
1920	1103	99	343	783	76	77	–
1921	1033	172	333	832	40	25	–
1922	943	172	340	712	63	30	–
1923	857	179	349	611	76	44	–
1924	795	171	349	595	22	−3	–
1925	801	189	348	626	16	−24	–
1926	781	211	366	652	−26	−54	–
1927	795	234	345	644	40	−36	–
1928	799	246	357	652	36	−53	–
1929	794	254	363	673	12	−56	–
1930	784	266	354	711	−15	−98	40
1931	809	249	334	752	−28	−113	92
1932	867	231	332	743	23	−48	120
1933	825	232	295	737	25	−25	162
1934	831	239	277	753	40	11	147
1935	842	244	277	798	11	40	99
1936	878	251	272	841	16	−43	50
1937	939	257	278	918	0	−55	7

[a] Before depreciation and stock appreciation. Excludes public corporations. Except for columns (6) and (7) all figures apply to the combined public authorities

Source: columns (1)–(5) calculated from Feinstein (1972, table 14, p. T35); column (7) is calculated by adjusting the figures in Middleton (1981) to a calendar year basis. The 'constant-employment basis' corresponds to unemployment rates of 10.95 per cent of the insured and 7.8 per cent of the civilian labour force. Column (6) is from London and Cambridge Economic Service, *The British Economy: Key Statistics, 1900–1970* (n.d.), p. 12.

Thus the return to gold, and ensuing exchange rate and balance of payments difficulties, severely restricted the range of permissible options for dealing with unemployment. Even Keynes and the few others who had opposed the return to gold in 1925 accepted \$4.86 as an economic fact of life and framed their subsequent recommendations accordingly. The only proposal to command widespread support was the call for rationalization of industry, an inadequately defined plan to restructure industry so as to produce an 'export breakthrough' much like that hoped for in the 1960s.

Initial difficulties

Such were the circumstances and the policy orientation when Britain experienced the first hint of exchange market difficulties in 1927. Compared with what followed, 1926 had not been a difficult year for the Bank of England. Sterling's strength had resulted from the combined effects of a high Bank rate in London and continued flight from the French franc. However, French political uncertainty was largely resolved in the summer of 1926. With the stabilization of the franc in December of that year at a rate that, if anything, undervalued the French currency, France suddenly was perceived as an attractive haven for funds. By the end of 1926, the Bank of France was forced repeatedly to sell francs to prevent the exchange rate from appreciating.[58]

The exchange market difficulties of 1927 marked the first of three critical junctures in the history of the interwar gold standard. Each successive episode – 1927, 1929 and 1931 – was of increasing severity, and the last, of course, proved fatal. As a prelude to 1931, it is instructive to analyse these earlier episodes and to examine the authorities' response to each.

The 1927 exchange rate difficulties had both internal and external origins. The stability of sterling was undermined initially by the sudden decline in British exports that accompanied industrial unrest in 1926. Even more unsettling was the manner in which domestic and foreign developments contrived to create a temporary deterioration in the capital account of the balance of payments. The General Strike and attendant political uncertainties rendered London a less desirable repository for short-term funds, while currency stabilization abroad provided an alternative to sterling deposits by making available an elastic supply of foreign government securities combining relatively low risk with high yield.[59] Investment in the New York stock market came to

[58] Eichengreen (1982, p. 76).

[59] Although stabilization of the French franc is the most important example, by 1926 some 35 currencies had been stabilized for at least a year: see Yeager (1966, p. 286).

appear increasingly attractive over the course of 1927. Although the Bank of England was disturbed by the steady transfer of funds abroad, Governor Norman was reluctant to use Bank rate to stem the outflow because of the anticipated effects of a high discount rate on a slowly growing economy.

Superimposed upon an intrinsically difficult situation were unanticipated financial manoeuvres by the Bank of France. Following *de facto* stabilization of the franc in 1926, the Bank of France had initiated steps to augment its gold reserve by liquidating its holdings of convertible foreign exchange. Above all, the French authorities wished to avoid any repetition of their experiences with depreciation in 1923 and 1926 by building up an unassailable gold reserve. Yet, at the same time, exchange rate appreciation was not desired. The dominant contingent within the Bank of France remained concerned with the defence of French industry's competitive position. Moreau's objective was to deter speculative purchases of the franc which might create pressure for revaluation.[60] The potential for speculative inflows was considerable, for there were still those who questioned whether the franc should be stabilized *de jure* at its current level and argued in favour of a return to the prewar parity.[61] However, the majority view was that speculative purchases of French assets should be discouraged by shifting the burden of adjustment to London. Once conditions in the London money market were tightened, British loans to Amsterdam and Berlin would be recalled, and Paris would be relieved of the inflow of funds both from London and from other continental financial centres. In part to induce a Bank rate increase by the Bank of England, the Bank of France began to convert large blocks of its sterling balances, which probably matched in value the Bank of England's entire gold reserve. In May, Emile Moreau, the governor of the Bank of France, requested that the Bank of England undertake to acquire £3 million weekly in gold to be made available for export to France.

The Bank of England had reason to resist any proposal for an increase in Bank rate. Partly in response to pressures exerted by Winston Churchill, the Conservative Chancellor of the Exchequer, the Bank had only just managed to reduce Bank rate to 4½ per cent in April. Suddenly to reverse that decision threatened to create grave political difficulties.[62] This conflict provided the backdrop for Norman's visit to Paris on 27 May 1927.[63] Two aspects of Norman's discussions with French officials are revealing. Norman pointedly warned Moreau of the possibility that

[60] See Moreau (1954, p. 601).

[61] *Ibid*. Poincaré was among those who argued for appreciation. See Sauvy (1965, volume 1, pp. 88–92); Clarke (1967, p. 110).

[62] See Boyce (1982, p. 2); Moreau (1954, p. 324).

[63] For accounts of this episode, see Clay (1957, pp. 228–31); Clarke (1967, pp. 117–18); Kindleberger (1973, pp. 65–6); van der Wee and Tavernier (1975, p. 236).

the Bank of France's actions could force Britain to abandon the existing parity and thereby undermine the entire gold standard edifice. He also indicated that the Bank of England felt constrained in its response by the difficulties experienced by British industry.[64] It was clear that the Bank of England was unwilling to sacrificc British industry on the altar of the gold standard. And although the Bank of France wished to shift the burden of adjustment abroad, it had no desire to force Britain off gold. Eventually Moreau became convinced of the precariousness of the British position. The Bank of France redirected its demand for gold to New York and decided for the moment to maintain a diversified portfolio of gold, dollars, sterling and other assets. This, along with a not entirely unrelated shift in short-term capital flows, relieved the pressure on London.[65]

This episode had demonstrated sterling's susceptibility to external pressure and revealed the Bank of England's reluctance to defend the exchange rate at any cost. It led D. H. Robertson to warn,

> In the judgement of the present writer, conditions might arise in which it would be imperative to take the bull by the horns and to remind our creditor classes that their contracts are in terms of pounds sterling and not of gold: but for this autumn of 1928 he is not prepared to plump boldly for such a course.[66]

These lessons were driven home by the next exchange market crisis. The Bank of England's battle with the exchange rate effects of the New York stock market boom and the drain of French balances from London began in earnest in the summer of 1928. From January to June the Bank gained £20 million of gold, especially once *de jure* stabilization in France eliminated any remaining hope for an appreciation of the franc. However, the entire increment to the gold reserve was lost by the end of the year. After a period of strength which lasted through July, spot sterling in New York hovered between \$4.85½ and \$4.84¾ during the last five months of 1928. Sterling commanded a premium on the forward market, reflecting speculators' confidence that these pressures were largely seasonal and that the Bank of England remained committed to the defence of the existing parity. Yet the Bank's response was noteworthy primarily for the absence of a rise in Bank rate. Out of concern for the state of industry, Norman relied instead upon moral suasion and direct intervention in the market to stabilize the exchange rate, and

64 Moreau (1954, pp. 324–5). The Bank's desire to protect British industry from the effects of restrictive credit conditions is similarly described in Sayers (1976, volume 1, pp. 218–21). Norman's awareness of the political ramifications of a rise in Bank rate is discussed in Brown (1940, p. 457).

65 Bouvier (1981, p. 15).

66 Robertson (1928, p. 128).

Bank rate remained steady throughout the year at 4.5 per cent. Repeatedly, Norman drew upon the Bank of England's hidden foreign exchange, selling off more than £20 million worth of its dollar reserves in return for sterling to assist the Federal Reserve in its attempts to control the dollar–pound rate.[67]

As the effects of the New York Stock Exchange boom spread to other financial centres, pressure on sterling continued to mount. In the face of the New York market's seemingly insatiable appetite for capital, London was forced to satisfy German and French demands for finance. High interest rates in New York induced Berlin to borrow from London and Paris, leading Paris to withdraw balances from London in order to place them in Berlin. The crisis continued to intensify despite the decline in primary commodity prices that led to an improvement in Britain's terms of trade and helped to maintain the strength of her current account.

Eventually, illiquidity in the world's primary producing regions intensified the pressure on sterling. A disturbing development in international commodity markets in the 1920s was the tendency of the supply of many agricultural products to grow more rapidly than demand.[68] As with Britain's staple trades, the war had disrupted normal channels of international trade and induced many countries, including the United States, which traditionally had relied on imports for a large proportion of supply, to expand domestic production. The problem of excess supply was particularly severe after 1927, and in consequence downward pressure on primary product prices was considerable. Not all primary product prices moved together: for example, the market for industrial materials and animal products generally remained buoyant.[69] However, the prices of many important foodstuffs trended downward, wheat, sugar, wool and lard being prominent examples.

The declining prices of agricultural commodities forced large current account deficits on most members of the outer sterling area. The Bank for International Settlements presents estimates of £81 million in 1928 and £99 milllion in 1929 for the current account deficits of the outer sterling area. For 1928 the deficit of the outer sterling area erases more than 80 per cent of the UK's current account surplus, while for 1929 it more than offsets the surplus of the UK, rendering the entire sterling area dependent for balance of payments equilibrium on capital inflows from other

[67] Jones (1935, pp. 26–7); Clay (1957, p. 238). Under the Currency and Bank Notes Act of 1928, the Bank had an obligation to inform the Treasury only of foreign exchange held in the Issue Department. The Bank's hidden reserves, listed under 'Other Securities' in the Banking Department, contained foreign assets (primarily US dollars in the form of bank balances and US Treasury bills) acquired surreptitiously for the purpose of facilitating exchange market intervention.

[68] For statistics, see League of Nations (1945, pp. 85–6).

[69] See Lewis (1949, p. 45).

countries.[70] While these estimates are only approximate and are subject to a wide margin of error, the implication that the sterling area's current account position was continuing to weaken seems beyond dispute. Moreover, many of these nations had borrowed abroad in order to ease the transition to peace time production and in the absence of capital inflows found it difficult to make interest payments without depleting their reserves of foreign exchange, which they usually held as sterling balances in London. According to the Bank for International Settlements (BIS), the independent countries of the sterling area other than the UK ran deficits on invisibles account in the range of £100 million per annum in this period, which represented primarily interest payments on outstanding debt. Before 1928–29, earnings from commodity exports rendered these debt service payments manageable. In 1929, by all indications, the slump in primary commodity prices moved the trade balances of the independent sterling area countries into deficit, although earnings from gold exports, amounting to roughly half the value of debt service, were maintained.

The case of Australia is illustrative. Between 1923 and 1928, Australia ran trade balance deficits of £69 million, and the nominal value of her external debt rose by 35 per cent.[71] With the collapse of the world prices of wool and wheat, Australia was again forced to approach London brokers for loans. Eventually, one such request, which coincided in April 1929 with the height of the New York stock market boom, was not taken up by the market. Fears of default rendered the market willing to make new loans only at interest rates the Australian authorities considered prohibitive; in 1929–30 Australia's net borrowings amounted to a mere £1.7 million, in comparison with net additions of more than £33 million per annum over the preceding three years. Despite measures to restrict gold export and ration sterling, with the collapse of primary commodity prices the Australian authorities found it increasingly difficult after December 1929 to maintain their peg against the pound, and devaluation ensued. In several such instances, liquidity crises caused governments to liquidate sterling balances traditionally maintained in London, thereby aggravating the drain of gold and foreign exchange arising from the deficits of the independent countries and dependent territories of the sterling area.

These developments created growing concern within the Bank of England for the future of the gold standard. In February 1929 Norman visited New York, but was unable to convince the American authorities that a rise in the Federal Reserve's discount rate was needed to check

[70] Williams (1963, p. 97); Bank for International Settlements (1953, p. 28). Pressnell (1978) is more cautious in his assessment of the position of the sterling area, suggesting only that sterling area countries moved into deficit in 1929.

[71] See Harris (1931, pp. 475–92); Dalton (1931, pp. 6–7); Clay (1957, pp. 357–8); Kindleberger (1973, chapter 4).

the stock market boom and lay the groundwork for an eventual reduction in market interest rates. The failure of these negotiations rendered Norman increasingly pessimistic about the viability of the existing parity.[72] However, Norman and his colleagues in the Bank bore these fears alone; there is little evidence that their concern for the future of the gold standard parity was shared by officials in the Treasury and the Board of Trade, or by ministers. The warnings that Norman communicated to government officials and to George Harrison, the newly appointed governor of the Federal Reserve Bank of New York, that Britain might be forced off the gold standard, instigated no substantive change in policy at home or abroad.[73]

With Norman's failure to obtain a rise in American discount rates, the drain on British reserves mounted. Allegiance weakened within the Bank to the 4.5 per cent Bank rate, and expectations of higher interest rates rendered difficult the Treasury's attempts to place its bill issue. In February this finally forced upon the Bank a one percentage point increase in Bank rate. While half a point might have helped some months earlier, the one point increase in February succeeded in stemming gold losses only temporarily. With the contraction of the new issue market and the reimposition of controls on foreign issues, a number of countries began to liquidate their sterling balances.[74] Negotiations over reparations at the Hague Conference and new manoeuvres by the Bank of France heightened the uncertainty. A further rise in Bank rate was widely anticipated, and the fact that it did not occur has been attributed to political pressures.[75]

The dollar–pound rate remained at or only slightly above the gold export point from June through much of September, and the Bank of England lost £27 million of gold in the third quarter of 1929. The Bank of France continued to absorb gold at an alarming rate. In September and October the Bank of England's gold and foreign exchange reserves reached their lowest level prior to the September 1931 crisis. For much of the summer, political considerations again led the Bank to delay raising Bank rate, forcing it to make large purchases of successive issues of Treasury bills and to intervene with sales of hidden dollar reserves. However, in September the Hatry scandal (involving the collapse of an industrial empire built with loans backed by fraudulent collateral) and Snowden's return from the Hague Reparations Conference provided the occasion for a one point increase to 6.5 per cent, which proved effective owing largely to its fortuitous coincidence with the collapse of the New York stock market boom.[76]

[72] Moggridge (1972, p. 137).
[73] Clay (1957, p. 252); Boyce (1982, p. 2).
[74] Clarke (1967, p. 150); Sayers (1976, volume 1, p. 228).
[75] Clarke (1967, p. 167); Moggridge (1972, p. 138); Sayers (1976, volume 1, pp. 226–7).
[76] *The Economist*, 28 September 1929, pp. 362–3. See also Hatry (1938).

Once more, the period of crisis was followed by an interlude of calm lasting approximately a year. Following the collapse of the New York market, interest rates, commodity prices and industrial activity all declined rapidly, first in North America but soon in other parts of the world as well. This reduction in economic activity relieved the pressure on London. Between October 1929 and October 1930 spot sterling frequently traded at a premium in New York. From November 1929 onward the Bank of England was able to re-acquire gold, and by May 1930 the gold reserve, which had dipped to an alarming £129 million the previous October, was again comfortably above the 'Cunliffe minimum' of £150 million. From May 1930 the Bank was also able to augment its foreign exchange reserves. Bank rate was reduced in successive steps to 3 per cent, but no further reductions took place after May 1930, owing to concern for the long-term stability of sterling. Although the foreign exchange market was never far from Norman's mind, not until the final three months of 1930 did fears for the future of sterling again reach the point where they would dictate the Bank's actions.[77]

We must understand the authorities' perception of the exchange rate crises of 1927 and 1929 before we can attempt to interpret their actions during the period leading up to devaluation in 1931. In retrospect, the interwar gold standard system exhibited obvious weaknesses which rendered it vulnerable to destabilizing shocks and drastically reduced its resiliency. However, many of these changes in the operation of the gold standard were imperfectly appreciated by ministers and by Bank and Treasury officials. There was a tendency to attribute each crisis to exceptional circumstances: to unreasonable demands for gold by foreign central banks in 1927; to the coincidence of a stock market boom in a foreign financial centre and illiquidity in primary producing regions in 1929; and to the combination of global economic depression and European financial instability in the summer of 1931.

Treasury and Bank of England officials were aware that the war had transformed the structure of British financial markets and sharpened the division between Bank and Treasury objectives. No longer was the London money market dominated by commercial paper. The war had been responsible for the rise of the Treasury bill: prior to 1914 the annual issue of Treasury bills rarely exceeded £30 million, whereas it fluctuated for most of the 1920s in the range of £600–£800 million annually.[78] In earlier periods, Treasury bills amounted to less than 1 per cent of total bills outstanding, but in the 1920s the value of Treasury bills

77 Sayers (1976, volume 1, p. 233). Howson (1975, p. 67) paints a somewhat bleaker picture of the Bank's directors' perception of exchange market conditions. See also Clarke (1967, pp. 175–8).

78 Dacey (1958, p. 60); Balogh (1947, p. 191); Sir Ernest Harvey's Macmillan Committee Evidence (1930), Q465. See also Lord Bradbury's Minute of Dissent from the Macmillan Committee Report: Committee on Finance and Industry (1931, pp. 274-5).

in circulation consistently exceeded the value of commercial bills. This change in the composition of personal and clearing bank portfolios had implications for the conduct and co-ordination of policy.

Under normal circumstances the large quantity of Treasury bills in circulation provided the Bank a convenient instrument for intervening in the London market, but in periods of stress it rendered monetary control difficult. Whenever exchange market difficulties arose, the Bank of England contemplated its option of raising Bank rate. However, if such a rise in Bank rate was anticipated by the market, commercial banks hesitated to purchase new Treasury issues until it actually took place, so as to avoid the capital losses that would result from a rise in market interest rates. At the same time, foreigners switched out of sterling bills and into bank deposits. In such instances, the Bank of England was forced to purchase Treasury issues, injecting sterling into the banking system and compromising the intent of its own restrictive policy.[79] In the words of a contemporary, 'The existence of Treasury liabilities of this character upon so substantial a scale in the period following the return to gold in 1925 complicated very greatly, if it did not render practically impossible, the task of the monetary authorities in administering the gold standard.'[80]

The Labour government's economic advisors were aware that Great Britain's capacity to withstand speculative crises was weaker than had been the case under the classical gold standard. Before the war, Britain had been a net creditor in long-term securities to an extent that dwarfed any net liability in short-term obligations. But to finance the war effort, between £200 and £300 millions' worth of short-term assets had been liquidated. The basic balance deficits of the 1920s further increased the ratio of short-term liabilities to short-term assets. The Macmillan Committee's incomplete estimates indicated that in March 1931 British short-term liabilities to foreigners included at least £407 million of sterling bills and deposits held in London. The ready availability of sterling bills and deposits was particularly attractive to foreign investors, since there was little danger of a capital loss over the relevant holding period. Britain's known short-term assets included £153 million of sterling bills accepted on foreign account, plus a comparable amount of gold in the hands of the Bank of England (although only a small portion of this gold reserve normally was available to defend sterling against speculation).[81] Thus Britain was known to be a net debtor on short-term account to the extent of £100 million. Had the approximately £350 million of sterling bills held by foreign banks and investors in their own custody, less £33.3 million of Bank of England hidden foreign exchange

[79] Pollard (1969, p. 222); Sayers (1976, volume 1, pp. 298–313); Dimsdale (1981, pp. 307–8); Brown (1940, pp. 652–3).

[80] Hall (1935, pp. 10–11).

[81] Committee on Finance and Industry (1931, p. 112).

reserves, been added to this total, Britain's net short-term position would have appeared even more alarming.[82] While London's short-term liabilities did not by themselves undermine the stability of the gold standard, their existence rendered confidence essential to the maintenance of the system.

The anatomy of crisis

When the second Labour government took office in June 1929, the burning issue of the day was not the stability of the exchange rate but the level of unemployment. By June the number of insured persons recorded as unemployed had fallen to 1.16 million (9.6 per cent of the insured labour force) from a peak of more than 1.42 million (12.2 per cent of the insured labour force) reached in January 1929.[83] While this effect was largely seasonal, unemployment increased only slightly over the summer, providing grounds for hope within the government that the worst was over. Labour ministers had no reason to anticipate the effects of the Great Depression, which found reflection in Britain's unemployment statistics in the final quarter of 1929. According to the National Bureau of Economic Research, Britain passed the peak of its reference cycle in July of that year.[84] Within 12 months of that turning point, the numbers unemployed nearly doubled.

The exchange rate frequently occupied the attention of Labour ministers and their advisors, but only as a constraint upon policies for dealing with internal problems. Although one might assume that Labour ministers, with socialist principles in hand, would be less inclined than their predecessors to adhere strictly to financial orthodoxy, there is no evidence that the heterodox possibility of devaluation was ever contemplated.[85] In part, this mirrored the inflexibility of Philip Snowden, Labour's Chancellor of the Exchequer. To a large extent, however, it reflected the ministers' belief that allegiance to sound finance was necessary to reassure the financial community of the new government's reputability.

Attitudes toward devaluation changed little over the two-year period preceding the 1931 financial crisis. The unanimity of public and private opinion at the beginning of 1930 is apparent in the evidence heard by the Macmillan Committee. Set up to carry out Labour's electoral pledge to inquire into the relations between finance and industry, the Macmillan Committee opened its hearings at a time when sterling was exhibiting

[82] Sayers (1976, volume 2, p. 389). These developments are further discussed by Kindleberger (1937, pp. 127–30). See also Keynes (1932, p. 148).
[83] Ministry of Labour (1934, p. 52).
[84] Burns and Mitchell (1946, p. 79).
[85] Skidelsky (1967, pp. 248–9).

unusual strength. Of the Committee's witnesses, only Keynes and Hawtrey seriously questioned whether the goal of exchange rate stability might properly be subordinated to price stability. Keynes played a prominent role in the proceedings of the Committee, in examining witnesses and ultimately in shaping its report. He introduced into the record a variety of iconoclastic proposals for dealing with unemployment. These included import duties, export bounties, import boards, tax cuts, public investment, subsidies to private investment, an embargo on foreign loans and measures to reduce interest rates. Keynes argued that Britain's economic troubles could be traced to the high interest rates that central banks maintained to defend their exchange rates. These high interest rates depressed investment, particularly residential construction and fixed investment in industry, while, to a somewhat lesser extent, they encouraged saving, thereby reducing demand for both consumer and producers' goods. This resulted in downward pressure on commodity prices which, in conjunction with the limited flexibility of wages, gave rise to unemployment.[86]

A noteworthy aspect of Keynes's evidence is his rejection of devaluation as a solution to the unemployment problem. Despite his earlier opposition to the return to gold, in 1930 Keynes was unwilling to advocate abandoning the existing parity:

> If I were the drafter of the Report I should not recommend going off the gold standard at this moment; not until I had tried other expedients, but I should not have complete confidence in the efficacy of these alternatives. Meanwhile I think the dangers of going off are such, that I would not even talk about it.[87]

In Keynes's view, devaluation would undermine Britain's international financial position and hinder the fight against deflation. For once Keynes and the rest of the profession were in agreement: in G. C. Allen's canvass of economists in the summer of 1930, he encountered only two – Hawtrey of the Treasury and J. W. F. Rowe of Cambridge – who considered devaluation a permissible option. As time passed, devaluation was increasingly discussed. In a letter composed while he was involved in drafting the Macmillan Committee's report, Keynes commented with surprise on 'for the first time in my experience . . . a good deal of more or less open talk about devaluation of sterling'.[88]

To understand just how strongly Keynes opposed devaluation at this point, it is instructive to recall that his evidence included an admission of

[86] Keynes's fullest exposition of these views (further elaborated in Keynes, 1930), is in PRO T200/4, pp. 38–46, 21 February 1930, recently reprinted in Keynes (1981, pp. 66–93).

[87] Ibid., p. 29.

[88] Allen (1975, p. 42); 'Letter to Walter Case', 21 February 1931, in Keynes (1981, p. 485).

hesitant support for a tariff. The idea of restricting international trade was antithetical to a free trade tradition that stretched back to Britain's abolition of the Corn Laws in 1846. One reason Keynes was identified with the Free Trade cause was the position he had taken in the 1923 general election. In an article published that year in the *Nation and Athenaeum*, Keynes had labelled the claim that a tariff can be used for employment purposes 'the Protectionist fallacy in its grossest and crudest form'.[89] In February 1930 Keynes acknowledged a change of heart. His analysis of British unemployment led him to conclude that the solution lay in any measure that would stimulate the demand for domestic goods and raise producers' prices relative to costs. None the less, given his opposition to devaluation, the range of permissible options was limited by the balance of payments constraint. The proposals Keynes presented to the Macmillan Committee fell into four broad categories: 'a great National Treaty among ourselves' to reduce the general level of wages and other production costs; a system of subsidies or 'bounties' for domestic industry; measures to promote productive efficiency, known as 'rationalization'; and an across-the-board tariff on imports into Britain.

Throughout the Committee's deliberations, the issue of protection served as a litmus test of the strength of sentiment opposing devaluation. During the drafting discussion of November 1930, Ernest Bevin, soon to emerge as the leading advocate of devaluation, found that both he and Lord Bradbury, a staunch defender of economic orthodoxy, preferred devaluation to tampering with free trade.[90]

When Governor Norman appeared before the Macmillan Committee in March 1930, devaluation was alluded to only indirectly. Upon being asked by Macmillan, 'In your opinion, I gather, the advantages of maintaining the international position outweigh in the public interest the internal disadvantages which may accrue from the use of the means at your disposal?' Norman replied:

> the disadvantages of the internal position are relatively small compared with the advantages to the external position. . . . we are still to a large extent international bankers. We have great international trade and commerce out of which I believe considerable profit accrues to the country; we do maintain huge international markets . . . and the confidence and credit which go with them are in the long run greatly to the interest of industry as well as to the interest of finance and commerce.[91]

Even less consideration was devoted to the possibility of devaluation

[89] *Nation and Athenaeum* (1 December 1923, p. 336). Keynes's own reflections on his early views appear in Keynes (1936, p. 334). For further discussion of Keynes's views on this issue, see Eichengreen (1981a, pp. 5–9).

[90] Moggridge (1972, p. 99).

[91] PRO T200/8, 26 March 1930, pp. 212–13. Alternatively, see Sayers (1976, volume 3).

in the deliberations of the Economic Advisory Council (EAC) in 1930.[92] Alternative policies were most thoroughly explored by the EAC's Committee of Economists, which numbered among its members A.C. Pigou, Lionel Robbins and Hubert Henderson, under Keynes's chairmanship. In July, when MacDonald solicited from the EAC views as to the causes of the slump and recommendations for government action, there ensued a lively debate over the merits of a tariff but no serious discussion of devaluation. The same was true of responses to Keynes's subsequent questions to the Committee of Economists.[93] Towards the end of September, Keynes put to the Committee a scheme for tariffs plus export bounties, but this plan's equivalence to devaluation was acknowledged only obliquely. Bevin and G.D.H. Cole used the tariff question as an opportunity to recommend devaluation when the EAC considered the Committee's report in November, but their proposal garnered no support. Hubert Henderson was alone in warning that devaluation might prove inevitable if world prices continued to fall while British costs proved inflexible.[94]

It is unclear how much influence the economists' analyses had on ministers. By the autumn of 1930, when the Committee's briefs were issued, the Labour government was under intense pressure to respond actively to the rise in unemployment. It was generally agreed that Britain's economic difficulties were at least partially domestic in origin, and that the government had means at its disposal for dealing with the problem.[95] Disagreement centred upon how best to cope with the depression in trade and industry, given the balance of payments constraint. Members of the Conservative opposition, under the direction of Neville Chamberlain, organized a campaign for a tariff that increased in intensity along with Britain's growing industrial difficulties. In response to pressure within the party and to the crusade for Empire Free Trade mounted by the press lords Beaverbrook and Rothermere, Stanley Baldwin, leader of the Conservatives, adopted an increasingly protectionist position. Proposals for a tariff continued to be received with disfavour in Labour and Liberal circles. As a party in opposition, the

92 The EAC, set up by Ramsay MacDonald to provide the Cabinet with assessments of economic conditions and alternative policy responses, discussed a variety of other issues. See Howson and Winch (1977).

93 Section B of Keynes's draft report stated only that there were 'obvious objections' to devaluation, carrying such 'very great weight' that the Committee was not prepared to recommend it. See Keynes (1981, pp. 436–7). The Prime Minister's questions can be found in PRO Cab 58/10 EAC (H) 98, 8 July 1930, p. 417. Keynes's questions appear in Cab 58/150 EAC (E) 8, 'Questionnaire Prepared by the Chairman', 15 September 1930. For further discussion of the questions and the economists' replies, see Eichengreen (1981a, pp. 9–13).

94 'Memorandum by Mr H. D. Henderson on the Drift of the Draft Report', in Keynes (1981, p. 455).

95 McKibban (1975, pp. 102–7).

Liberals had considerable room for manoeuvre, which they used to advocate an ambitious scheme to combat unemployment, involving large-scale public works and capital expenditure. The Liberal plan was based upon a programme constructed prior to the 1929 general election by Keynes, Hubert Henderson and others.[96] The Liberals' proposals were pressed on the government in a series of two-party conferences held in the summer of 1930. There was considerable support for their approach within the Labour Party, but the ministers were largely preoccupied by their responsibility for financial affairs and unwilling to embark upon a course involving additional public spending. This had in May culminated in a dispute between a small group of activists, most visibly Oswald Mosley, and the majority of ministers, who were much swayed by the stubborn orthodoxy of Snowden. Mosley had paid a visit to the Prime Minister in December 1929 to express his dissatisfaction, and in January 1930 he had composed a long memorandum on the economic situation outlining his suggestions for public policy. His resignation on 20 May 1930 symbolized the majority's 'failure of nerve', and it was left to the government to appease its supporters by citing its efforts to liberalize the provisions of the dole. In January 1930 the level of dependents' benefits had been raised and rules governing qualification were relaxed.[97] By redeeming its pledge to ensure adequate maintenance for the unemployed, the Labour government modified the insurance acts in a way that threatened to force the budget deeper into deficit in times of depression. In 1930 alone, the deficit in the unemployment insurance scheme amounted to £75 million, and for 1931 a £100 million deficit was anticipated.[98] As the number of unemployed rose toward 2.5 million, the size of the budget deficit emerged as a crucial determinant of the state of confidence.

Any imbalance between government expenditure and receipts appeared particularly alarming in the light of Britain's delicate balance of payments position, recent estimates of which are presented in table 3.2. These figures show how the healthy current account surplus of more than £100 million achieved in 1928 evaporated over the subsequent three years. Neither the figures in table 3.2 nor the Board of Trade's contemporary figures for the current account, made available in

[96] The origins of these proposals can be traced to the Liberal Industrial Inquiry of 1925: see Keynes and Henderson (1929), and Lloyd George (1929). In fact, by the summer of 1930 the Liberal proposals had taken on a slightly different form from the electoral platform of the previous year, with greater emphasis on budgetary economies and a ligher tax burden for industry: see Skidelsky (1967, pp. 220–1).

[97] Under the 1930 revision of the 1927 Unemployment Insurance Act, the 'genuinely seeking work' clause was eliminated, and transitional benefits were made available to claimants in need of assistance but otherwise unable to qualify. The debate over these measures is analysed by Skidelsky (1967, chapters 8–11). See also Baake (1935), Mosley (1968) and Skidelsky (1975).

[98] Royal Commission on Unemployment Insurance (1931, ii, p. 381).

September 1931, suggest that the slight deterioration in Britain's trade balance was responsible for this trend. The volume of manufactured and semi-manufactured exports fell slightly during the year, but this trend was largely offset by (and perhaps itself partly due to) a sharp improvement of nearly 9 per cent in Britain's net barter terms of trade.[99] The significant change in the current account was in invisibles. Falling interest rates were associated with declining rates of return which depressed Britain's earnings from overseas investment, while at the same time the contraction of world trade reduced her income from shipping and financial services rendered to foreigners. Between 1929 and 1931 there was a swing in Britain's invisible balance of more than £130 million, a figure roughly double the concurrent deterioration in the trade balance.

The stability of the sterling parity again became a matter for public concern in May 1930, when gold losses to the Bank of France unexpectedly resumed. To a considerable extent, concern for the stability of sterling in the months following the New York stock market boom originated with foreign sources. The Federal Reserve Bank of New York had been preoccupied by sterling's weakness since September 1930. Between 14 October and the end of the year, the New York Reserve Bank acquired £7.2 million through open market sales of dollars. The Bank of France also intervened, purchasing sterling sporadically in November. At least one prominent figure, Pierre Quesnay, previously general manager of the Bank of France and then general manager of the BIS, suggested measures the British authorities might take to reduce the resources at the command of foreign exchange speculators. French readers of the *Revue d'economie politique* were alerted to the danger of a sterling crisis in the first issue for 1931.[100]

Within the Labour government, expressions of concern for the future of sterling became commonplace by the end of the year. The EAC had been aware of the danger of a convertibility crisis for some time; its staff issued the first of a series of successively stronger warnings about the status of the balance of trade and payments in November 1930. The Treasury and Bank of England had also been preoccupied with the possibility of a crisis since the end of 1930, especially once the gold reserve had again dipped below the 'Cunliffe minimum' in December. In January 1931 Snowden alerted the Cabinet to the disturbing implications of the persistent transfer of funds abroad, warning that this could lead to panic flight from the pound.

At the beginning of 1931, the British commercial press took little if any notice of the prospect of a crisis. By February, however, public officials in both Britain and America had begun to consider this very

[99] Lipsey (1963, p. 415). See his table 4 for monthly export and import values. Figures for the volume of trade appear in table 3.7 below, p. 76.

[100] Clarke (1967, pp. 175–8); Sayers (1976, volume 1, pp. 233–4); Sauvy (1965, volume 1, p. 121).

possibility. Forward sterling quotations on Paris and several other foreign bourses fell below the normal gold export point, as speculators began to gamble on the probability of devaluation.[101] Spot sterling in New York fell from \$4.86 ¼ to \$4.85 ½ over the course of the month and continued to trade at a discount, a development that *The Economist* termed 'ominous'.[102] At the 2 February meeting of the EAC, the Prime Minister raised the issue of a speculative run. In answer to the Prime Minister's question, Sir Alfred Lewis, a banker and EAC member, remarked that there existed abroad an 'unfavourable feeling' about Britain which had not been in evidence before the turn of the year. Lewis reminded MacDonald that 'It was not fully appreciated how dependent Great Britain was for its liquid assets on the free flow of money in payment of debts from foreign countries.' On 11 February, the same day that Snowden acquiesced to Liberal pressure to establish a Committee on National Expenditure (ultimately known as the May Committee, after its chairman Sir George May), the Chancellor warned that foreigners had reservations about the budgetary position that might have 'very disastrous consequences'.[103]

While foreign exchange speculators already were acting upon expectations of devaluation, the government took few steps to support the external position. In its defence, there were a number of reassuring indications outside the foreign exchange markets. By the end of January, the Bank of England had successfully stemmed the drain of gold which had resulted in a loss of £19 million since the previous November, although it was some time before the success of its operations was

[101] The term 'normal gold point' is from Einzig (1961, p. 297). There was in the second half of 1930 some confusion about the current location of the gold points owing to the effects of Bank of England operations. Since 1925 the Bank of England had delivered gold in fine (.996) bars unless otherwise requested and bought most of its gold in sovereigns of standard (.916) fineness. By 1930 the Bank found itself running short of fine gold. Unable to secure capacity at the mint to refine sovereigns into fine bars, the Bank of England fulfilled its legal obligation by paying out gold of standard fineness only, which the Bank of France was not permitted to accept by virtue of its regulations. It was necessary to refine bars withdrawn from the Bank of England for shipment to France, subject to additional expense and possible delay. From June 1930, this caused the operational gold point to fall on balance and to vary with the expense of refining and the interest cost of financing any delay. As Einzig puts it, 'nobody quite knew [the gold point's] new figure.' See also Einzig (1931, chapter 12) and Moggridge (1972, pp. 174–5). In January 1931 these differences among central banks were resolved in consultations among the directors of the BIS, and the gold export point returned to its normal level. See Bank for International Settlements (1931). Throughout the period, however, the normal gold export point retained psychological significance.

[102] *The Economist*, 7 February 1931, p. 278.

[103] PRO Cab 58/2, EAC 11th Meeting, 'Conclusions', 2 February 1931, p. 8; Bassett (1958, p. 45). Official appointment of the Committee of National Expenditure came some five weeks later, on 17 March.

apparent to all. Consultations among the Board of Directors of the BIS achieved an agreement that succeeded in stabilizing the gold export point. Although the volume of British exports declined in the first quarter of 1931, this was accompanied by a fall in import volume. The only readily available indicator of the external accounts, the trade balance deficit, showed a slight improvement over the previous year, when the monthly deficit had averaged £32 million. Little was known about the development of the invisible balance or the capital account.

Although Governor Norman had been sufficiently alarmed to warn the Committee of Treasury in the first week of March of the danger of forced devaluation, these fears were temporarily allayed.[104] By the third week in April, Clay reports, sufficient confidence had been restored that among Norman and his colleagues 'there was as yet no urgent sense of crisis'.[105] Apart from some movement in the Cabinet towards the position that expenditure cuts and tax increases were needed to bolster confidence, little was done before the situation reached its flash point in July.[106] The small size of the Bank of England's reserves provided little room to manoeuvre, and the credibility of the government's commitment to the existing parity was undermined by its hesitation to act decisively. Ministers found themselves hemmed in by political considerations: although several alternatives for defending the exchange rate were available in theory, in practice few were politically palatable. Foreign borrowing would have been possible, although there was the danger that it would be interpreted as a sign of financial weakness and political ineptitude; in any case, there is little indication that it was contemplated until there remained no alternative. Coordinated international reflation, advocated by Keynes, or at least monetary expansion abroad, hoped for by several members of the Labour government, might have been sufficient to support sterling, but the co-operation of American and French authorities was not forthcoming. The other expansionist remedies, devaluation and protection, either were ruled out of order without benefit of serious consideration or remained overly controversial. The only option remaining to a government committed to maintaining the existing parity was concerted deflation.

The fact that the authorities turned to deflation rather than devaluation at a time when unemployment was creeping towards 22 per cent of the insured labour force reveals the depth of their commitment to the existing parity. Among the government's economic advisors, instinctive support for maintenance of the gold standard parity was weakening, although no one was willing openly to advocate devaluation. Certain members of the EAC opposed devaluation for the adverse effect it

[104] Sayers (1976, volume 1, pp. 233–4).
[105] Clay (1957, p. 375).
[106] Moggridge (1972, p. 195).

would have on London as a financial centre and on sterling as a vehicle currency. On 16 April, Bevin reminded the EAC that the gold standard was not sacred and proposed the adoption of a floating rate indexed to the domestic price level. Keynes's response at the time was that the adoption of a floating rate would have a disastrous impact on Britain's international banking receipts. While Keynes continued to argue that the exchange rate could be successfully defended, he recognized that circumstances might change for the worse. But in contrast to his public statements, Keynes privately acknowledged that the government might be forced to consider Bevin's suggestion sometime in the future.[107] Although the effect of exchange rate changes on Britain's invisible receipts remained an important concern, Keynes's opposition to devaluation was based largely upon political considerations. By opposing the one alternative that had little popular support, Keynes hoped to encourage the government to cling to the existing parity and thereby occupy 'the vacant financial leadership of the world'.[108]

Unfortunately, in the absence of international co-operation, many of the expansionary remedies Keynes had presented to the Macmillan Committee were incompatible with maintenance of the existing exchange rate. Therefore Keynes pressed the case for a tariff, the single viable alternative that might succeed in reducing unemployment without forcing Britain to devalue. In a controversial 7 March 1931 article in the *New Statesman*, he proposed the imposition of a non-discriminatory revenue tariff, with one or two flat tax rates and exemptions for certain important categories of raw materials and imported inputs. Keynes argued that a tariff would stimulate employment by switching demand away from imports and towards domestically produced goods, and that, in so far as it relieved the pressure on Britain's trade balance, it would enhance the stability of the exchange rate. Moreover, the government could use the resulting revenues to augment its expenditure without increasing the size of the budget deficit.

The parallels between protection and devaluation were highlighted in the Report of the Macmillan Committee, which was finalized in June and published on 13 July.[109] The Report summarized the expansionist case as it stood in the spring of 1931. A variety of measures designed to increase international liquidity and raise the domestic price level were discussed in the most general of terms, but devaluation was rejected by

[107] PRO Cab 58/2 EAC 13th Meeting, 'Conclusions', 16 April 1931, p. 4. After devaluation, Keynes advocated a scheme similar to Bevin's, indexing sterling to the prices of the principal commodities entering into international trade. See Moggridge (1980, pp. 89–90).

[108] J. M. Keynes, 'Mitigation by Tariff', *New Statesman*, 7 March 1931, reprinted in Keynes (1931, p. 276).

[109] Committee on Finance and Industry (1931).

the majority on the grounds that Britain's 'international trade, commerce and finance are based on confidence.' The signatories warned:

> in the environment of the present world slump the relief to be obtained from a 10 per cent devaluation might prove to be disappointing. It is not certain that, with world demand at its present low ebb, such a measure would serve by itself to restore our export trades to their former position or to effect a radical cure of unemployment. On the contrary, in the atmosphere of crisis and distress that would inevitably surround such an extreme and sensational measure as the devaluation of sterling, we might well find that the state of affairs immediately ensuing on such an event would be worse than that which had preceded it.[110]

A minority of six, including Keynes, McKenna, Bevin and Thomas Allen, attached to the Report an addendum drafted by Keynes in which they went on to suggest measures that might be taken if the principal foreign governments could not be convinced to co-operate in reflation. After identifying the target of policy as stimulating output and employment by raising producers' prices relative to wages and other costs, the minority listed three options: devaluation, tariffs plus bounties, and Keynes's scheme for a national treaty to adjust all nominal incomes simultaneously. The last of these was dismissed on grounds of the great political difficulties involved in implementation. Devaluation was judged '[t]heoretically the most obvious and comprehensive method of effecting the desired object' but rejected because it would create uncertainties that might interfere with international trade and finance.[111] Another special circumstance that discouraged thoughts of devaluation was the fact that, to a considerable extent, the sums the government was owed from abroad were fixed in terms of sterling while the amounts it owed other countries were denominated in foreign currencies. The obvious examples were war debts: Britain's debt to the United States was denominated in dollars, while interallied debts owed the United Kingdom were denominated in sterling. Thus, devaluation would raise the sterling value of debt payments to the United States while leaving unchanged sterling receipts arising from interallied repayments. It might seem odd that in 1931 such weight still was attached to the remote possibility that these debts might one day have to be paid; none the less, the impact of devaluation on the government's international position was a matter of real concern to Treasury officials.[112]

[110] Ibid., paragraph 257.

[111] Bevin and Allen attached a reservation to the addendum, in which they expressed a preference for devaluation. None the less, they signed the addendum in recognition of the insurmountable political difficulties standing in the way of devaluation: Ibid., p. 210.

[112] For subsequent reflection of this concern see PRO T172/1768, 'Capital Items in the International Balance of Payments', 15 December 1931. See also Eichengreen (1981a, p. 27).

This left the minority one alternative: Keynes's scheme for uniform import tariffs plus matching export bounties. The authors of the addendum noted that the great virtue of tariffs plus bounties was that they would stimulate supply and restrict demand for traded goods in precisely the same way as devaluation, while leaving the value of Britain's international obligations unchanged in terms of gold.[113] Although the economic costs of altering the exchange rate still were seen as prohibitive, the recommendations put forth by government advisors took on an increasing resemblance to devaluation.

It has been said that the main impact of the Macmillan Report was that it came out firmly against devaluation, but it also has been suggested that the form of the Report – with each committee member except the chairman submitting addenda or reservations, and with its emphasis on London's illiquidity – left investors uncertain about the government's resolve and reluctant to maintain funds in the City.[114] In fact, the Report was very much overshadowed by events. It 'had the undeserved misfortune', according to *The Economist*, 'to be published during a week in which public interest has been too greatly engrossed by the dramatic development of the world financial crisis. . . .'[115]

While for Britain the final struggle to defend the exchange rate began in the middle of July, financial difficulties had commenced much earlier on the Continent. The European banking crisis began in May, as evidenced by the growing difficulties facing the Credit-Anstalt, the most important commercial bank in Austria. With its collapse in the wake of protracted negotiations for credits, more than £5 million of British deposits in Austria were suddenly rendered illiquid. The Austrian crisis set off a chain reaction, as bankers and depositors alike sought to increase the liquidity of their positions. Banks in Germany and throughout Eastern Europe were subjected to large-scale withdrawals. This scramble for liquidity, plus continued French resistance and mixed reaction elsewhere to Hoover's proposal on 20 June for a debt moratorium, proved to be fatal blows to the German banking system. The Darmstadter Bank, one of the largest German financial institutions, failed on Monday 13 July, the day the Macmillan Report was published. It was able to reopen three days later only under the protection of exchange control and with the benefit of government guarantees.[116] This time £70 million of German debts to British banks were frozen.[117]

[113] Committee on Finance and Industry (1931, p. 199).
[114] Howson and Winch (1977, p. 86) present both views. See also Lloyd (1970, p. 164); Sayers (1976, volume 1, pp. 372–3); Clarke (1967, p. 202).
[115] *The Economist*, 18 July 1931, p. 106.
[116] Morton (1943, p. 23); Bennett (1962, chapter VI); Kindleberger (1973, p. 156); Kirby (1981, p. 61).
[117] The estimate is Snowden's. See Morton (1943, p. 31).

Financial pressure surfaced next in London. On 13 July the Bank of England first lost gold for export. On 15 July sterling fell sharply against both the dollar and the French franc, and gold losses resumed. George Harrison, Governor of the Federal Reserve Bank of New York, was sufficiently alarmed by these events to cable Norman for an explanation. Over the two-and-a-half weeks from 13 July to 1 August, the Bank of England lost more than £33 million in gold and at least £21 million in foreign exchange, more reserves than it was to lose in any comparable period of the crisis.[118] Of the more than £38 million of UK gold exports in July to the United States, France, Holland, Belgium and Switzerland, approximately 60 per cent went to France and 30 per cent to Holland.[119]

With hindsight, one might argue that the Bank of England should have raised Bank rate at the first opportunity in order to signal to the market its commitment to the parity. The Bank was reluctant to raise Bank rate, owing to concern for the state of industry, out of sensitivity to political pressure, and because of doubts that a higher discount rate would succeed in stemming the gold outflow. In part, the decision to delay reflected a belief that the weakness of sterling would disappear with the resolution of the liquidity crisis on the Continent. A rise in Bank rate was considered on 16 July but rejected in deference to the Seven-Power Conference held on 20–23 July, in the hope that the delegates might make sufficient progress on the issue of credits to restore confidence in Germany's finances.[120] Bank rate finally was raised by one point to 3.5 per cent on 23 July, and after this failed to halt the loss of reserves it was raised by another point on 30 July. This was the final change in Bank rate until devaluation.[121] The question of why no further increase in Bank rate took place remains a mystery.[122] It may be that the Bank had no wish to add to British industry's already heavy burden in the light of doubts about the effectiveness of Bank rate increases. There is also the possibility that the Bank withheld further

[118] PRO P 1/97, '£ Sterling, Strictly Private and Confidential', not dated. For the period 13 July – 1 August, only totals are presented; however daily figures are available for the subsequent seven weeks (see table 3.5). By all indications, these figures were sent to C.P. Duff (the Prime Minister's private secretary) by C.J. Mahon (Comptroller at the Bank) in two summaries transmitted toward the end of August and beginning of September. Figures for subsequent dates were added in the Prime Minister's office on the basis of subsequent letters from the Bank.

[119] Hurst (1932, p. 640).

[120] Sayers (1976, volume 2, p. 391).

[121] Sayers (1976, volume 2, pp. 392–3) suggests that there existed some division within the Bank in the last week of July over whether further Bank rate increases or attempts to secure foreign credits were the appropriate response, but by 30 July the importance of both had been generally accepted.

[122] Sayers (1976, volume 2, p. 405) finds no record after 6 August of actual proposals to raise Bank rate.

increases in its discount rate as a way of bringing pressure to bear on the government to balance the budget.[123]

In the British financial press, there was still little awareness of crisis conditions.[124] In its report dated 21 July, the London and Cambridge Economic Service mentioned the abnormal size of gold outflows only in passing. On 25 July *The Economist* stated reassuringly that 'The Bank of England still possesses a wide margin out of which to meet further gold losses, and foreign withdrawals to date have still left the money market reasonably well supplied with funds.'[125] There seems to have been little awareness of the extent of Bank of England intervention in the foreign exchange market. It was tempting to identify the problem as a temporary symptom of illiquidity on the Continent rather than as a fundamental loss of confidence in sterling. But this surely was not the view of Hopkins or Snowden. In the last week of July, Hopkins sent the Chancellor a memorandum in which he spoke of the danger that Britain would be driven off the gold standard unless dramatic action was taken:

> We are the victims of many circumstances. Some we cannot in the least control. One – a vital one – can be controlled but only if the nation will stand up to it.
>
> We cannot control that we are in the midst of an unexampled slump, nor the fact that Germany is bankrupt, that great assets of ours are frozen there, and that foreign nations are drawing their credits from there over our exchanges. Nor can we control the fact that foreign nations have immense sums of money in London and will try to get them away if distrust of the pound extends. . . . the first thing at which foreigners look is the budgetary position. Whether it is reasonable that they should do so may be open to debate. That they do so is beyond question. When on Monday the Governor sounds J. P. Morgan as to the possibility of an American loan to support the pound, the first question the latter will ask, in my belief, is: 'Will steps be first taken about the dole and the budgetary position?'[126]

As Hopkins's memo emphasizes, continental observers looked immediately to the budget when confidence in sterling weakened. Many had had vivid recollections of the great central European inflations and depreciations of the early 1920s, which had been driven by budget deficits financed by the issuance of government bills and unbacked currency. The French drew similar lessons from their experience with

[123] See Boyce (1982); Clay (1957, p. 384); Morton (1943, p. 44).

[124] According to Sayers (1976, volume 2, p. 392), in the last week of July ministers were 'almost unaware' of the Bank of England's problem of reserve losses.

[125] London and Cambridge Economic Service, *Monthly Bulletin*, 21 July 1931, p. 208; *The Economist*, 25 July 1931, p. 158.

[126] PRO T 175/51, Hopkins to Snowden (untitled and undated, but probably 24 July 1931), pp. 5–7.

budget deficits and exchange depreciation in the mid-1920s.[127] The May Report on National Expenditure, received by Snowden on 24 July and published on 31 July, contained an alarming prognosis for Britain's own budgetary position.[128] The reserve losses of the last week in July may have been exacerbated by rumours concerning its contents. If Britain's budget deficit had begun to affect foreign opinion as early as May, it had become a factor of critical importance by August.[129]

Given its reluctance to raise Bank rate, the Bank relied heavily on direct intervention in the foreign exchange market, both spot and forward. Such a strategy required that the Bank have ample reserves. On 25 July Sir Robert Kindersley, a director of the Bank, was sent to Paris to arrange a £25 million credit with the Bank of France. On 30 July a matching amount was obtained from the Federal Reserve Bank of New York.[130] With credits in hand, the Bank of England initiated open market operations which offset the deflationary impact of gold losses on the domestic money base. The fiduciary issue – that portion of the Bank's note issue that did not have to be backed by gold – was raised by £15 million on 1 August as a condition of the American credit, New York being concerned that London have gold available when repayment came due.[131] There was provision for such an increase under the Currency and Bank Notes Act of 1928, which permitted the fiduciary issue to be raised in times of need in order to release additional gold for the defence of sterling.[132] The Bank may have welcomed the additional room to manoeuvre and also may have wished to accommodate the normal seasonal rise in currency demand as reinforced by the bank holiday. In any case, such an initiative, clearly defensible in the face of an internal drain, had unfortunate effects in the presence of an external drain. Coming on the same day as release of the May Report and in the wake of such serious reserve losses, the mere existence of this option to increase domestic credit could not have reassured speculators, particularly foreign ones, of the strength of the Bank of England's commitment to the defence of sterling.[133]

[127] The Governor of the Bank of France made the comparison explicitly (Clay, 1957, p. 386).

[128] Committee on National Expenditure (1931).

[129] Sayers (1976, volume 2, p. 390).

[130] Credits offered by other sources, such as the National Bank of Belgium, were declined. See van der Wee and Tavernier (1975, p. 237).

[131] Sayers (1976, volume 2, p. 394, and volume 3, p. 261).

[132] The government's intention was that this authority could be employed not only in time of crisis but in the ordinary course of events. See Clarke (1967, p. 139); Committee on Finance and Industry (1931, pp. 30, 139–40). The Currency and Bank Notes Act is reprinted in Sayers (1976, volume 3, pp. 108–12).

[133] Sayers (1976, volume 2, p. 294) suggests that the increase in fiduciary issue 'would be interpreted abroad as a sign that the UK authorities had lost their grip and were resorting to the very devices they had always condemned'. Clay (1957, p. 386) suggests that foreigners took it as 'evidence of inflation'.

TABLE 3.4 American and French credits: amounts spent, August 1931

	American £25m.	*(£ million)*	*French £25m.*
7 August	2.3		–
8 August	0.5		1.5
10 August	4.6		0.75
11 August	2.85		1.7
12 August	0.3		0.1
13 August	2.2		0.75
14 August	3.35		0.9
15 August	0.85		0.2
17 August	0.75		0.65
	−5.15	transferred between accts	5.15
18 August	1.0		0.05
19 August	1.25		1.3
20 August	2.55		0.8
21 August	1.65		0.55
22 August	1.55		0.85
24 August	4.05		2.2
26 August	3.3		1.0
27 August	0.45		0.25
	−3.3	transferred between accts	3.3
Total (net of transfers)	25.05		22.00

Source: PRO P 1/97, 'American and French Credits', not dated. Both spot and forward market operations are included.

The American and French credits were rapidly drawn down over the remainder of August (see table 3.4). The Bank of England succeeded in supporting the pound and preventing any further loss of gold to the end of the month, but only at the expense of £15 million of its hidden foreign exchange reserves (over and above the £50 million of American and French credits). There are a number of explanations of why the credits were not more helpful. Their very existence was viewed by some as a sign of weakness.[134] Confidence may have been further undermined when the credits were used only intermittently upon the opening of the foreign exchange markets on 4 August. As *The Economist* explained on

[134] Clay (1957, p. 386).

8 August, 'There may have been a mistaken idea that a hitch had developed in obtaining the credits.'[135]

Market observers also were perturbed by what they perceived to be the Bank of England's curious reluctance to use its own reserves in support of sterling.[136] In fact, reports provided to the Prime Minister indicate that the Bank was continuing to sell off foreign exchange at its customary pace.[137] Over the second half of July it had sold foreign exchange at a rate slightly in excess of £1.4 million per day. On 4 August, the day the markets reopened, the Bank sold £1.65 million of foreign exchange, and it followed this with sales of £1.40 and £2.5 million the next two days (see table 3.5). However, Bank of England operations may have sent confusing signals to the market; early on 4 August the Bank apparently withdrew its support for the pound in both Paris and London, which may have undermined confidence in the parity.[138] In any case, only on 7 August, when it finally was able to draw on the American credits, did the Bank's reliance on its own foreign exchange reserves decline, although the overall level of intervention – the sum of drawings on the credits and on the Bank's own reserves – remained steady. Once the French credits became available the following day, the Bank stepped up the level of intervention.[139] The daily figures on foreign exchange drawings in tables 3.4 and 3.5 suggest that what the markets interpreted as an absence of intervention may have been nothing more than erratic behaviour.

The conjunction of the May Report, the foreign credits and the continued loss of reserves caused opinions about the future of sterling to crystallize. MacDonald reserved judgement on the whole affair, but his advisors now volunteered some provocative opinions. Keynes for one had been convinced by the events of July of the inevitability of devaluation. When asked by the Prime Minister for his assessment of the May

[135] *The Economist*, 8 August 1931, p. 254.

[136] Similarly, Skidelsky (1967), Clay (1957) and Sayers (1976) comment on the absence of intervention on 5 August. Clarke (1967, p. 207) finds records in the archives of Federal Reserve Bank of New York of dollar sales by the Bank of England. He comments only that the Bank of England failed to support the pound 'firmly'. Actually, it may have been the termination of Bank of France support for sterling on the Paris market immediately prior to the opening of the credits that alarmed the market. See *The Economist*, 8 August 1931, p. 254; Kooker (1976, p. 114).

[137] PRO P1/97, '£ Sterling, Strictly Private and Confidential' (not dated).

[138] Sayers (1976, volume 2, p. 395).

[139] The delay in using the credits was due to disagreement with the French about the timing of withdrawals from the Bank of France and French commercial banks, plus the fact that the credits were extended with the understanding that American and French accounts would be drawn down at an equal rate. The delay may not have been entirely unwelcome to the Bank of England, which had hopes that, as in 1925, the mere acquisition of foreign credits would make their actual use unnecessary. See Kindleberger (1973, p. 159); Clarke (1967, p. 207).

TABLE 3.5 Change in Bank of England gold and foreign exchange reserves, August–September 1931

		(£ million)	
	Gold	*Foreign exchange reserves*	*Total*
4 August	0.15	−1.65	−1.50
5 August	1.2	−1.4	−0.2
6 August	−2.55	−2.5	−5.05
7 August	0.35	−2.25	−2.20
8 August	0.3	−2.6	−2.3
10 August	−0.2	−5.35	−5.55
11 August	0.35	−4.55	−4.20
12 August	0.2	−0.4	−0.2
13 August		−2.95	−2.95
14 August	−0.01	−4.30	−4.31
15 August	1.0	−1.05	−2.05
17 August	0.2	−2.25	−2.05
18 August	0.35	−1.10	−0.75
19 August		−4.05	−4.05
20 August		−3.45	−3.45
21 August	−0.01	−2.25	−2.26
22 August		−2.2	−2.2
24 August	−0.01	−11.9	−11.91
25 August	0.35	−6.00	−5.65
26 August	−0.55	−0.6	−1.15
27 August	0.05	−2.55	−2.4
28 August		−4.35	−4.35
29 August		−0.5	−0.5
31 August		−0.7	−0.7
1 September	0.92	−1.70	−0.78
2 September	0.03	−2.00	−1.97
3 September	0.01	−1.97	−1.96
4 September	0.10	−3.76	−3.66
5 September		−1.87	−1.87
7 September	0.28	−3.36	−3.08
8 September	1.03	−2.48	−1.45
9 September	0.12	−1.91	−1.79
10 September	−0.05	−3.34	−3.39
11 September	−0.05	−3.28	−3.33
12 September		−1.78	−1.78
14 September	−0.31	−3.03	−3.34
15 September	0.42	−3.22	−2.80
16 September	−0.35	−3.55	−3.90
17 September	−0.48	−5.74	−6.22
18 September	−1.78	−16.05	−17.83
19 September	−0.91	−9.54	−10.45

Source: PRO P 1/97, '£ Sterling, Strictly Private and Confidential', n.d.; *The Economist*, various issues. Throughout, the public records are taken as definitive. Entries smaller than 0.01 are omitted.

Report, in a letter dated 5 August, Keynes contrasted its proposals for deflation with the options that would be open after devaluation:

> it is now nearly certain that we shall go off the existing parity at no distant date. Whatever may have been the case some time ago, it is now too late to avoid this. We can put off the date for a time, if we are so foolish as to borrow in terms of francs and dollars and so allow a proportion of what are now sterling liabilities to be converted into franc and dollar liabilities. . . . But when doubts as to the prospects of a currency, such as now exist about sterling, have come into existence, the game is up. . . .[140]

Having decided that devaluation was inescapable, Keynes saw no reason for delay in implementing expansionary measures. He proposed an immediate devaluation of at least 25 per cent with an invitation to interested countries to form a currency area with Britain.

Hubert Henderson, while equally critical of the May Report, did not consider devaluation inevitable. In a memorandum to the Prime Minister dated 7 August, he argued that drastic budgetary economies were required to save the existing parity. Neither the Treasury nor the Bank would admit that the case was lost, although events threatened to escape their control. Sir Ernest Harvey, deputy governor of the Bank, wrote Snowden to warn that, unless the budgetary position was rapidly adjusted, 'we cannot maintain ourselves long'.[141] Keynes announced his opinion of the May Report in an article in the *New Statesman* on 12 August. While the article made no mention of devaluation, in a cover letter to MacDonald, Keynes warned that there would 'be a crisis within a month unless the most drastic and sensational action is taken'. The following day, in a letter to Richard Kahn, he expressed doubt that the government would take the necessary steps.[142]

On the Continent, parallels were drawn between the instability of the French franc before Poincaré and the plight of the pound. The implication was that only by balancing the budget could Britain suceed in restoring confidence in sterling. Budgetary economies were the price to be paid for the continued assistance of French and American central banks. Therefore, from the first week in August until the fall of the Labour government, the struggle to defend the gold standard centred upon measures to balance the budget. The May Committee had estimated the budget deficit for 1932 at £120 million, recommending £24 million of increased taxation and £97 million of spending cuts, including £67 million of expenditure reductions on unemployment insurance. These recommendations formed the benchmark for the negotiations that followed.

The Cabinet established an Economy Committee to construct an

[140] Howson and Winch (1977, p. 89).
[141] Marquand (1977, pp. 611–12).
[142] Howson and Winch (1977, p. 90).

alternative to the May Committee's recommendations. At its first meeting on 12 August, Snowden announced that, in light of the deepening depression and increased spending on unemployment insurance, a more realistic figure for the budget deficit was £170 million. In response to objections registered by several Labour ministers to reductions in the standard rate of unemployment benefit, the Economy Committee trimmed the value of expenditure cuts to £79 million. The Committee tentatively proposed £89 million of new taxation, the composition of which Snowden reserved as his own prerogative.

The Cabinet considered these proposals on 19 August. The run on sterling did not appear to be worsening: the Bank of England continued to stabilize the spot rate and to minimize reserve losses while drawing down the French and American credits at the rate of £1 – £3 million a day. On the other hand, by the end of business on 19 August, more than £28 million of the foreign credits had been used. Any sense of urgency did not prevent the majority of Labour ministers from holding firm to principle and rejecting a proposal for deep cuts in unemployment insurance outlays. The Economy Committee's proposed £44 million reduction in unemployment insurance was halved, leaving a package that was at once too much for labour's representatives, led by Bevin and Citrine, and too little for the financial community.[143]

The Cabinet met again on Saturday 22 August to seek a compromise. The Chancellor of the Exchequer reminded the Cabinet of the precariousness of the position and the consequences of inaction. The position of the Bank of England was that, 'if the economies suggested represented the Government's final word, the scheme would be of no value.' Snowden spoke of the disastrous consequences he believed would follow from devaluation. Given the 50 per cent devaluation-induced rise in the cost of living he envisioned, Snowden had no doubt that the Labour Party could better serve its constituency by further economizing on unemployment outlays.[144] The Cabinet discussed the possibility of re-imposing half the unemployment cuts that previously had been eliminated, but a minority of ministers was opposed. Even these proposed cuts fell short of balancing the budget. By the close of business on Saturday, 22 August, scarcely a third of the foreign credits were left. Thus the government's continued ability to support the exchange rate hinged upon its success in obtaining further credits. On Sunday a cautiously worded and pessimistically interpreted response to a request for credits was received from J. P. Morgan and Co., the British government's agent in the United States. Support within the

[143] For a detailed analysis of the negotiations, see Bassett (1958, chapter 4). For a partisan account, see also Snowden (1934, volume 2).

[144] PRO Cab 23/67, Cab 44(31), 'Conclusion of the Meeting of the Cabinet on 22 August 1931', pp. 343, 347.

Cabinet for the proposal to cut the standard rate of unemployment benefit then effectively dissipated. The Labour Ministry resigned on Sunday and a National Government took its place on Monday, 24 August.

Initially, 'a general feeling of nervousness' surrounding the intentions of the National Government gave new impetus to the run on sterling.[145] On 24 August, the Bank of England was forced to sell nearly £12 million of foreign exchange, a new high for one day. More than half came from the American and French credits (table 3.4), while the remainder was drawn from the Bank's own coffers (table 3.5). The markets were disturbed by a report in *The Times* that the French and American credits were approaching exhaustion.[146] By Wednesday, the foreign exchange markets had settled down, as investors gained confidence in the new government's commitment to defence of the existing parity.[147] On 27 August the National Government agreed on a package of expenditure cuts, and two days later the news was released that fresh credits of $200 million each had been arranged in Paris and New York. But speculation continued undiminished, and the Bank of England was forced to intervene to the extent of £2 million on each of the first three days of September. On 3 September, Harvey warned the new Cabinet that the Bank's gold and foreign exchange losses showed no signs of abating.[148] The proximate cause of the crisis was still lack of confidence abroad in the government's overriding commitment to the parity.

The National Government's own plan for budget economies was unveiled on 10 September. While this Emergency Budget differed in detail from the final proposals before the Labour Cabinet, its fiscal impact and its reception were the same. The new budget did not inspire confidence. On 10 September the final run on the Bank of England's reserves began. That day Keynes made his views public: in an article in the *Evening Standard* he admitted that he 'personally now believed [devaluation] to be the right remedy', but he continued to offer tariffs plus bounties as an alternative for the reluctant.[149] On 16 September he told an all-party group of MPs that the new budget was insufficient to

145 *The Economist*, 29 August 1931, pp. 377–8. It was notable that the difficulties of Monday, 24 August, occurred despite the fact that they fell three months to the day after a bank holiday, which meant that no Treasury bills matured on that day. With new Treasury bills to pay for, this created a considerable stringency in the market and led to a rise in day-to-day money rates.

146 Sayers (1976, volume 2, p. 399). Market psychology was not helped by reports of a £485,000 purchase of South African gold on Tuesday in London by a mysterious buyer.

147 *The Economist*, 29 August 1931, p. 378.

148 PRO Cab 23/68, 'Secretary's Notes of a Conversation between Sir Ernest Harvey and Mr. Peacock and Members of the Cabinet', 3 September 1931, p. 2.

149 Kahn (forthcoming). Other economists, such as T.E. Gregory, spoke out in favour of devaluation once they came to believe that protection was the only alternative under consideration.

solve the confidence problem.[150] Given the difficulty of co-ordinating international reflation, the only alternatives remaining to the government were import restrictions and devaluation. The next day the Cabinet Committee chaired by MacDonald acknowledged that import controls had been rendered impractical by the lack of time to marshall support for the necessary legislation. The question of 'whether it was time to stop defending the rate' was raised, but the idea was scotched almost immediately. The causes of the crisis were then summarized as a lack of confidence on the part of foreign nationals, an adverse balance of trade, and some internal flight from the pound.[151] Further credits were seen as the only alternative to devaluation. Enquiries in Paris and New York did not yield immediate results. Meanwhile, the Bank of England's reserve losses continued to mount.

The Bank was intervening in both spot and forward markets, doing its utmost to peg both rates within a narrow margin.[152] On Saturday, 19 September, the pound was supported at $4.86 in New York, while the one-month forward rate was at a discount of only ½ cent and the three-month forward rate was at a discount of only 2 cents. The same was true in every major foreign market except Rome, where sterling sold forward at a premium. The appearance of stability thus created is reflected in the market analysis published by *The Economist* on 19 September: 'Conditions were quiet in the exchange market. Sterling outwardly remained steady, and the undertone of the markets seemed to indicate some return of confidence. . . .'[153] Hopes for a return of confidence were soon dashed. The reserve losses of 18 and 19 September were massive, and the Bank of England was forced to give up its battle to support sterling above the gold export point. On the evening of Sunday, 20 September, the government released the press notice officially announcing the suspension of the gold standard.

Banking crisis or balance of payments crisis?

With over 50 years of hindsight, how should we view the sequence of events culminating in the 1931 devaluation of sterling? Contemporaries saw the run on sterling as the result of a combination of unfortunate

[150] Howson and Winch (1977, p. 93). Keynes's notes for this speech are in Keynes (1981, pp. 607–11).

[151] In addition, he mentioned unrest in the ranks of the Navy which had given rise to reports of a mutiny. See PRO Cab 27/462, FSC (31), 'Minutes of the Second Meeting of the Committee on the Financial Situation', 17 September 1931, pp. 14–28. Some accounts of developments in September place great weight on these sensational events, whose importance may have been somewhat exaggerated.

[152] Its forward market operations, which are discussed in Einzig (1937, pp. 371–2), are estimated by Sayers (1976, volume 2, p. 408) to have amounted to approximately £20 million between 8 and 19 September.

[153] *The Economist*, 19 September 1931, p. 502.

circumstances. In the first instance, the low ratio of Bank of England reserve assets to outstanding UK short-term liabilities rendered defence of the exchange rate inherently difficult. The slump had led to an alarming deterioration in the current account of the balance of payments, a development that could not have come at a less opportune time. The scramble for liquidity on the Continent intensified the pressure on London, and when the Labour and National Governments were unable to decide upon a concerted response, the banking crisis was transformed into a political crisis. As confidence continued to erode, events developed more quickly than did British officials' capacity to respond to them.

Traditionally, historians have emphasized the role of confidence, bank failures and international political turmoil in the 1931 crisis. Britain's balance of payments position is portrayed as weak but not untenable. What transformed a shaky balance of payments position into an uncontrollable speculative run that ultimately exhausted the Bank of England's capacity to defend the exchange rate was the collapse of the Austrian and German banks, the ensuing scramble for liquidity, and the Labour and National Governments' unwillingness, or inability, to respond quickly and convincingly to the erosion of confidence in sterling.

Since the time of the crisis itself, there has coexisted another interpretation of the events of 1931 in Britain. This interpretation focuses not on foreign bank failures but on the fundamental determinants of Britain's own deteriorating balance of payments position. There was considerable discussion at the time, in the Economic Advisory Council and elsewhere, of fears that the nation's declining balance on current account was causing a loss of gold and undermining confidence in sterling. In 1940 W.A. Brown argued that Britain's shrinking surplus on invisibles account had been at fault in the 1931 sterling crisis. Recently, Donald Moggridge has again attempted to shift the emphasis from foreign bank failures to Britain's deteriorating invisibles position. Moggridge does not dispute that bank failures abroad precipitated the sterling crisis, but he raises the question of whether a convertibility crisis would have occurred even in their absence. After four straight years of surpluses, he points out, in 1931 Britain's current account balance moved into deficit. This was due not to any pronounced change in her trade balance but to a serious deterioration in the balance of invisibles resulting from the contraction of world trade. In conjunction with other balance of payments trends, Moggridge argues, this development would have culminated eventually in the exhaustion of reserves even had foreign bank failures not intervened. The confidence crisis inspired by international political turmoil, and the scramble for liquidity associated with banking collapses in Austria and Germany, only 'brought matters to a head'.[154]

[154] Moggridge (1970, pp. 832–3). See also Brown (1940, pp. 999–1001), Howson (1975, p. 77), and Howson and Winch (1977).

Thus, there exist two views of the 1931 sterling crisis: one that characterizes this episode as an unfortunate and perhaps unavoidable consequence of the unanticipated financial and political developments of the summer of 1931, and a second that, while conceding that the liquidity crisis was the proximate cause of the run on sterling, suggests that long-term trends in market variables, such as relative prices, relative incomes and other determinants of the balance of payments, would have eventually driven Britain from gold even in the absence of the liquidity crisis. It is difficult to distinguish between these views of the crisis on the basis of existing data on the balance of payments. The annual figures in table 3.2 indicate only that a large current account deficit had emerged by the end of the year, and that the invisible balance had declined by some £90 million between 1930 and 1931.[155] This change in external accounts might equally well be attributed to unfavourable movements in prices and incomes or to political developments that undermined confidence in the exchange rate. However, the fact that the value of both Britain's current account and invisibles balances fell each year from 1929 to 1931 is suggestive of some cumulative deterioration in the economic determinants of those accounts. Monthly figures are available for the trade balance only. Those presented in table 3.6 reveal that Britain's trade balance deficit increased in value between the first and second quarters of 1931, but that the magnitude of this change was not particularly alarming. Data in table 3.7, on the composition of British exports, indicate that the growth of the trade deficit was due largely to a decline in the volume of Britain's exports of manufactured goods. In the absence of explicit counterfactual estimates of prices and incomes at home and abroad, it is impossible to say whether, had Britain managed to stay on gold in September 1931, her balance of payments would have deteriorated sufficiently in the period that followed to drive her off the gold standard.

A limitation of the preceding discussion is its neglect of the capital account of the balance of payments. Capital moved between Britain and other countries in response to changes in expectations about the relative rate of return and riskiness of domestic and foreign assets. Such expectations would have been formed on the basis of both long-term trends in prices, incomes and profits and the unusual political and financial developments of the summer of 1931. Here again it is difficult to discriminate between the two views of the 1931 crisis.

155 The Board of Trade's provisional 1931 estimates, presented in September 1931, slightly overestimated the trade balance deficit but correctly predicted the size of the deterioration of the invisibles account. See PRO Cab 58/18, Economic Advisory Council, Committee on Economic Information, 'Provisional Board of Trade Estimates of Changes in the Balance of Trade', 3 September 1931; 'Balance of Trade, Memorandum by the Board of Trade', 21 September 1931. A summary of these figures appears in Moggridge (1970, p. 833).

TABLE 3.6 Exports of UK goods minus total net imports, 1930–31[a]

	(£ million) 1930	1931
January	−35.4	−31.9
February	−27.7	−26.0
March	−31.9	−31.3
April	−29.2	−30.9
May	−31.0	−30.0
June	−32.8	−33.2
July	−27.8	−30.9
August	−30.8	−32.3
September	−30.6	−34.7
October	−36.8	−42.6
November	−28.5	−46.4
December	−45.9	−39.4

[a] Seasonally unadjusted
Source: Tinbergen (1934, p. 110); Methorst (1938, pp. 208–10)

Historical narrative alone, even one that makes use of considerable detail on the pattern of reserve gains and losses, does not enable us to distinguish among the various views of the 1931 sterling crisis. One approach to assessing these alternative interpretations is to model them formally and then to see whether historical time series conform to the predictions of the model. The strategy adopted here is to specify a small model of the balance of payments in which reserve flows depend on prices, incomes, interest rates and other fundamental determinants, and then to see whether it provides any indication of a weakening in Britain's balance of payments.

By estimating this model over the period when confidence in the stability of the exchange rate dominated the market (from the beginning of 1926 to the beginning of 1931), we can examine the extent to which Britain's reserve gains and losses under the interwar gold standard are explicable in terms of the fundamental determinants of the balance of payments. Then, by simulating the model for subsequent portions of 1931, we can construct some evidence bearing on the question of whether those fundamental determinants continued to evolve in such a way as to generate a loss of reserves. If so, then support is lent the view that the events precipitated in 1931 by bank failures abroad would have resulted eventually from balance of payments trends even if foreign financial difficulties had not intervened. If not, then the conventional view, that the 1931 crisis is properly understood as a consequence of a

TABLE 3.7 The volume of UK trade, 1930(I)–1932(III) (Average of quarterly volume for 1929 = 100)

Groups	*1930*				*1931*				*1932*		
	(I)	*(II)*	*(III)*	*(IV)*	*(I)*	*(II)*	*(III)*	*(IV)*	*(I)*	*(II)*	*(III)*
Imports											
Food, drink and tobacco	91.2	91.2	97.3	125.8	99.0	101.2	109.6	128.7	104.2	99.4	103.6
Raw materials and articles mainly unmanufactured	103.7	86.3	74.6	94.0	85.5	79.5	75.0	96.4	97.8	82.3	76.4
Articles mainly or wholly manufactured	102.4	103.9	96.8	97.5	91.4	97.3	103.0	115.8	70.6	59.7	64.1
Total	97.9	93.4	90.8	109.0	93.0	94.4	98.6	116.3	92.3	83.3	84.6
Exports (domestic produce)											
Food, drink and tobacco	88.1	82.9	102.2	101.6	82.3	72.2	67.5	88.7	75.2	69.9	70.5
Raw materials and articles mainly unmanufactured	97.7	85.0	75.3	79.5	66.9	71.3	65.7	73.5	62.0	64.9	60.9
Articles mainly or wholly manufactured	91.2	79.4	77.2	72.8	61.0	57.8	59.3	59.6	61.5	63.9	57.7
Total	91.8	80.2	79.0	76.6	63.6	60.6	61.0	64.5	63.0	64.4	58.8

Source: League of Nations (1932, p. 28)

scramble for liquidity only indirectly related to the fundamental determinants of Britain's balance of payments position, remains the logical candidate.

One approach to modelling the balance of payments is to specify separate equations for the trade balance, the invisible balance, the long-term capital account and the short-term capital account. The virtue of this approach is that the results can be linked readily to contemporary accounts of the crisis; its weakness is that any such model will be complex and must place a heavy burden on the data, particularly upon crude estimates of the short-term capital account. An alternative approach is to specify a monetary model that focuses on the bottom line: the official settlements balance. The strengths of this approach are simplicity, since only the overall balance need be considered; reliance on figures for official reserves, which are accurate in comparison with other balance of payments statistics; and compatibility with alternative models, since accounting identities require monetary models to be consistent with disaggregated approaches to balance of payments analysis.[156] However, these advantages are obtained at the expense of imposing a number of restrictive assumptions.

Thus, the model does not focus directly on the invisibles balance. It looks instead at determinants of the official settlements balance, since it is that balance, rather than any one of its components, that determines the extent of reserve flows. That there occurred a striking deterioration in the invisibles balance is relevant only in so far as that development was not offset by a strengthening of the trade balance or, more likely, the capital account. Indeed, it is common to observe offsetting movements in the components of the balance of payments in periods of external imbalance. Therefore, it is important to focus on the official settlements balance rather than any one of its components. None the less, the knowledge that a particular component of that account (in this case the invisibles balance) exhibited a large swing prior to the crisis may be helpful for interpreting the results.

The model is kept to essentials. It contains one relationship determining the demand for money, two relationships that together determine the supply of money, an identity and an equilibrium condition.

$$\frac{\mathrm{M}}{P} = y^{a_1} e^{a_2 I}. \qquad (1)$$

Equation (1) relates the demand for real balances M/P to a scale variable (in this case output) Y and the market interest rate I. The supply of money M is the product of the money multiplier V and the

[156] On the compatibility of this asset market view with approaches that focus instead on import demands and export supplies, see Polak (1957) and Tsiang (1961).

monetary base H. The base has two components: domestic credit C and the Bank of England's international reserves R.

$$M = VH = V(R + C) \tag{2}$$

Invoking the equilibrium condition that money supply equals money demand:

$$\frac{V\,(R + C)}{P} = Y^{a_1}e^{a_2 I}. \tag{3}$$

In what follows, a lower-case letter denotes the log of the variable represented by the corresponding upper-case letter. A circumflex over a variable denotes its growth rate per unit of time (that is, $\hat{X} = d\,ln\,X/dt = dx/dt$), -1 and -2 subscripts signify variables lagged one and two periods respectively, and Δ denotes a first difference ($\Delta X = X_t - X_{t-1}$). Taking the logarithm of (3) and differentiating with respect to time yields:

$$\frac{R}{H}\hat{R} = \hat{P} + a_1\hat{Y} + a_2(\Delta I) - \hat{V} - \frac{C}{H}\,\hat{C}. \tag{3'}$$

This is the reserve flow equation.[157] The rate of change of Bank of England reserves, adjusted for the reserve-to-monetary-base ratio, is a function of rates of change of prices, output, the money multiplier, the domestic credit component of the monetary base and of the change in interest rates.

We turn now to the money supply process. The authorities are assumed to control the domestic credit component of the monetary base, while the banking system determines the money multiplier as a function of the gap between the market interest rate I and the Bank of England's discount rate J:[158]

$$v = m - h = a_3\,(I - J). \tag{4}$$

Recasting (4) in terms of time derivatives:

$$\hat{V} = a_3\,(\Delta I - \Delta J). \tag{4'}$$

Allowing for the possibility that the Bank of England intervened in financial markets through open market operations, we posit a simple

157 See also Zecher (1976).
158 Here we follow Obstfeld (1980).

reaction function:

$$\Delta C = a_4 \Delta R. \tag{5}$$

Had the Bank of England played by the 'rules of the game' by reinforcing the impact of gold flows on the monetary base, $a_4 > 0$. Had it chosen instead to sterilize reserve flows, $a_4 < 0$. Equation (5) can be transformed into:[159]

$$\frac{C}{H}\,\hat{C} = a_4 \frac{R}{H}\,\hat{R}. \tag{5'}$$

For purposes of estimation, lagged left- and right-hand-side variables are included as additional determinants of the rate of domestic credit creation.

Equations (3′), (4′) and (5′) comprise a three-equation system determining the rate of change of reserves, domestic credit and the money multiplier (where the first two variables are weighted by the shares of reserves and domestic credit in the monetary base, respectively). The remaining variables are exogenous or predetermined by assumption. In particular, output and prices are assumed to be exogenous to contemporaneous events in financial markets, and the market interest rate is assumed to be related to the exogenous foreign interest rate I^* by open interest parity:

$$I = I^* + E\,(\hat{\varepsilon}) \tag{6}$$

Here ε denotes the exchange rate (the sterling price of one unit of foreign exchange), and E is the expectations operator. If capital is perfectly mobile internationally, incipient capital flows ensure that the domestic interest rate equals the foreign interest rate plus the expected rate of depreciation of exchange rate. So long as expectations of the maintenance of the gold standard parity dominate the market ($E\,(\hat{\varepsilon}) = 0$), domestic and foreign interest rates on equivalent assets will be equal. The impact on the British economy of deteriorating conditions abroad will be reflected in the paths of P, Y and I.

A further simplification is the decision not to distinguish gold from foreign exchange in the reserves of the Bank of England or to model the speculative demand for gold as distinct from foreign exchange. This simplification seems reasonable, since for most of the period the two assets were extremely close substitutes from the point of view of their risk characteristics. Foreign exchange dominated gold in terms of trans-

159 We multiply the left-hand side by C/C, multiply the right-hand side by R/R, and divide both sides by H.

port costs, but only gold was available upon demand from the Bank of England.

Equations (3′) and (5′) form a simultaneous system to be estimated by two-stage least squares, while the recursive block (4′) is estimated by ordinary least squares.[160] The data are described in the Appendix, but the price and output series deserve further comment. The price data used throughout are the Board of Trade's index numbers of wholesale prices. It is not clear whether wholesale or retail prices provide the appropriate deflator for nominal money balances, but the wholesale price index is chosen on the grounds that it is more closely tied to foreign commodity prices. The index of industrial production, constructed by the London and Cambridge Economic Service, while incomplete in coverage provides a consistent quarterly series spanning the period 1925–31. (The difficulty of constructing an adequate monthly series for the level of economic activity dictates the use of quarterly data.) To take into account the possibility that the seasonal pattern of activity in the omitted sectors differed from the seasonal pattern of activity in the sectors considered, seasonal dummy variables are included in equation (3′). Seasonal dummy variables also are included in equation (4′) to provide for the Bank of England's tendency to vary domestic credit conditions in response to the seasonality of currency demand.

Empirical results are presented in the Appendix. The estimated coefficients all have the expected signs. The money supply equation shows that a rise in Bank rate relative to market interest rates reduces the money multiplier. The central bank reaction function suggests the existence of partial sterilization by the Bank of England.[161] In other words, the Bank does not appear to have consistently obeyed the 'rules of the game' in its open market operations under the interwar gold standard. Whether or not this violation of the rules is sufficient in magnitude to undermine Britain's balance of payments position can be answered by simulating the model.

The reserve flow equation shows that reserve losses and gains experienced by the Bank of England under the interwar gold standard are largely explicable in terms of a few determinants of money supply and money demand. Equation (3′) predicts that an expansion of domestic credit should lead to a loss of reserves. The predicted coefficient on $(C/H)\hat{C}$ is -1, and the estimated coefficient of -0.83 is insignificantly

[160] Disturbance terms in (3′), (4′) and (5′) are assumed to be serially independent and to have zero covariance.

[161] When domestic credit and foreign reserves both account for half of the monetary base ($C/H = R/H = \frac{1}{2}$), approximately half of the impact of a change in foreign reserves is offset by the Bank of England's adjustment of domestic credit. Over the sample period, R/H ranged from 0.38 to 0.56. As a rule, however, it was less than 0.5, in which case the offset coefficient also would be less than 0.5.

different from −1. The coefficient on $\hat{V}$ is negative as anticipated, but significantly different from −1. The coefficient on the interest rate also is negative, as predicted, and significantly less than zero at the 95 per cent level using the appropriate one-tail test. The coefficient on the rate of change of prices, although positive and insignificantly different from unity, is imprecisely estimated. The coefficient on the rate of change of output also is imprecisely estimated, but it is significantly less than unity.[162]

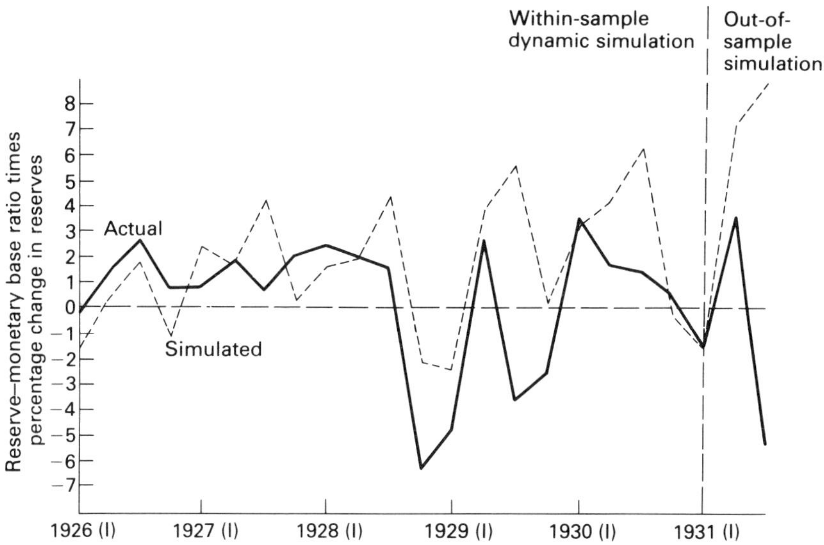

Figure 3.1 Actual and simulated reserve flows, 1926(I)–1931(III)

Source: see text. Vertical scale is in percentage points.

With these parameter estimates, we can use this model to perform simulation experiments. Figure 3.1 presents actual and simulated values of $(R/H)\hat{R}$, where the hypothetical values are derived from dynamic simulation. Dynamic simulation is a demanding test of a model, yet the model replicates the reserve losses and gains of the Bank of England with some success. The simulation shows the Bank of England continuing to accumulate international reserves during the 1927 exchange market difficulties. It replicates the loss of reserves that took place in the fourth quarter of 1928 and the first quarter of 1929, coincident with the effects of the New York stock market boom. It tracks the balance of payments' recovery in the second quarter of 1929 and its relapse in the fourth quarter of 1929, but not the effects of the intense speculation that took place at the height of the boom in the third quarter of that year.

162 Further discussion of these results appears in the Appendix to this chapter.

The simulation then shows reserves flowing back into Britain over the first three quarters of 1930, followed by a weakening of the balance of payments. Thus balance of payments trends of the period 1926 (I)–1931 (I) are to some extent explicable in terms of the fundamental determinants of the official settlements balance.

To test whether the underlying determinants of the balance of payments warranted a continued outflow of reserves during the second and third quarters of 1931, we simulate the model out of sample, using actual values of the exogenous variables, with the following results.

Dependent variable: $\frac{R}{H}$ $\hat{R}$

	Actual value	Simulated value
1931 (II)	3.62	7.06
1931 (III)	−5.14	8.76

The simulation does not support the view that the 1931 financial crisis is explicable in terms of the fundamental determinants of Britain's balance of payments. The model succeeds in tracking the reserve gains experienced by the Bank of England in the second quarter of 1931. Between the first and second quarters of the the year, the deepening of the worldwide depression caused market interest rates to fall. In Britain, this increased money demand and, by lowering the money multiplier, at the same time reduced money supply, thereby strengthening the balance of payments. Between the first and second quarters of 1931, the Bank of England also reduced the domestic credit component of the monetary base, thereby encouraging an inflow of reserves. These factors appear to have been more than sufficient to offset the deterioration in Britain's balance of payments arising from the continued fall in output and prices.

For the third quarter of 1931, the story is radically different. The model does not generate the loss of reserves that culminated in devaluation. The model points to several factors tending to undermine the balance of payments position: falling prices, which raised the real value of money balances, domestic credit creation by the Bank of England and higher interest rates which reduced the demand for money and led to a further reserve outflow. According to the simulation, however, other factors, notably the two increases in Bank rate in July, were more than sufficient to neutralize the influence of variables making for a loss of reserves. The rise in Bank rate caused the money multiplier to decline again between the second and third quarters of 1931, and a marked increase in industrial production augmented the demand for money. On the basis of this simulation, therefore, there is no evidence that, in the absence of foreign financial difficulties, the reserve losses experienced by the Bank of England in the third quarter of 1931 would have resulted eventually from the development of the fundamental determinants of the balance of payments.

Relaxing the restrictive assumptions upon which the model is based would only reinforce this conclusion. It could be argued that the financial crisis in Austria and Germany depressed economic activity on the Continent, putting downward pressure on prices and output in Britain as well. Had British prices and output been higher in the absence of the continental bank failures, then money demand would have been augmented, further increasing the extent of Britain's balance of payments surplus. Similarly, in so far as market interest rates in the second and third quarters of 1931 already incorporated doubts about the stability of sterling, those market rates would have been lower in the absence of the continental financial crisis. Lower interest rates also would have augmented money demand and led to larger balance of payments surpluses. All these effects merely reinforce the conclusions reached above. However, the argument that, in the absence of the crisis, Bank rate would have been lower works in the opposite direction. The conclusion of this section is not, therefore, that no balance of payments pressures other than those associated with the foreign financial difficulties can be discerned, but that there is no evidence of balance of payments pressures of a magnitude that could not have been offset by the level of Bank rate actually maintained.

Few readers need to be reminded that the results of this section derive from a model based on restrictive assumptions. In addition to the exogeneity of a number of crucial variables, it is assumed throughout that bonds denominated in different currencies are perfect substitutes and that capital is perfectly mobile; that fluctuations in the exchange rate between the gold points can be safely neglected; and that the Bank of England's response to international reserve flows takes an especially simple form. The virtue of restrictive assumptions, so long as they do no violence to historical circumstance, is that they render the model tractable and eliminate confusion about the channels through which influences are transmitted. More complex models incorporating less restrictive assumptions may lead to a modification of this section's conclusions, but at the very least the simple model analysed here yields preliminary evidence contrary to the balance of payments view.

Macroeconomic effects of devaluation

Britain's macroeconomic performance following the 1931 devaluation of sterling reflects the peculiar mix of positive and negative elements so characteristic of the economy's interwar record. On the negative side, throughout the 1930s the problem of widespread unemployment continually confronted British policy-makers. Between 1931 and 1936 the total unemployed as a percentage of all employees, on an annual average basis, never once fell below 10 per cent. Among insured employees, unemployment remained above 13 per cent over the entire period. Another economic problem of some concern to the authorities was the persistent deficit on the current account of the balance of payments. Until 1938 that deficit never approached half the staggering £114 million incurred the year Britain left the gold standard; but only in 1935, when the current account was in surplus by £13 million, did Britain escape deficit.[163]

On the positive side, at no time after 1931 does the balance of payments appear to have constituted a binding constraint on the rate of growth of domestic production. The stability of British growth in the 1930s was in marked contrast to the pronounced fluctuations of the 1920s.[164] The cyclical upswing that began at the end of 1932 was an exceptionally long one, and for the remainder of the 1930s real gross domestic product grew steadily, with investment demand providing much of the impetus for the economy's expansion. By 1937 British manufacturing production had expanded by nearly 50 per cent over a period of only six years. Although recovery started from an artificially low level, providing considerable room for expansion, the achievement was impressive none the less.

The stimulus provided by depreciation in 1931 and the flexibility imparted by the retention of a floating exchange rate thereafter were not the only factors contributing to the cyclical upswing of the mid-1930s. Economic recovery abroad and restoration of a semblance of international financial normality played important roles in providing a favourable climate for British growth. At the same time, the exchange rate played an equally important role in the macroeconomic trends of the 1930s.

Exchange rate fluctuations

In contrast to the devaluations of 1949 and 1967, following the 1931 devaluation the pound continued to float. Thus it is impossible to discuss the effects of depreciation without considering also the policies that influenced the exchange rate's subsequent course. There were a number of significant changes in British policy after 1931 with implications for the path of the exchange rate, including the advent of cheap money and the imposition of a general tariff.[165] Without depreciation, cheap money would not have been possible, while in the absence of

[163] Statistics are from Feinstein (1972, p. T128) and table 3.2, above.
[164] Burns and Mitchell (1946, p. 371).
[165] On the implications of tariff protection for exchange rate determination, see Eichengreen (1981b, 1983a).

cheap money, as in the absence of the tariff, a smaller depreciation probably would have ensued. Hence the effects of exchange rate changes cannot be discussed in isolation from the policies that were associated with those changes.

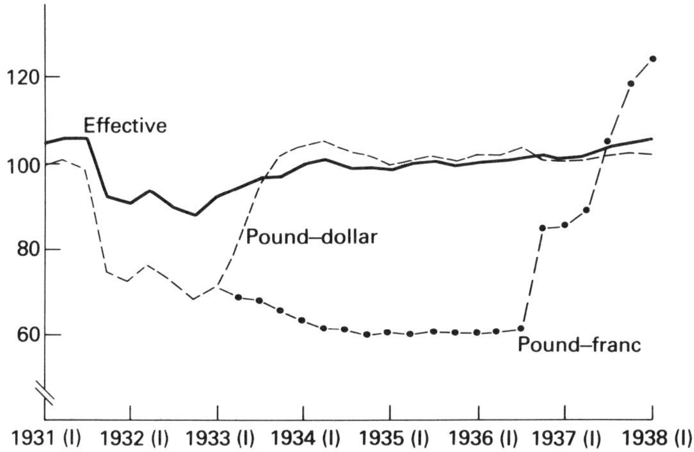

Figure 3.2 Bilateral and effective exchange rates, 1931–38 (1929/30=100)

Source: Redmond (1980)

The initial depreciation of sterling against the currencies of Britain's trading partners was far from uniform. Against the dollar and the currencies of other countries that continued to peg to gold, the initial depreciation was 25 per cent, from \$4.86 to \$3.75 at the end of the first week of floating. Following a brief upturn, the pound's descent continued, reaching a low of \$3.25 at the beginning of December, after which it recovered to \$3.40 at the turn of the year.[166] In February, massive speculative inflows drove sterling up temporarily to a peak of \$3.70. More than two dozen countries allowed their currencies to depreciate along with sterling. These included most of the Empire, Scandinavia and Eastern Europe, along with other traditional trading partners such as Portugal, Argentina and Egypt. Subsequently, other countries, such as Turkey and Japan, attached their currencies to the pound. All this renders it somewhat misleading to summarize fluctuations in sterling in terms of movements in the bilateral pound–US dollar rate. This is evident in figure 3.2, where the pound–dollar and the pound–franc exchange rates are plotted along with Britain's effective exchange rate (a weighted average of bilateral rates, where the weights equal the share of each country in Britain's total imports and exports).[167] In contrast to

[166] This 'overshooting' phenomenon is discussed by Hall (1935, p. 3).
[167] For details on the construction of this index, see Redmond (1980, pp. 85–7).

the 25 per cent depreciation of the pound against the dollar and the franc, Britain's quarterly average effective exchange rate fell by only 13 per cent between the third and fourth quarters of 1931. Ensuing fluctuations in the effective rate can be understood in terms of the pound's movements against the dollar and the European currencies that remained on gold. For the first four months of 1932 the pound appreciated against currencies on the gold standard, and for the remainder of the year it tended to depreciate against gold. In each period Britain's effective exchange rate moved in parallel fashion.

The United States broke with the gold bloc in 1933. Roosevelt proclaimed a bank holiday on 6 March 1933, and four days later he extended restrictions on foreign exchange dealings and gold and currency movements. On 5 April an executive order was issued requiring individuals to deliver their gold coin, bullion and certificates to federal reserve banks. With the issuance on 20 April of another order extending the gold embargo, the dollar price of gold began to fluctuate.[168] This created a situation in which sterling appreciated against the currency of the United States, a country that accounted for around 12 per cent of Britain's trade, while continuing to depreciate against the currencies of the gold bloc, whose share of Britain's trade was approximately equal in size. Because of the magnitude of its depreciation, the movement of the dollar dominated Britain's effective exchange rate, which appreciated over the second half of 1933 and for much of the subsequent year. Devaluation of the dollar set off another round of currency depreciation; in January 1934, when the dollar was stabilized at 59 per cent of its former gold content, the only major currencies that remained pegged to gold at traditional parities were those of Belgium, Czechoslovakia, France, Germany, Holland, Italy, Poland and Switzerland.

Figure 3.3 depicts Britain's bilateral exchange rates against the dollar and the French franc along with ratios of foreign to domestic prices. These series provide limited support for the purchasing power parity doctrine, which suggests that we should observe parallel movements of exchange rates and relative national price levels.[169] In the 1930s, exchange rates and relative prices moved together, but exchange rate fluctuations often tended to be larger than relative price movements. Sizeable deviations from purchasing power parity thus can be observed. For instance, the 23 per cent depreciation of the quarterly average pound–dollar and pound–franc exchange rates that took place between the third and fourth quarters of 1931 was accompanied by a mere 7 per cent fall in American wholesale prices relative to British wholesale prices. Similarly, when the dollar was devalued in 1933, and when the franc depreciated in 1936, British prices declined relative to foreign

[168] Friedman and Schwartz (1963, pp. 463–5).
[169] See Frenkel (1978, pp. 169–92).

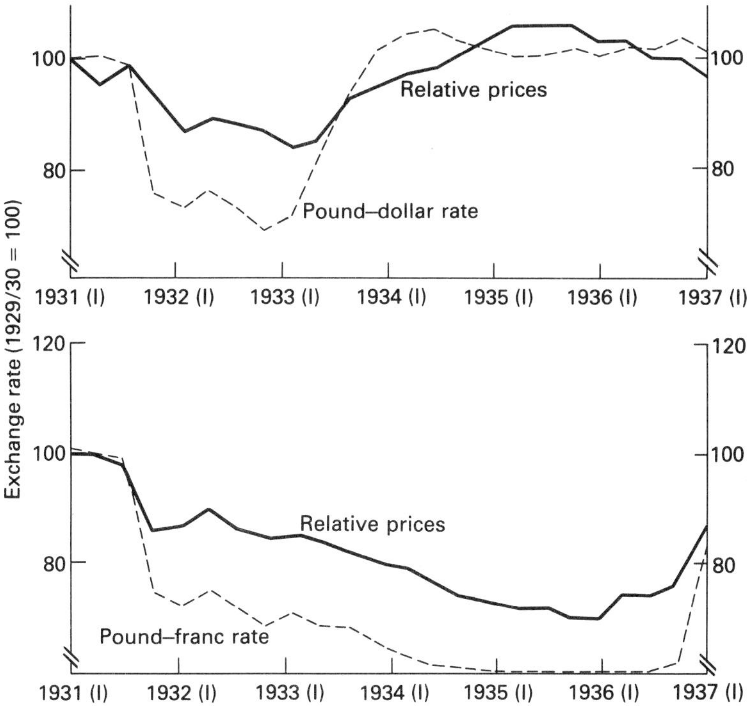

Figure 3.3 Exchange rates and relative prices, 1931–36

Source: Methorst (1938); Einzig (1937)

prices, but not to the extent of the appreciation of the pound. Empirical tests reported in the Appendix are broadly consistent with the purchasing power doctrine, but they indicate that wholesale price movements account for only a part of sterling's fluctuation.

Intervention played an important role in foreign exchange markets throughout the 1930s. A measure of the magnitude of British intervention can be obtained by considering the role of official financing and short-term capital movements in accommodating Britain's balance of payments. Table 3.8 shows Britain's basic balance, short-term capital movements and reserve gains. The influence of short-term capital flows can be gauged by asking whether they were helpful in financing the basic balance or added to external imbalance. Although short-term capital movements have been accused of having 'little relation to current balance of payments situations',[170] in every year from 1932 to 1937 short-term capital helped finance Britain's basic balance, and in many years those flows were quite substantial.

170 Richardson (1967, p. 63); see also Aldcroft (1970, p. 268).

TABLE 3.8 Capital transactions and official financing, 1931–38

	(£ million)			
	Basic balance	*Short-term capital*[a]	*Change in reserves*[b]	*External borrowing*
1931	−119	85	−34	82
1932	−53	82	29	−114
1933	−30	152	122	0
1934	−68	78	10	0
1935	−5	84	79	0
1936	−42	253	211	0
1937	−60	189	129	0
1938	−45	−223	−268	0

[a] Short-term capital flow includes change in British government stocks
[b] Change in reserves is exclusive of external borrowing

Source: Computed from table 3.2

Table 3.8 indicates that throughout the 1930s official financing reached significant proportions. In many years intervention nearly matched self-financing through capital flows. In Britain, the mechanism for this intervention was the Exchange Equalisation Account.

The British authorities' attitudes toward exchange rate fluctuations underwent considerable change following devaluation. After initial efforts to push down the pound, the Treasury and the Bank agreed on a hands-off policy on sterling.[171] Despite the government's own description of the gold standard's suspension as temporary, any attempt to peg the exchange rate was rendered impractical by the depleted state of Bank of England foreign exchange reserves.[172] Although continental observers took for granted the presumption that Britain's return to the gold standard was imminent, discussions within the government and the Bank of England were steadily moving towards other conclusions.[173] In official statements issued soon after devaluation, the Bank described its responsibility as discouraging speculation, preventing inflation and strengthening London's position as an international financial centre. Within the Bank, new committees were established to consider the question of a desirable level for sterling and to determine the Bank's role in its achievement. At first, these discussions were much coloured

[171] See Howson (1975, pp. 173–6); Howson (1980a, pp. 54–5).

[172] See the text of the press notice announcing suspension of the gold standard, in Sayers (1976, volume 3, pp. 264–5).

[173] So Keynes reported to Walter Case in his letter of 2 November 1931. See Keynes (1982, pp. 10–11).

by the fact that a sizeable depreciation would generate powerful inflationary pressures, a danger that was foremost in the minds of Treasury officials as well.[174] With time, the spectre of inflation receded, and the Bank was increasingly swayed by the attractions of a low exchange rate. By March of 1932, the decision in favour of a low exchange rate and a policy of cheap money had been made, and the Bank of England undertook to replenish its stocks of gold and foreign exchange. The Exchange Equalisation Account (EEA) was established to provide a convenient vehicle for exchange market intervention. The EEA, endowed initially with more than £170 million in sterling (an endowment more than doubled in the Budget of 1933), held a portfolio composed of gold, foreign exchange, and British Treasury bills. These assets were controlled by the Treasury, but the Account's day-to-day operations were the responsibility of the Bank of England. Its activities reflected the results of continuous discussions of exchange rate management between Treasury and Bank officials.[175]

There exists some dispute concerning the authorities' motives in establishing the EEA. Traditionally, it has been argued that the EEA was created in order to provide a convenient mechanism for smoothing fluctuations in exchange rates without interfering in the development of long-term trends.[176] That is, the EEA is seen as a vehicle for 'leaning against the wind', when that wind took the form of gusts that blew the exchange rate off course. Recently, Howson has argued that from the start the EEA was a means 'to keep down the pound'.[177] It may be that there was a difference of opinion within official circles: while the Bank of England saw the EEA as a mechanism for neutralizing the impact of disturbances, the Treasury correctly anticipated that for the most part intervention would be needed to prevent appreciation. Whatever the rationale for creating the EEA, there is no doubt that it was soon intervening to prevent exchange rate appreciation. By the middle of 1932 the Treasury had decided in favour of a cheap money policy designed to promote employment and domestic investment, and a low value of the pound was viewed as a necessary concomitant to that policy. Thereafter, whenever sterling exhibited a tendency to appreciate to an undesirable extent, the EEA responded by purchasing gold and foreign exchange in return for sterling obtained from the release of Treasury bills. It first did so in the summer of 1932. When sterling

174 Cab 58/169, Keynes, 'Notes on the Currency Question', 16 November 1931; T 175/57, Hopkins, 'Note on Mr Keynes' Memorandum of 16 November', 15 December 1931; Eichengreen (1981a, pp. 25–8).

175 Sayers (1957, p. 74); Richardson (1936, p. 40).

176 See for example Bank of England (1968, pp. 378–81). Hall (1935, p. 4) describes the purpose of the EEA as 'to prevent changes in foreign balances moving the exchange away from the equilibrium rate. . . .'

177 Howson (1980a, p. 54). See also Waight (1939, chapter 5); Dimsdale (1981, p. 330).

weakened the following November, the EEA sold off considerable quantities of foreign exchange yet was unable, or perhaps unwilling, to prevent the pound from falling to $3.15.

This intervention appears as official financing in table 3.8. In six of the seven years from 1932 to 1938, the government accumulated gold and foreign exchange through the sale of sterling.[178] There were also a number of periods like November 1932 when the EEA purchased sterling on balance. Howson's figures on UK gold and foreign exchange reserves, based largely on Treasury records, indicate that between October 1932 and April 1936 British reserves rose in three out of every four months. Yet on the basis of a survey of the financial press, Whitaker and Hudgins find a consensus of opinion that the EEA was intervening to support the exchange rate in 26 out of 78 months from July 1932 to December 1938, and a consensus of opinion that it was intervening to depress sterling in 20 of those months.[179] Apparently the Bank of England and the EEA had some success in disguising their operations.

Several reaction functions based upon Howson's figures for changes in UK gold and foreign exchange reserves are presented in the Appendix. These equations suggest that intervention by the British authorities was related to changes in the exchange rate and to Britain's balance of trade. There is no evidence of leaning against the wind; to the contrary, these estimates support Howson's view that the authorities intervened so as to reinforce exchange rate movements. However, the authorities also appear to have taken Britain's trade balance into account. When the size of the trade balance deficit increased, they intervened to depress the pound with all the more vigour.

External balance

For calendar year 1931 Britain's current account deficit amounted to an unprecedented £114 million. Following devaluation, the current account eventually righted itself, with the deficit falling by nearly 50 per cent from 1931 to 1932 and by a further 75 per cent between 1932 and 1933. Much of this improvement was due to the effect of depreciation on the trade balance. With the depreciation of sterling, the persistent fall in the volume of exports was halted, and import volume declined absolutely in the first quarter of 1932. There also occurred a pronounced shift in the geographical pattern of British trade. Britain's imports were drawn increasingly from the Dominions and less so from other regions. Her export trade shifted towards the sterling area and away from other

[178] On the Fund's gold holdings, see Paish (1937, p. 348) and Howson (1980b, table A–1).

[179] Whitaker and Hudgins (1977, p. 1484); Howson (1980b, table A–1).

foreign countries. However, tariff protection at home and abroad, rather than exchange rate changes, was largely responsible for these shifts on the export side.[180]

While depreciation ultimately succeeded in strengthening the trade balance, its favourable effects were not immediately apparent in the months following devaluation. As in 1968, the trade balance deficit, valued in sterling, continued to grow following the devaluation, and only in January 1932 did it fall below its pre-devaluation level. To some extent this effect was seasonal: Britain's deficit typically increased between the third and fourth quarters of the calendar year. The increase in 1931 was not greatly in excess of average. However, import demand functions based on monthly data suggest that Britain's price elasticity of demand for imports varied from approximately 0.1 in the very short run to 0.7 in the long run.[181] Assuming similar values for the foreign price elasticity of demand for Britain's exports, depreciation would have worsened the trade balance in the very short run but improved it subsequently.[182] Another factor contributing to the rise in imports was anticipatory purchases designed to forestall expected import duties. As shown in table 3.7, not just the value but the volume of British imports rose between the third and fourth quarters of 1931.

Following their initial divergence, the exchange rate and the trade balance moved together. This is apparent in figure 3.4, where Britain's effective exchange rate and trade balance are plotted. The trade balance improved with a lag when the effective exchange rate depreciated, and it deteriorated following an appreciation of the exchange rate. A notable feature of the figure is the manner in which the two series diverge after 1933, when continued appreciation of the effective exchange rate was not accompanied by successively larger trade balance deficits. Through 1935, British exports expanded more rapidly than those of Germany and the United States: imperial preference and the continued growth of the new industries both contributed to this trend.

The figures in table 3.9 on Britain's balance on invisibles tell a vastly different story. Relative to its pre-devaluation level, the surplus in invisible trade declined in 1932 and recovered only slowly thereafter. Shipping receipts provide a good example of delayed recovery; they declined steadily from 1929 to 1933 while improving markedly in later

180 See Eichengreen (1979) for details on the tariff's effects.

181 These equations are reported in the Appendix. There are several reasons, described by Orcutt (1950), to assume that these elasticity estimates are biased downward. The long-run price elasticity of 0.7 is indistinguishable from the estimates of 0.64 obtained by Chang (1951), 0.60 for 1931 estimated by Friedman (1974), and 0.5 estimated by Thomas (1975) and assumed by Moggridge (1969).

182 Estimates of the price elasticity of demand for British exports in this period range widely, but 0.5 is a representative figure. See Cheng (1959), Kaliski (1961) and Thomas (1975).

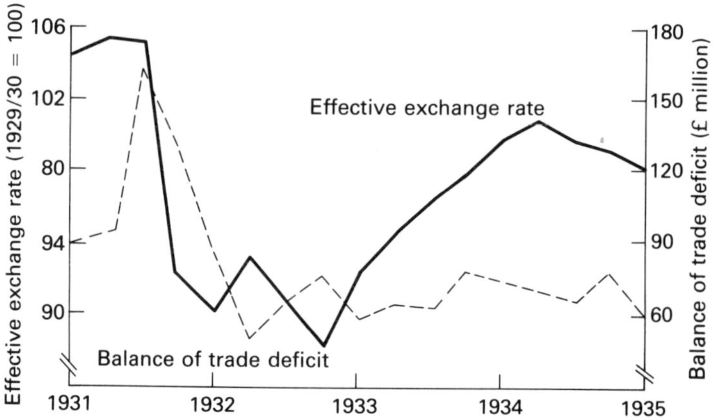

Figure 3.4 Effective exchange rate and trade balance deficit, 1931–35

Source: Methorst (1938) and Redmond (1980)

TABLE 3.9 UK balance of trade in invisibles, 1925–38

	(£ million)			
	Exports of services	*Imports of services*	*Property income from abroad*	*Property income paid abroad*
1925	215	149	318	67
1926	223	152	323	67
1927	245	142	324	67
1928	234	140	325	69
1929	242	152	328	69
1930	214	147	295	67
1931	168	140	221	53
1932	153	123	182	52
1933	146	120	194	34
1934	145	116	208	33
1935	149	124	226	36
1936	174	135	246	40
1937	229	144	264	43
1938	193	152	247	43

Source: Feinstein (1972, table 15, pp. T38–9)

years. This deterioration in the invisible balance undoubtedly was due to a combination of factors: devaluation, the erection of tariff barriers, and economic stagnation abroad. However, the effects of exchange rate uncertainty and trade restraints in depressing Britain's income from shipping and financial services rendered to foreigners accounted for only a small part of the decline in invisible receipts. Britain's exports of services, measured in constant prices, fell by about 5 per cent between 1931 and 1932; meanwhile, imports of services declined by a considerably greater proportion. To the extent that it had any effect, therefore, it is likely that devaluation had a favourable impact on the service account.

The critical factor underlying the deterioration in the invisible accounts was the fall in property income from abroad. Table 3.9 indicates that property income was by far the largest component of the invisible balance, and that British receipts fell by 18 per cent between 1931 and 1932. Figures on British income from overseas investment are summarized in table 3.10. The property income component of the current account includes interest and dividends paid by British companies operating abroad, interest on loans to Empire and non-Empire governments, and returns on investments in foreign companies. Income on loans to Empire governments remained steady over the entire period. This is not surprising in the light of the relatively low incidence of default on these loans and the fact that overseas loans were denominated in sterling. In contrast, the rate of return on loans to non-Empire governments declined steadily over the first part of the 1930s, in large part owing to defaults resulting from the contraction of trade and the effects of worldwide depression. If anything, depreciation of sterling may have reduced the incidence of default by making it easier for some debtor countries to repay their sterling obligations.

The other factor contributing to the decline in income from investment abroad was the falling rate of return on the debt and equity of foreign companies and British companies operating abroad. As always, the profitability of these investments moved with foreign business cycles. The secular decline in the rate of return to these enterprises between 1930 and 1933 can be linked to the downward trend in primary commodity prices; once the prices of primary products in general and of gold in particular recovered after 1933, so did the profitability of Britain's direct foreign investments.[183] Only the fall in the value of British investments in foreign companies can be linked to exchange rate fluctuations. Uncertainty surrounding the value of the pound in 1932 and 1933 may have discouraged British residents from holding the securities of foreign companies.

These various components of the current account of the balance of payments are summarized in table 3.2. They reveal the familiar tendency of the UK to run deficits in visible trade and surpluses in invisible trade. For years Britain had been able to finance consumption

[183] Kahn (1946, pp. 186–7).

TABLE 3.10 Investment and income from abroad, 1930–35

(*£ million*)

	Loans to Empire governments		*Loans to non-Empire governments*		*Investment in British companies*		*Investment in foreign companies*	
	Value of assets	*Rate of return*	*Value of assets*	*Rate of return*	*Value of assets*	*Rate of return*	*Value of assets*	*Rate of return*
1930	1080	4.3	357	5.0	1209	6.3	785	6.7
1931	1104	4.2	337	5.2	1210	4.0	766	5.3
1932	1109	4.4	323	4.2	1191	3.6	717	5.5
1933	1147	4.3	333	3.6	1210	3.3	698	5.0
1934	1163	4.2	336	3.6	1216	3.7	690	5.8
1935	1157	4.2	346	3.6	1229	4.2	697	6.2

Source: computed from annual articles by Kindersley in the *Economic Journal*: see Kindersley (1932, 1933, 1934, 1935, 1936)

of imported merchandise well in excess of her export sales out of interest earnings from abroad. In contrast to the 1920s, however, in the 1930s, as a consequence of the decline in overseas lending, income from overseas investments and from services rendered to foreigners no longer was sufficient to cover the deficit arising from trade in goods. Thus, on balance the current account was weaker after 1932 than it had been in the 1920s.

TABLE 3.11 Geographical distribution of exports, 1929–35

	1929(I)	*1932(I)*	*1935(I)*
	%	%	%
British countries	45.3	43.8	46.2
Sterling area foreign countries	11.5	12.4	15.9
Other foreign countries	43.2	43.8	37.9

Source: PRO Cab 58/30, EAC (SC) 21; *The Economic Outlook*, 20 July 1935

A notable characteristic of Britain's trade in goods following the 1931 devaluation was its changing geographical pattern. Table 3.11 presents a comparison of trade with British countries, sterling area foreign countries and non-sterling area countries.[184] Despite a share of world trade that remained almost exactly constant over the course of the 1930s, the share of Britain's export trade with sterling area countries grew at the expense of the share of exports destined for other foreign countries.[185] This is contrary to the anticipated effects of exchange rate depreciation: we would expect the demand for British products to have risen in foreign markets where the domestic currency had appreciated relative to sterling. However, by 1935 the dollar and other foreign currencies linked to it had been devalued relative to sterling for nearly two years, and this should have minimized any shift in the direction of the export trade. Another reason that the anticipated rise in the proportion of exports to non-sterling area countries never materialized was that many of these countries responded to Britain's devaluation by raising tariff barriers. A further explanation may lie in the fact that much of the sterling area shared in Britain's unusually rapid economic recovery.

[184] In table 3.11, the sterling area includes countries with currencies tied to the pound as of the beginning of 1935: Finland, Sweden, Norway, Denmark, Portugal, Egypt, Iraq, Iran, Siam and Argentina.

[185] Figures on world trade are from League of Nations (1938).

Over this same period, the share of British imports drawn from the Dominions rose relative to the share drawn from both sterling area and other countries. If effective exchange rate depreciation alone were to explain the shift in the geographical origin of Britain's imports, one would expect to find imports from the Dominions and from other sterling area countries both to have risen at the expense of imports from other foreign countries, whose currencies appreciated relative to sterling. That the share of imports from the Dominions rose so rapidly is evidence that the General Tariff of 1932, concessions made to the Dominions at Ottawa, and bilateral agreements concluded with other countries with which Britain traditionally ran trade balance deficits (such as the Scandinavian nations and Argentina) were as important as devaluation in explaining the changing geographical composition of British trade. According to Harris's calculations for six Dominions and 23 foreign countries, the share of imports from the Dominions in the UK's total imports rose from 19 per cent in 1930–31 to nearly 30 per cent in 1932–34.[186]

Given these relatively small changes in Britain's current account position, how was maintenance of balance of payments equilibrium consistent with such a strong exchange rate? A large part of the explanation lies in the controls placed on outward capital movements and the virtual cessation of long-term lending in the 1930s. Overseas capital issues were immediately prohibited upon the gold standard's suspension and remained under strict control for several years. In June 1932 the entire new-issue market came under regulation as part of the effort to convert the War Loan to a lower interest rate. This embargo was relaxed in January 1933, when freedom to lend to Commonwealth borrowers was once more extended, but foreign issues remained rigorously controlled. Of all new issues on the London market between 1932 and 1935, only 2½ per cent represented foreign issues, and these were nearly all for the purpose of helping sterling area countries replenish their reserves.[187]

Since capital controls had no statutory foundation, there was initially some question as to their effectiveness. In fact, their power was considerably enhanced by the virtual collapse of familiar patterns of international lending. As a whole, the creditor countries experienced a net inflow rather than an outflow of capital in the 1930s.[188] New overseas issues on the London market, which frequently had exceeded £200 million prior to the war, never approached £50 million between 1932 and 1938. Other overseas issues, including conversion and refunding issues, were considerably more important, but the total volume of

[186] Harris (1936, pp. 448–9).
[187] Cairncross (1973, pp. 56–7). For further details, see Stewart (1938, *passim*).
[188] Lewis (1949, p. 71).

long-term lending channelled through the London market still remained depressed by historical standards.[189]

Internal balance

Annual rates of growth of real GDP following devaluation were not unprecedented by interwar standards. However, in comparison with the 1920s, the persistent, uninterrupted nature of the growth that followed the 1931 devaluation is noteworthy. By the end of the decade, British observers could look back on a sustained cyclical upswing marked by a growth of manufacturing production unparallelled in Britain's twentieth century experience.

Devaluation could have sustained the economy's expansion through its impact on either aggregate supply or aggregate demand. The most important increment to aggregate demand was associated with the investment boom induced by the introduction of 'cheap money'. However, devaluation also had expenditure-switching effects. By reducing the price of British goods relative to the price of foreign goods, the devaluation switched expenditure towards British output. In figure 3.5 the competitiveness of British and American goods is plotted along with the dollar–pound exchange rate. The measure of competitiveness shown is the real (wholesale price adjusted) exchange rate. Whenever the price of American goods rose relative to the price of British goods, this measure of competitiveness declined, making British goods more attrac-

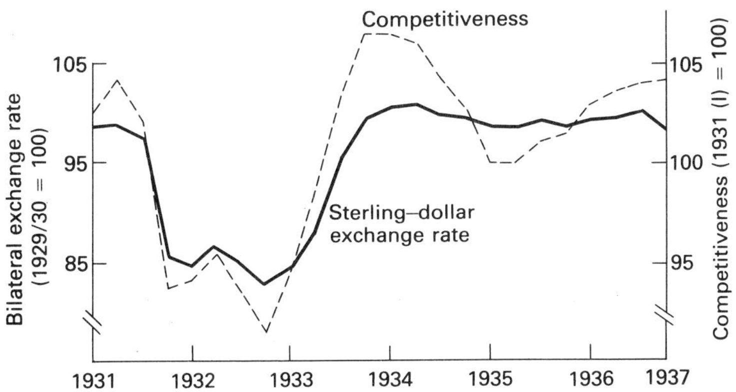

Figure 3.5 The exchange rate and competitiveness, 1931–36

Source: Methorst (1938) and Einzig (1937)

189 See Sayers (1976, volume 3, pp. 310–11). These are Midland Bank estimates, reworked by Kindersley and reported in his annual *Economic Journal* articles.

tive to consumers and switching expenditure towards the products of British industry.

The movement of this index suggests that the 1931 devaluation of sterling enhanced the competitiveness of British goods relative to American goods in the short run.[190] The exchange rate and the competitiveness index follow one another closely, because short-term changes in competitiveness were due almost entirely to exchange rate changes. The adjustment of domestic currency prices at home and abroad eroded this devaluation-induced improvement in the competitive position only slowly. Thus, it is not surprising that the 1933 devaluation of the dollar, which restored the bilateral rate to its gold standard level, largely eliminated the short-term gain in British competitiveness.[191] The devaluation of the dollar makes it difficult to judge how long, in the absence of further initiatives, the change in competitiveness arising from the 1931 devaluation of sterling would have endured. By the time the United States devalued in 1933, six quarters subsequent to the 1931 devaluation of sterling, the improvement in British competitiveness had shown few signs of dissipating.

These changes in international competitiveness switched expenditure first towards British goods in 1932 and then away from them in 1933. A plausible upper bound for the relative price elasticity of demand for British goods in 1931 is 2.2; that is, on an annual basis, a 1 per cent rise in the relative price of imports led to a 2.2 per cent increase in the demand for British goods.[192] Owing to the movement of relative prices, the devaluation should have provided significant stimulus to demand in 1932 and over the first half of 1933. This stimulus worked its way through to output and employment with a lag. In terms of domestic production, 1932 was a year of continued stagnation, while 1933 marked the start of recovery; similarly, the number unemployed reached a peak at slightly less than 3 million in the first quarter of 1933.

Supply-side effects of the 1931 devaluation are more difficult to discern. The figures in table 3.12 indicate little if any rise in output prices relative to wage costs. Output prices rose by 2 per cent relative to the cost of raw materials in the year following devaluation, but this effect was only temporary. The wage and price equations reported in the Appendix suggest the following explanation: wages rose or fell gradually in response to conditions in the British labour market, but given the amount of slack present in that market, wage demands were not particularly sensitive to changes in purchasing power. In so far as

[190] The behaviour of this index is much the same when exchange rates are adjusted for changes in retail prices or money wage rates instead of changes in wholesale prices. Data sources are described in the Appendix. Exactly the same pattern emerges when British and French prices are compared. See Sauvy (1965, p. 343, figure 37).

[191] Morton (1943, p. 151).

[192] This estimate is from Eichengreen (1979, p. 231).

TABLE 3.12 Product wages, 1931–36 (1931 = 1.00)

	Wages relative to total final output deflator	*Wages relative to prices of domestically producted plant and equipment*	*Wages relative to wholesale prices*
1931	1.00	1.00	1.00
1932	1.01	1.01	1.01
1933	1.02	1.00	1.00
1934	1.02	1.02	0.97
1935	1.02	1.00	0.97
1936	1.03	0.98	0.93

Source: Wholesale prices from Methorst (1938, pp. 206–13); all other series from Feinstein (1972, p. T140)

devaluation raised the cost of living by increasing the domestic price of imported foodstuffs, this led to little discernible rise in the general level of wage rates. In any case, the impact of devaluation on the cost of living was swamped by other influences. Import prices denominated in sterling continued to fall despite devaluation; Keynes for one labelled the stability of British prices in the wake of devaluation as 'remarkable'.[193] Money wages were by no means fixed; to the contrary, in so far as devaluation promoted recovery and stimulated the demand for labour, it put upward pressure on wage rates from the demand side. From 1933 up to the Second World War, the annual rate of money wage increase averaged 2½ per cent. But once wages were determined by conditions in the labour market, prices were marked up over wages and other costs in a standard fashion, with little attention paid to the prices set by foreign competitors. Given domestic prices, the exchange rate adjusted gradually in the direction of purchasing power parity.

A final important aspect of the 1931 devaluation of sterling was the relationship between the exchange rate and domestic policies pursued by the authorities. The long-term benefits of devaluation derived principally from the lower interest rates and increasingly expansionary monetary policies adopted in the 1930s. Prior to the 1931 devaluation, the monetary and fiscal options open to the authorities were limited by the necessity of defending the exchange rate. Under the interwar gold standard, British interest rates were closely related to the general level of world interest rates, and the money supply could not be determined independently of those interest rates and the level of income.

193 'Letter to Walter Case', 2 November 1931; in Keynes (1982, pp. 4–5).

The 1931 devaluation of sterling and the decision to allow the pound to float provided the authorities with an opportunity to alter their monetary stance. With the advent of a floating exchange rate, the rigid link between British interest rates and foreign interest rates was disrupted, and the British authorities were able to exercise increased control over the growth of the money supply. Initially, fears that exchange rate depreciation would lead to rapidly rising wages and a panic flight of foreign capital caused the authorities to raise Bank rate to 6½ per cent. However, when the vicious spiral failed to materialize and foreign funds began to flow back into sterling, the authorities were able to reduce Bank rate and use open market operations to expand the money supply without destabilizing the exchange rate.

'Cheap money' was introduced early in 1932, when Bank rate was lowered in successive steps to 2 per cent.[194] To prevent the emergence of a sizeable gap between Bank rate and market rates, the Bank of England expanded the banks' cash reserves through open market operations. These operations were not sufficient to prevent capital inflows: total reserves expanded by 18 per cent over the course of the year, the largest jump occurring in May. Owing to the combined effects of capital inflows and open market operations, total deposits of the ten London clearing banks rose by more than 10 per cent between 1931 (IV) and 1932 (IV). Cheap money was introduced, despite the Bank of England's fears of inflation, in the hope that domestic economic activity would be stimulated. A low interest rate was part and parcel of the effort to keep the exchange rate down: open market sales increased the supply of sterling on domestic and foreign markets alike.[196] Perhaps the overriding factor swaying the authorities in the direction of low interest rates was the Treasury's preoccupation with the cost of debt service.[197] The financial crisis had reinforced the belief that maintenance of a balanced budget was critically important for confidence, so efforts to reduce the cost of debt service, notably by engineering the massive War Loan conversion of 1932, provided a further incentive to reduce interest rates.[198] In the presence of capital controls and tariff barriers, the danger that monetary expansion might lead to uncontrollable exchange rate depreciation seemed less threatening.

Converting the War Loan meant inducing the market to accept 3½ per cent securities in place of the government's outstanding 5 per cent obligations. By the end of September 1932, all but 8 per cent of the £2,086 million loan had been converted, and the remainder was paid out

[194] On the introduction of cheap money, see Nevin (1953) and Howson (1975).

[195] *Bank of England Statistical Summary*, various issues.

[196] See Nevin (1953).

[197] Howson (1975, p. 89).

[198] Subsequent conversion operations took place in 1934, 1935, 1936 and 1938. See Peacock and Wiseman (1967) and Howson (1975).

in cash at the end of the year. This successful conversion operation contributed to the fall in debt service as a percentage of national income from 8.3 per cent in 1932 to 4.6 per cent in 1935.[199]

The effects of cheap money soon were evident. For the remainder of the interwar period, the rate of interest on gilt-edged securities fluctuated below a ceiling of 3½ per cent. Associated with the decline in interest rates was the recovery in share prices: these rose by more than 20 per cent over the second half of 1932, and between 1932 and 1936 the index of ordinary industrial share prices more than doubled. The restoration of confidence provoked an increased demand for securities, much of which can be traced to insurance companies and investment trusts. For larger firms, retained earnings remained the most important source of finance for new investment. Smaller firms relied to a greater extent on bank loans and, in some cases, on new issues on the London market.[200] The attractiveness of raising funds through the issue of new gilt-edged securities was enhanced by the maintenance of capital controls discouraging the acquisition of foreign securities and by the growth of uncertainty about foreign political conditions, both of which channelled demand towards the home market. The share of investments in bank portfolios rose substantially after 1932. But it was not until 1937 that the ratio of advances to deposits began to rise, and not until 1939 that total advances regained their 1929 level.

Residential construction was the activity most frequently cited as benefiting from cheap money.[201] The decline in mortgage rates from 6 to 4.5 per cent provided considerable stimulus to housing demand. Residential construction began to revive within six months of the reduction in Bank rate. Compared with the two preceding quarters, housebuilding was more than 25 per cent higher on average in the final quarter of 1932 and the first quarter of 1933.[202] With dwellings accounting for two-thirds of all new construction, the building industry remained buoyant through 1936: nearly three-quarters of all houses built in Britain during the interwar period were constructed between 1932 and 1939.

The case should not be overstated: industrial investment in sectors such as iron and steel also was stimulated by the fall in interest rates, and cheap money was but one factor, along with rising real incomes, contributing to the building boom.[203] Between 1931 and 1937, residential construction expanded at only 60 per cent of the rate of growth of manufacturing production. Yet compared with residential construction, gross domestic manufacturing investment recovered at a relatively late

199 See Howson (1975, chapter 4) for details.
200 Hodson (1938, p. 181); Nevin (1953, p. 25). See also Aldcroft (1970) and Dimsdale (1981).
201 See for example Stolper (1941).
202 Howson (1975, pp. 115–16).
203 Richardson (1967, p. 195); Kirby (1981, p. 75).

date. After bottoming out in 1932–33, manufacturing investment began to climb only in 1933–34, some six months to a year after the initial spurt in building activity. Investment in heavy industries such as steel revived only in 1934–35, a lag that reflected in part the higher costs of installing new equipment and disrupting ongoing production. In subsequent years, investment in the engineering, aircraft and vehicle industries was stimulated by rising government expenditures on rearmament. This staggered pattern of investment activity provides one explanation for the long duration of the cyclical upswing that characterized the British economy in the 1930s.

Conclusion

The 1931 devaluation of sterling, foreseen by few and desired by fewer, had sustained and far-reaching effects. Since the depreciation of the exchange rate was offset only gradually by changes in national price levels, devaluation enhanced the competitiveness of British goods in domestic and foreign markets. This ultimately strengthened the trade balance and stimulated demand for the products of British industry. However, the reaction of foreign governments, which took the form of trade barriers imposed against imports of British goods and depreciation of their own currencies, eventually neutralized the impact of devaluation on the competitive position and dimmed earlier hopes for an export-led recovery. Hence, the impressive expansion of the economy in the wake of the 1931 devaluation must be understood in terms of the new opportunities for stimulating domestic investment that it provided the British authorities.

Freed from the constraints imposed by sterling's gold standard parity, the authorities turned to a policy of cheap money and intervened in the foreign exchange market to depress the exchange rate. Lower interest rates stimulated investment and final demand without leading to any significant increase in the general level of money wages. Over the remainder of the decade, manufacturing production expanded at a rate unparallelled in modern British history.

A further question is how the 1931 devaluation affected the world economy in general and the speed of its recovery from the Great Depression in particular. One view is that the devaluation of sterling transmitted 'powerful deflationary pressure' to countries remaining on a gold standard.[204] Freed from the rigours of the gold standard, the United Kingdom was relieved of any remaining obligation to respect freedom of trade and foreign lending. The import duties and capital controls imposed by the British reinforced similar tendencies previously

[204] Kindleberger (1973, p. 171); see also Robbins (1933, pp. 112–13).

manifested abroad. The fall of sterling disrupted familiar financial arrangements between traders and financiers and impeded the recovery of international trade. Central banks incurred capital losses on their sterling reserves, and the scramble for liquidity was on once more. According to this view, the downward spiral of exchange rates provided much of the impetus for the continued contraction of international commerce and lethargic recovery of world prices.

It is beyond dispute that tariff retaliation and competitive devalution were unfortunate features of international economic relations in the 1930s. However, it appears unlikely that the 1931 devaluation of sterling and subsequent devaluations abroad had a deflationary impact on balance. Another view is that, by devaluing their currencies, Britain and countries that followed her example were able to counteract the deflationary pressures resulting from the banking crisis of preceding years.[205] The unprecedented expansion of the British economy over the remainder of the 1930s certainly helped to stimulate the economies of her trading partners. With the removal of exchange rate constraints, central banks around the world were able to pursue cheap money policies like that of the Bank of England. As prices rose relative to costs, a stimulus was provided to industrial production and, indirectly, to international trade as well. Perhaps here lies an explanation of why Britain's foreign trade in the 1930s expanded most rapidly with countries that had depreciated their exchange rates along with sterling.

[205] Harris (1936, pp. 469–70).

Appendix to Chapter 3

This appendix provides regression results cited in the text, along with variable definitions and data sources. Throughout, numbers in parentheses are *t*-statistics, a dot above a variable denotes its percentage rate of change, and lower-case letters are used to denote natural logarithms of the corresponding upper-case variables. When a variable appears in an equation with and without an asterisk, the presence of an asterisk denotes the British value and the absence of an asterisk, the foreign value. OLS and CORC indicate the use of ordinary least squares with and without the Cochrane–Orcutt correction for autocorrelation. IV indicates the use of instrumental variables, and FAIR appears before equations in which Fair's method is used to correct for autocorrelation when instruments are employed.

Definitions of variables

Money supply: currency outside banks plus clearing bank deposits. Source: Moggridge (1972, pp. 148–9).
Total reserves: Bank of England gold reserve plus foreign exchange reserves. Source: Moggridge (1972, pp. 148–9).
Monetary base: currency outside banks plus bankers' and other private deposits in the Bank of England's Banking Department. Source: Moggridge (1972, pp. 148–9); Committee on Finance and Industry (1931, pp. 302–3); and *The Economist* (1931, various issues).
Output: final industrial production index (London and Cambridge Economic Service index numbers of production, average 1924 = 100). Source: London and Cambridge Economic Service *Monthly Bulletin* (various issues).
Prices: Board of Trade general wholesale price index (quarterly average of monthly figures where needed, 1913 = 100). Source: Tinbergen (1934, p. 104); Methorst (1938, p. 206).
Interest rate: day-to-day money rate (quarterly average of monthly rates). Source: Tinbergen (1934, pp. 106–7); Methorst (1938, p. 206).
Bank rate: quarterly averages. Source: Moggridge (1972, pp. 148–9).
Bilateral exchange rates: bilateral sterling–dollar and sterling–franc exchange rates, defined as units of foreign currency per pound sterling. (Quotations are for the final Saturday of the month or, when that quotation is unavailable, the latest prior quotation.) Source: Einzig (1937, pp. 470–81).
Import value: total net imports in current pounds sterling. Source: Methorst (1938, pp. 208–11).

Balance of trade: total net imports minus exports of UK goods. Source: Methorst (1938, pp. 208–11).
UK gold and foreign exchange reserves: £ million at current prices. Rate of change computed as a percentage of beginning of month level. Source: Howson (1980b, table A–1).
Average weekly wages: index of average weekly wages (December 1924 = 100). Source: Methorst (1938, pp. 207–8).
Retail prices: Ministry of Labour retail price index (1924 = 100). Source: Methorst (1938, pp. 207–8).
Unemployment: percentage of insured persons unemployed, men and women. Source: Methorst (1938, pp. 212–13).

Reserve flow model

Appendix table A3.1 presents the estimates of the reserve flow model referred to in the text. The money supply equation is estimated with ordinary least squares, while the reserve flow equation and central bank reaction function are estimated with two-stage least squares. All coefficients are estimated freely.[206]

Using ordinary least squares to estimate the reserve flow equation yields the following:

$$\text{OLS}\ \frac{R}{H}\hat{R} = \underset{(1.15)}{0.007} + \underset{(0.44)}{0.005\hat{Y}} + \underset{(0.46)}{0.038\hat{P}} - \underset{(2.20)}{0.008\Delta I} - \underset{(3.34)}{0.572\hat{V}} - \underset{(12.96)}{0.929}\frac{C}{H}\hat{C} \qquad \text{(A1)}$$

plus seasonal dummies

$R^2 = 0.96 \quad DW = 2.02$ sample period: 1926 (I)–1931(I).

The coefficients are quite similar to the two-stage least squares estimates reported in table A3.1. In the presence of sterilization, ordinary least squares produces estimates of a coefficient on domestic credit that are biased towards minus unity. This is evident from a comparison of coefficients in the equation above and in table A3.1. As in the table, the coefficients on the rate of growth of prices and output are insignificantly different from zero at the 5 per cent level of confidence. Since this is a problem that afflicts all of the results in this chapter, we look directly at the money demand function through which these variables enter into the model. Taking the logarithm of the demand for money equation (1):

$$m - p = a_0 + a_1 y + a_2 I \qquad \text{(A2)}$$

[206] An alternative approach, which relies more heavily on the predictions of the theory, would entail constraining the coefficients on P, V and C to unity.

TABLE A3.1 Estimates of the reserve flow model, 1926(I)–1931(I)

Reserve flow equation

$$\frac{R}{H}\hat{R} = \underset{(1.12)}{0.007} + \underset{(0.43)}{0.005}\hat{Y} + \underset{(0.53)}{0.051}\hat{P} - \underset{(1.79)}{0.009}\Delta I - \underset{(3.10)}{0.58}\hat{V} - \underset{(2.83)}{0.83}\frac{C}{H}\hat{C} + \text{seasonal dummy variables} \qquad (3')$$

$R^2 = 0.96$ $DW = 1.64$

Money supply equation

$$\hat{V} = \underset{(2.67)}{0.008} + \underset{(2.67)}{0.036}\,(\Delta I - \Delta J) \qquad (4')$$

$R^2 = 0.26$ $DW = 2.41$

Central bank reaction function

$$\frac{C}{H}\hat{C} = \underset{(0.48)}{0.003} - \underset{(2.14)}{0.523}\frac{R}{H}\hat{R} - \underset{(0.95)}{0.32}\left(\frac{R}{H}\hat{R}\right)_{-1} - \underset{(1.13)}{0.397}\left(\frac{C}{H}\hat{C}\right)_{-1} + \text{seasonal dummy variables} \qquad (5')$$

$R^2 = 0.91$ $DW = 1.83$

Note: Figures in parentheses are *t*-statistics. The money supply equation is estimated by ordinary least squares, and the remaining equations are estimated by two-stage least squares. Note that the Durbin–Watson statistic is biased towards 2 when it is applied to an equation such as (5′) containing a lagged dependent variable. Applying the Cochrane–Orcutt correction to this equation yields an autocorrelation coefficient insignificantly different from zero at the 95 per cent level of confidence, thus failing to reject the hypothesis that the residuals are serially uncorrelated.

Estimation yields

$$m - p = 1.77 + 0.19\, y - 0.10\, I \qquad \text{(A3)}$$
$$(2.74) \quad (1.98) \quad (5.16)$$

$R^2 = 0.56$ $\quad DW = 0.50$ $\quad$ Sample period: 1926 (I)–1931 (I).

Here the output term is marginally significant at the 95 per cent confidence level, but the presence of positive autocorrelation suggests that its standard error is underestimated. Since the money demand equation enters (3′) in first difference form, we can take the first difference of (1′) and re-estimate:

$$\hat{M} - \hat{P} = 0.02 + 0.03\, \hat{Y} - 0.02\, (\Delta I) \qquad \text{(A4)}$$
$$(3.61) \quad (0.97) \quad (2.32)$$

$R^2 = 0.24$ $\quad DW = 1.66$ $\quad$ Sample period: 1926 (I)–1931 (I).

As in the table, the scale variable in the money demand and reserve flow equations y has an estimated coefficient insignificantly different from zero at the 5 per cent level of confidence. This may reflect the limitations of industrial production as a measure of economic activity.

Purchasing power parity equations

These equations regress the log of the exchange rate against the log of relative wholesale prices.

$$e = p - p^* \qquad \text{(A5)}$$

where e is the log of foreign price of £1 sterling and p is the log of the wholesale price index.

The sample is monthly data for the period October 1931–December 1936. Following Krugman (1978), Fair's method is employed to correct for autocorrelation by using the Cochrane–Orcutt technique and to account for the endogeneity of prices by using a time trend and lagged variables as instruments:

OLS

$$e_{US} = 0.004 + 1.92(p - p^*) \qquad \text{(A6)}$$
$$(0.39) \quad (12.55)$$

$R^2 = 0.72$ $\quad DW = 0.17$ $\quad$ sterling–dollar

FAIR

$$e_{US} = 0.082 + 0.91(p - p^*) \qquad \text{(A7)}$$
$$(1.30) \quad (1.80)$$

$\rho = 0.94$ $\quad DW = 1.93$ $\quad$ sterling–dollar

OLS

$$e_{FR} = 0.002 + 0.82(p - p^*) \qquad \text{(A8)}$$
$$(0.22) \quad (6.94)$$
$$R^2 = 1.28 \qquad DW = 1.28 \qquad \text{sterling–franc}$$

FAIR

$$e_{FR} = 0.007 + 0.76(p - p^*) \qquad \text{(A9)}$$
$$(0.05) \quad (4.13)$$
$$\rho = 0.36 \qquad DW = 2.01 \qquad \text{sterling–franc}$$

The coefficients on relative prices in equations (A7) and (A9) are insignificantly different from unity at the 5 per cent confidence level.

Reaction functions for the Exchange Equalisation Account

These equations relate the EEA's intervention to exchange rate movements and the balance of trade. When measures of domestic economic conditions, such as unemployment rates, industrial production indices and price changes, were added to these equations, they were uniformly insignificant and had little effect on the coefficients reported below. All equations are estimated on monthly data for the period November 1932–April 1936, using ordinary least squares with a Cochrane–Orcutt correction for autocorrelation.

CORC

$$RES = 10.97 - 381.2E_{US} \qquad \text{(A10)}$$
$$(2.92) \quad (2.30)$$
$$R^2 = 0.25 \qquad DW = 2.01 \qquad \rho = 0.33$$

CORC

$$RES = 10.55 - 693.8E_{US} - 1031.16E_{FR} \qquad \text{(A11)}$$
$$(2.70) \quad (2.68) \quad (1.54)$$
$$R^2 = 0.30 \qquad DW = 2.05 \qquad \rho = 0.36$$

CORC

$$RES = -20.17 - 493.1E_{US} - 0.14BAL \qquad \text{(A12)}$$
$$(1.31) \quad (2.79) \quad (2.11)$$
$$R^2 = 0.33 \qquad DW = 2.01 \qquad \rho = 0.38$$

where *RES* is the change in total UK gold and foreign exchange reserves, and *BAL* is the balance of trade in current sterling prices.

Import demand functions

The import demand functions relate the log of import volume to the log of relative prices, the log of real income and a lagged dependent variable. They are estimated on monthly data for the period October 1931–December 1936 using ordinary least squares, with and without a correction for autocorrelation. The coefficient on the relative price term is the sum of coefficients on a 12-month distributed lag constrained to follow a second order Almon polynomial.

OLS

$$n = 4.47 - 0.33prel - 0.68y + 0.36n_{-1} \quad \text{(A13)}$$
$$\quad (1.40) \quad (2.24) \qquad (1.42) \quad (2.28)$$
$$R^2 = 0.36 \qquad DW = 2.07$$

CORC

$$n = 3.66 - 0.32prel - 0.56y + 0.49n_{-1} \quad \text{(A14)}$$
$$\quad (1.26) \quad (2.47) \qquad (1.28) \quad (3.20)$$
$$R^2 = 0.38 \qquad DW = 1.99$$

where n = log of import value deflated by British wholesale prices, and

$prel = p - e_{US} - p^*$, where p is the log of US wholesale prices, e is the log of the pound–dollar exchange rate, and p^* is the log of British wholesale prices.

The coefficient on relative prices is significant at the 5 per cent confidence level and has the predicted sign: a rise in American prices relative to British prices, expressed in units of common currency, reduces British import demand. The coefficient on British income is insignificant. The remarks on the Durbin–Watson statistic at the foot of table A3.1 apply to (A13) as well. Once again, the autocorrelation coefficient is insignificantly different from zero at the 95 per cent level.

Wage and price equations

The wage and price equations are estimated on monthly data for the period November 1931–December 1936. They form a recursive system, so, assuming the disturbance terms to be serially uncorrelated and to have zero covariance, they can be estimated using OLS. In the price equation, the coefficients on the percentage change in wages and import prices are sums of eight-month distributed lags constrained to follow a second-order Almon polynomial.

OLS

$$\hat{W} = 0.006 - 0.00003U + 0.011\hat{Z}_{-1} \quad \text{(A15)}$$
$$\quad (3.20) \quad (3.13) \qquad (0.28)$$
$$R^2 = 0.17 \qquad DW = 2.12$$

OLS

$$\hat{Z} = 0.0005 + 1.94\hat{W} - 0.18\hat{P}_{imp} \quad \text{(A16)}$$
$$\quad (0.40) \qquad (2.00) \qquad (1.75)$$
$$R^2 = 0.22 \qquad DW = 1.41$$

where $\hat{W}$ is the percentage change in average weekly wages, $\hat{Z}$ is the percentage change in retail prices, $\hat{P}_{imp}$ is the percentage change in US retail prices divided by the dollar price of a pound sterling, and U is the percentage of insured persons unemployed.

While wages rise and fall with the level of unemployment, they seem insensitive to changes in the cost of living. Retail prices appear to be marked up over wages and insensitive in the short run to the prices of competing imports.

4

The 1949 Devaluation of Sterling[1]

To those who took part in it, the devaluation of sterling in September 1949, from \$4.03 to \$2.80 to the pound, was one of the most dramatic episodes in the post-war history of the United Kindom. It seemed likely at the time that it would also prove one of the most important in terms of its effects. There might be room for disagreement as to the need, the purpose, the wisdom or even the significance of the devaluation. But it was unmistakably a turning-point. So rare and startling an event as a fall of 30 per cent in the parity of sterling, the currency in which well over a quarter of the world's commerce was conducted, could not fail to exercise a powerful influence on international transactions of all kinds.[2]

Yet many of those who have looked back on the devaluation have doubted whether it accomplished any lasting changes and have concluded that it was of quite minor importance in post-war economic development. Ralph Hawtrey dismissed devaluation as an inappropriate and costly response to a temporary recession in America. He saw no need for it when imports were already rigorously controlled and British industry was apparently competitive at the existing parity but was 'over-employed' because of long order books, for which excess liquidity was ultimately to blame.[3] Roy Harrod took much the same view. Devaluation was 'an unfortunate incident' that had 'very severe adverse effects, both on demand and on cost inflation', and he doubted whether 'even in

[1] The main official source used in the preparation of this chapter was the collection of Treasury papers contained in PRO 269 and labelled 'Devaluation 1949 and Consequent Measures'. Of these five volumes, the first covers the period before devaluation up to 6 September 1949; the second consists of Cabinet and Economic Policy Committee papers from mid-June to 29 August; the third contains material on the discussions in Washington; the fourth relates to cuts in government expenditure beginning with Bridges's minute of 6 July; and the fifth deals with the dollar import programme and the cuts in imports. These papers were probably assembled by William Armstrong – at that time private secretary to the Chancellor – after the devaluation. Other official papers when cited are given in the following footnotes.

[2] Bank for International Settlements (1953, p. 4).

[3] Hawtrey (1954, pp. 31, 44–5).

1960' the full effect on costs and prices had worked through the whole economy. No lasting improvement in the balance of payments had resulted. It would have been wiser to wait until, say, 1952 when there was capacity to spare, and make a smaller devaluation of 10 per cent.[4] An American economist, after reviewing the effect of devaluation on market shares and the volume (but not, unfortunately, the direction) of exports, concluded, like Harrod, that it would have been better to wait a year or two until the competition from Germany and Japan had begun to make itself felt more strongly.[5] Others again have written of the devaluation as 'a bad piece of tactics'.[6] How does it look now in retrospect, after 30 years that have seen one more major devaluation of sterling as well as day-to-day fluctuations that rob devaluation of its drama?

We begin with a narrative that describes how the decision was actually taken. We then turn to the economic background to devaluation and the trends underlying it. The main question for consideration here is how far the pressures that led to devaluation were ephemeral, reversible and resistible, and how far they were enduring and likely to be cumulative.

This discussion leads naturally into a consideration of its effects. These effects are not easily assessed because of their submergence from the middle of 1950 onwards once the outbreak of war in Korea sent the world economy out of balance. But so far as they can be assessed after the event, they have to be looked at in the framework of expectations when the decision to devalue was taken. The wisdom of the decision has to be measured not just in terms of the effectiveness of the instrument – devaluation – but also in terms of its appropriateness to the circumstances and how correctly the circumstances were appreciated.

A narrative of events

The first postwar discussion of devaluation in Whitehall goes back to June 1945, when R.W.B. ('Otto') Clarke, who had recently moved to the Treasury, circulated a memorandum entitled 'Towards a Balance of Payments'.[7] In this memorandum he looked forward to a recovery of

[4] Harrod (1963, p. 130).

[5] Flanders (1963, p. 196).

[6] Brittan (1964, p. 160). The most penetrating contemporary assessment (in fact delivered *before* the devaluation) was that of James Meade (1948), in his inaugural lecture at the London School of Economics on 'Financial Policy and the Balance of Payments'.

[7] Clarke (1982, pp. 96–122). Clarke was echoing earlier memoranda on the United Kingdom's postwar balance of payments prepared in the Economic Section of the War Cabinet Office and going back as far as November 1941. (These are in the Public Record Office under T230/4 and T230/5, and were previously filed under EAS 29/01A and EAS 29/01B.) The Treasury view, as expressed in a letter from Sir Wilfrid Eady to Lionel Robbins, was that a depreciation of the pound at the end of the war would not

international trade to pre-war volumes by 1949–50 and argued that the United Kingdom should be able to get back into balance within five years if there were an early and modest devaluation of sterling. Keynes, who did not see 'any serious risk of an overall shortage of gold and dollars in the first three [post war] years', took issue with Clarke over the need for a devaluation. In his view, a comparison of inflation rates in Britain and America indicated some overvaluation of the dollar, and he concluded that British exporters would retain a residual cost advantage at the end of the war.[8]

A purchasing power parity test of competitiveness such as Keynes proposed does not, however, dispose of the issue. It pays no regard to capital flows on the one hand or to the scale of adjustment required in the balance of trade on the other. The United Kingdom had emerged from the war with enormous external debts such as no other belligerent had contracted, had sold a large proportion of her foreign assets, and was bound to come under pressure in due course to supply capital to Commonwealth and other countries; this affected the choice likely to be made by holders of assets between pounds and dollars. At the same time, the current account could be balanced or brought into surplus only if large changes occurred in the volume and pattern of British trade, and these changes in trade flows might well call for substantial changes in exchange rates, in favour of the dollar and against the pound.

On the other hand, however great the trade imbalance at the end of the war, and however necessary an eventual devaluation of sterling to its removal, there was a strong case for deferring an adjustment for some years. To have devalued immediately would have done little or nothing to accelerate the process of reconversion from war to peace. Price was not the significant limiting factor in the recovery of exports from the low level to which they had sunk. At the same time, imports were largely under the direct control of the government. The balance of trade would have responded very slowly and probably very little to a devaluation, while the terms of trade might have changed sharply for the worse. Higher import prices would also have given an additional fillip to inflation unless the government had intervened with higher subsidies; this would have been particularly awkward at a time when there was already an enormous budget deficit.

---

be of help because of sterling liabilities and the reactions of American bankers. In the January 1942 version of the Economic Section paper, devaluation was thought to be of limited value partly because overseas income was denominated in sterling and partly because imports were limited in other ways than by price. In a long memorandum on the postwar balance of payments in December 1943, with an annex on the exchange rate by James Meade, it was suggested that exchange rate variations might be contemplated in the 'transition' (then regarded as extending for four years from the end of the war in Europe – in other words, from 1945 to 1949). These references have been kindly supplied by Professor L.S. Pressnell.

[8] Keynes (1979, p. 367); Clarke (1982, pp. 108–9, 122–5).

In the early post war years not much was heard of devaluation. The immediate problem was how to cover an inevitable deficit by borrowing from the countries in surplus: to this end long-term loans totalling $5 billion were negotiated with the United States and Canada. In 1946 it looked as if these might prove sufficient, but the coal crisis of 1947 set back recovery, and the loans ran out unexpectedly early. A second problem, complicating the first, was that a deficit with one group of countries could not automatically be met out of a surplus with a second group of countries because of inconvertibility of currencies. A deficit with so-called 'hard' currency countries such as the United States had to be paid in gold or dollars, while a surplus with 'soft' currency countries was paid, if at all, in inconvertible currency. The drain on the gold and dollar reserves was thus larger than might appear from the balance of payments as a whole. The drain was further aggravated in 1947 by the move to convertibility of sterling in mid-July under the terms of the US Loan Agreement — a move that lasted only six weeks, during which the run-down in reserves reached alarming proportions.

In order to contain and eliminate the deficit, the government relied heavily on the continuation of wartime controls. These held down imports by a combination of rationing and licensing, supplemented by exchange control. The sterling area countries co-operated to minimize their outlay in hard currencies and to develop alternative supplies payable in sterling. Efforts were also made to encourage exports, for example through more liberal supplies of materials for this purpose, and exporters were asked to give preference to hard currency markets. All these controls could be tightened up in a crisis or loosened when the balance of payments permitted. They formed part of a quite deliberate and successful strategy to effect a major structural change that would raise British exports 75 per cent in volume above the prewar level while holding imports to or below their prewar volume. In the end it took ten years for imports to regain the level of 1936–38, while five years were enough for exports to grow to 65 per cent above that level.

By the time the loans were finally exhausted in the first quarter of 1948, Marshall Aid was coming to the rescue, and the first $89 million was received during the second quarter. Exports, too, were rising fast and in the course of the year grew by 25 per cent, bringing the current account back into balance for the first time since 1935 – one might almost say since 1929.

At the beginning of 1948 devaluation reappeared on the Treasury's agenda: officials began to prepare a contingency plan and opened a 'Sterling War Book'. In June Otto Clarke gave it as his view that 'We shall ourselves decide that we should devalue. I am myself very largely convinced of the desirability of this, as the only means of mobilizing ordinary commercial incentives for the task of righting our dollar balance of payments.'[9] But Clarke, who was at that time an assistant secretary, did not speak for the Overseas Finance Division of the Treasury under Henry Wilson Smith. Later in the year the Treasury abandoned all work on the contingency plan.

There were of course many people outside Whitehall who felt that sterling ought to be devalued. There were doubts about the continued use of exchange control in support of the parity. Some critics of government policy argued against a fixed rate on principle or took it for granted that a change in the rate would dispose of any balance of payments problem and remove the need for a whole catalogue of government controls.[10] Others thought that a floating rate would automatically put an end to an external deficit, but this, like the later idea that it would automatically allow convertibility to be restored, was never argued out. There was also a widely held expectation of devaluation in financial circles, which, however, did not come to the fore until the spring of 1949.

Financial opinion, especially in North America, regarded the gap between the official and black market rates for sterling as evidence of the need for a devaluation, and at a later stage the discount on the official rate was used by ministers as an indication of the size of the devaluation required. By 1949 'cheap sterling' had become an important preoccupation of the government, especially because of the commodity shunting operations that flourished because of its availability.[11] But in fact, 'cheap sterling' was probably more a reflection of the blocking of capital transfers through exchange control than a measure of the appropriate rate of exchange. Black market rates continued to show a discount on the official exchange rate even after a 30 per cent devaluation.[12]

[9] Hennessy and Brown (1980c).

[10] Jewkes (1948, p. 233).

[11] 'Cheap sterling' was sterling traded in irregular markets outside the jurisdiction of the Exchange Control at rates involving a discount in relation to the official rate of exchange. 'Commodity shunting' took the form of transactions in goods bought with cheap sterling and sold for dollars; or it might involve conversion into dollars from a sterling account through the unauthorized diversion of goods for disposal in a dollar market that had been acquired for use in a sterling market. Figures of transhipments assembled in the Treasury pointed to a diversion of some of the main primary products of the sterling area amounting in all to \$5 million in the sample month of April 1949. This represented 7 per cent of imports of these products into the United States from sterling area sources. Wool and hides from South Africa and rubber from Malaya were the largest items affected, the main centre of the trade being the Netherlands. See PRO T231/445, 'Cheap Sterling'.

[12] Hawtrey (1954, p. 45). The rate for what Pick (1955) calls 'hand payments' in London (illegal cash payments delivered by hand to the payee's residence) fell from \$3.09 to £1 at the end of March 1949 to \$2.83 at the end of August and to \$2.55 at the end of

The case for devaluation was seen by outside opinion largely in terms of the balance of payments deficit, and it was the re-emergence of a deficit in 1949 that gave urgency to the renewed talk of devaluation. It was arguable, however, that a decision to devalue should rest on long-term considerations that had assumed importance precisely because the deficit looked like disappearing. When it became apparent at the end of 1948 that the current account had already reached rough balance and was likely to be in surplus in 1949, it was suggested in the Board of Trade that the time was approaching when sterling should be devalued so as to redirect sterling area exports towards dollar markets and help to reduce the dollar deficit rather than generate larger balances of inconvertible currencies. It would be wise to act before the issue came to be publicly debated, and there might be at most six months for ministers to make up their minds.[13] The proposal when made in December 1948 had no effect then or when revived in March 1949. The senior officials in the Board of Trade were dead against the idea. The President, Harold Wilson, showed no enthusiasm and made no move to discuss it. About the same time, however, Robert Hall, then Director of the Economic Section of the Cabinet Office, persuaded Sir Edward Bridges, who was Head of the UK Treasury, to set on foot an inquiry into the case for devaluation and himself put the suggestion to Cripps, who was unconvinced. Once his mind was made up, Hall set about converting some of his colleagues, including Edwin Plowden (then Chief Planning Officer) and Roger Makins (Head of the Economic Division in the Foreign Office). This was the beginning of a long campaign at the official level. The Board of Trade, both at ministerial and official level, stuck to the other side. The Bank of England was also strongly against devaluation and the Treasury was doubtful and divided.

Had devaluation taken place in April, it could have been represented as a considered move, inevitable in the long run and necessary in the general interests of the world economy.[14] It certainly would have been a

---

September. The rate then fell to a low point of \$2.38 at the end of the year before rising again over the first half of 1950 to \$2.57. Thus, the discount, which had never been less than 23.5 per cent before devaluation, fell to a maximum of 15 per cent in the months immediately following devaluation and to 8 per cent in the middle of 1950. See also Bank for International Settlements (1953, p. 85).

13 [As Economic Adviser to the Board of Trade, I minuted the Permanent Secretary (Sir J. H. Woods) to this effect on 24 December 1948 and the President on 21 March 1949 setting out eight reasons in favour of devaluation. Later, at the end of March, Austin Robinson, who had recently returned to Cambridge University, told me that in his view the time had come for Britain and other Western European countries to consider what changes would be appropriate in their exchange rate and that this and other problems might suitably be discussed at a World Economic Conference. He also warned me that Dennis Robertson would be making a similar suggestion in an address in Brussels the following week and was likely to come out openly in favour of devaluation. A.K.C.]

14 Dow (1964, p. 41).

good deal smaller and less disruptive. Unfortunately, it occurred under pressure after vociferous public debate. By August it was reported that the almost universal belief in the City was that sterling would be devalued or allowed to float.[15] Similar expectations were entertained on the other side of the Atlantic. Although there is no evidence that the US administration put direct pressure on the UK government then or later, it was known to share the view that the pound was overvalued; the US Congress, in cutting down the appropriation for Marshall Aid in the spring, took the line that less aid would be needed if exchange rates were adjusted.[16] The International Monetary Fund, under American inspiration, was also campaigning for a sterling devaluation, and the Economic Commission for Europe concluded in May that 'European currencies in general are over-valued in relation to the dollar.'[17] It is hardly surprising that a speculative run on the pound should have developed, and this at a time when the reserves, at their lowest level since the war, were inadequate to withstand sustained pressure.

At the beginning of May, the Chancellor of the Exchequer, Sir Stafford Cripps, reacting to growing speculation and rumours of a forthcoming devaluation, had felt it necessary to scotch the rumours in a speech in Rome which seemed to leave no scope for any subsequent change of front. Nevertheless, a few days after Sir Stafford's speech, George Bolton, an executive director of the Bank of England, was cabling the Treasury on 12 May to warn them of 'the spate of rumour regarding exchange readjustment, sterling depreciation, etc.' in Washington.

Later in May the British ambassador in Washington, Sir Oliver Franks, reported to Cripps and Bevin that a number of influential American economists favoured a devaluation of sterling and that it would be desirable to engage in consultations with the US government before things got out of hand.[18] Official consultations started with the

[15] *The Banker*, August 1949, p. 71.

[16] Hawtrey (1954, p. 33). The US administration spoke with many voices. In September, for example, the US Executive Director of the IMF, who had enough votes in his pocket to be sure of a majority, took a position – almost certainly in agreement with the US Treasury – that was in flat contradiction with presidential statements and official assurances that internal policy, including exchange rate policy, was entirely a matter for the British government to decide. He insisted on the inclusion in the Fund report of a strong passage practically calling on the UK to devalue, and tried to override the efforts of his British colleague to secure an adjournment so that he could consult his government. This was agreed to only after a recess of an hour, presumably to allow the US Executive Director to consult his government, which happened to be in Washington, on the proposed adjournment.

[17] Dow (1964, p. 41).

[18] Hennessy and Brown (1980a). According to Robert Hall, the pressure to devalue, 'inspired at first by the US Treasury and ECA', had built up by the end of May into something like an international attack on sterling, which, once launched, was carried along by the facts themselves.

visit to Washington at the beginning of June of Robert Hall and Henry Wilson Smith. This was followed by ministerial consultations in London early in July attended by John Snyder, Secretary of the US Treasury, Averill Harriman and Ambassador Lewis Douglas.

At their first meeting with William McChesney Martin, who was at that time Assistant Secretary of the US Treasury, the British officials were reminded by him, 'in a kind but firm tone', that the United Kingdom had agreed to work jointly with the United States towards a world of free convertibility and non-discrimination but now seemed to be moving in the opposite direction, discriminating against the dollar and against dollar purchases.[19] If there had been a change in British policy, would it not be well to say so? This was fair criticism: British ministers, who were temperamentally in favour of controls, were not conscious of any apparent change of front, especially as few of them had had much to do with planning for the peace.

The talks in Washington had a powerful effect on Wilson Smith who, as the official in charge of the Overseas Finance Division of the Treasury, was in a key position and carried great weight with the Permanent Secretary, Sir Edward Bridges. Up to that point Hall and Plowden had been almost the only officials in favour of devaluation, but by the beginning of July Wilson Smith had come round and from then on a fairly solid front developed inside the Treasury, so that by the time Gaitskell came on the scene, official advice was no longer divided.[20]

Hall and Wilson Smith reported on their return that, according to William McChesney Martin, 'practically all officials of the US Government were firmly convinced that devaluation of sterling was inevitable.'[21] Hugh Dalton, then Chancellor of the Duchy of Lancaster, recorded them in his diary as telling the Economic Policy Committee on 17 June that, when they put the case against devaluation, the Americans 'admitted that if we did [devalue] they would follow suit and "quicker than last time" [1933]. . . Americans have now swung back to mood of 1945. Convertibility and non-discrimination are now their principal aim – not helping Europe or resisting communism.' The Secretary of the US Treasury, John Snyder, 'advised by some new economists, is quite sold on devaluation'.[22]

[19] Letter from Lord Roberthall, 22 October 1981.

[20] By this time Hall was treated by the Treasury as if he were a member of the Department, although the Economic Section, of which he was director, remained until 1953 in the Cabinet Office.

[21] Annex to 'Report on a Visit to the United States in June 1949' by H. Wilson Smith and R.L. Hall (EPC(49)63).

[22] Dalton's diary (MSS) in the Library of the London School of Economics, entry for 17 June. The fear of an American devaluation persisted. In a paper to the Cabinet on 10 November Cripps maintained that 'there were interests in the United States who might make a determined effort to compel the Administration to devalue the dollar.'

By this time there were indications of a recession in trade that might have a serious effect on sterling. Dalton quoted Wilson Smith as reporting at the same meeting that 'all Americans expect [the recession] to go deeper and to last at least a year'. The Committee's attention had been drawn by Cripps to

> a lot of items in [the] dollar balance sheet all going wrong at once . . . our exports to the US very low in April and recession will keep them low; colonial dollar surplus has vanished, US no longer buying Malayan rubber and tin: Commonwealth countries spending too much, especially Australia and South Africa; forestalling, postponement of orders, etc. on devaluation talk.[23]

The drain on the reserves was gathering speed. Between the first quarter and the second it rose from £82 million to £157 million and the reserves fell to just over £400 million. According to Dalton, Cripps warned the Economic Policy Committee that 'within twelve months all our reserves will be gone. This time there is nothing behind them and there might well be a "complete collapse of sterling"'. Attlee, not easily perturbed, turned to Dalton as they left the meeting with the words '1931 over again'. To which, recalling the convertibility crisis of two years previously, Dalton replied: 'It reminds me awfully of 1947.'[24]

But there was no sign at that stage that any member of the Cabinet was taking immediate devaluation seriously. As late as 7 July Cripps was reiterating in the House of Commons that 'the Government have not the slightest intention of devaluing the pound.' Harold Wilson, had gone out of his way, in a long report on his visit to Canada, to dismiss the idea of devaluing the pound.[25] Some ministers, including Wilson, were giving more thought to the possibility of an autumn election than to the merits of devaluation. For them the question was: could an election he held before devaluation or would devaluation delay an election until the spring?[26]

[23] Ibid.

[24] Ibid.

[25] His report claimed that 'the [Canadian] Government advisers . . . accept the view that devaluation would merely add to the difficulties in which the already adverse terms of trade have involved us'; and that 'practically all the leading Canadian financial advisers (unlike some of their opposite numbers in the United States) reject devaluation as a means of overcoming Anglo-Canadian economic difficulties.' Nevertheless he referred later in his report to 'the unfortunate and fairly general – though erroneous – expectation of devaluation'. While emphasizing that 'our prices of consumer goods are far too high' to compete with American goods in the Canadian market, he refrained from any suggestion that only devaluation could close the gap, and while in Canada 'repeated the Chancellor's recent clear statement on devaluation' (paras. 20 and 40 of EPC (49)65, dated 23 June 1949).

[26] Nye Bevan was arguing in favour of an early election in May, and in recording this in his diary Dalton added, 'Douglas Jay argued this way with me last week. If we have to

Cripps was anxious to be seen to be taking action to stop the dollar drain before the periodical statement of the reserve position due on 5 July was published. On 20 June he put round a paper to the Economic Policy Committee, which met every Friday morning, indicating that the dollar reserves would run out by January or at latest by March if current trends continued. His proposals for dealing with the situation included the summoning of a Commonwealth Conference in July, a cut of 25 per cent in dollar expenditure over the twelve months to July 1950 (to be announced on 5 July, when the next quarterly statement on the dollar drain was due), and the suspension of fresh dollar payments, apart from exceptional cases, until 30 September. This was not a strategy likely to appeal to all his colleagues and had the disadvantage that it meant reviving and tightening controls that could be dispensed with in the event of devaluation. While no one came forward to argue for devaluation, Aneurin ('Nye') Bevan, the Minister of Health, was no doubt speaking for others, at a meeting of younger ministers in Cripps's circle on 23 June, when he expressed himself in favour of 'something different from everlasting cuts'. Nevertheless the proposals were accepted. The Commonwealth Conference ending on 17 July, just before Cripps's departure to a sanatorium in Switzerland, agreed to make the cuts proposed. There was a sharp fall in sterling area imports from the United States in the third quarter, and over the 12 months July 1949–July 1950 the fall was in fact 25 per cent as planned.

At the meeting of the Economic Policy Committee on 1 July, Stafford Cripps (who had flown over from a meeting in Paris ending at 2 am that morning) came under attack for circulating a paper proposing a rise in Bank rate and cuts in food subsidies. Morrison, the Lord President and previous co-ordinator of economic policy, argued that devaluation might be the least of the evils to choose from, and he seems to have received some support from Attlee.[27] According to Dalton, Cripps got no support from any of the ministers present, least of all for a rise in Bank rate, and was himself half-hearted. In his account of the meeting, Dalton writes: 'I say "Montagu Norman walks again." I thought we had buried all this stuff about Bank rate. [Stafford Cripps] says: "You see I don't support it." I say: "I was surprised you even mentioned it. One gets a lot of advice one doesn't think worth mentioning.''[28]

---

devalue sterling the cost of living will jump up and that will lose us the election. (Dalton's diary, entry for 24 May). Much later, writing from Zurich to the Prime Minister on 8 August after seeing Cripps, Harold Wilson reported that the Chancellor felt it 'more necessary than ever to have an early election', and took the view that, if one were held, devaluation should not take place until later. The letter, which is manuscript, is in PRO PREM.8/1178 Part I, 'Financial Policy in 1949–50'.

27 Donoughue and Jones (1973, p. 438).

28 Dalton's diary, entry for 1 July 1949. There is no indication that the pressure for a higher Bank rate came from the Bank of England or that officials wanted 'a drastically

Douglas Jay is quoted to the same effect, denouncing 'awful old stuff like rise in Bank rate'.[29] Dalton himself was equally opposed to restrictive fiscal action and tighter monetary policy. The prospective budgetary surplus on revenue account in 1949–50 was nearly £500 million and there was 'no sense at all in increasing Bank rate or interest rates or interest rates generally since capital expenditure is not now determined by what people want but by what the government permits. Here at least we have effective planning.'[30]

Meanwhile, officials remained divided. Sir Edward Bridges, Permanent Secretary to the Treasury, summing up offical opinion on 18 June, told ministers that 'most of us, with differing degrees of emphasis, are opposed to devaluation *now*' but he did not exclude the possibility of a forced devaluation in the autumn or of devaluing some time later in more propitious circumstances. He was anxious that devaluation should be regarded not as a panacea but in the context of other measures designed to reduce the overload on the economy. It would be fatal if one devalution were followed by a second, and it should therefore not be attempted when conditions were too inflationary, as those opposed to devaluation were followed by a second, and it should therefore not be wages would rise and the initial competitive gains would speedily disappear. The disadvantages were certain, the advantages uncertain. Devaluation would contribute little, if at all, to the development of export earnings in the United States, especially when the outlook in the American market remained obscure. This uncertainty posed a further difficulty in deciding how far the rate should go in the event of devaluation, and the Bank of England insisted that there should be no question of a floating rate, even for a limited period.

Those who opposed devaluation were chiefly concerned to see immediate cuts in public expenditure. Without such cuts, devaluation would not work; with them, it would prove unnecessary. Bridges pointed specifically to the food subsidies, suggesting that they should be cut by £100 million. Supporting measures in the credit field would also be necessary and should include a rise in Bank rate, higher interest rates generally and restriction of bank credit. Those who favoured devaluation (named by Bridges as Edwin Plowden, Leslie Rowan and Robert

---

tighter monetary policy', as suggested by Donoughue and Jones (1971, p. 437). Some of them, however, urged a less accommodating monetary policy. In commenting on the governor's views as expressed in a letter to Bridges dated 23 June 1949, Robert Hall wrote, 'During the whole of this period [i.e. 1945–48] I have been in favour of a tighter monetary policy but there is little evidence that the Bank of England has shared this view.' He went on to argue that a cut on food subsidies would be 'the most certain way of launching the upward movement of wages which the Government [fears] . . . as a consequence of devaluation'.

29 Ibid.

30 Ibid. For a sceptical view of the claim that the planning of capital investment was effective, see Devons (1970, especially pp. 76–79).

Hall) recognized the need for some accompanying measures but thought in terms of milder cuts in government expenditure and efforts to contain the rise in costs by a form of incomes policy.

Robert Hall himself put the case rather differently. He pointed out that although the process of reconversion after the war was largely complete and was likely to be followed by the recovery of some of our most important competitors, there was no end to the dollar deficit in sight, not even in the so-called 'Four Year Plan' for the years 1948–52 recently submitted to the OEEC (Organization for European Co-operation, the European predecessor of the OECD). The country had run through borrowings and gifts from abroad at a rapid rate all through the post-war years and was still living on Marshall Aid without fully appreciating the precariousness of the situation. Moreover, there was plenty of evidence that exporters were handicapped by high costs. The Canadians were constantly complaining that American goods were cheaper, and in the markets outside North America there were similar complaints. How, if not by devaluation, was it proposed to close the gap, both in export prices and in the dollar balance of payments?

The Governor of the Bank of England, C. F. Cobbold, was strongly against devaluation 'at the present time and in present conditions'. It was not, he told Bridges on 23 June, 'an alternative solution' and would not remedy 'for any length of time . . . the main causes of the present malaise'. These he saw as the depression in the United States, excessive government expenditure and the burden of sterling liabilities. When he saw the Chancellor on 5 July he inisted that the main thing necessary in order to restore confidence in the pound was action to reduce public expenditure. The Chancellor, on the other hand, made it clear that no deflationary policy, such as cuts in expenditure would involve, stood any chance of acceptance by the government or, in his view, any other government. Undeterred, the Governor wrote to Bridges a week later that 'the two things that would really change the atmosphere in North America . . . would be a real attack on government expenditure and a deferment of further nationalisation plans.'

In the Governor's view the fundamental issue was whether, after devaluation, we could be 'reasonably certain of seeing equilibrium in our balance of payments and avoiding pressure against sterling at the new rate over, say, the next two years'. He wanted a new agreement with the United States and Canada to 'take some of the rest of the world's demand for dollars off our back' by assuming some of the burden of sterling liabilities. On the one hand, our cost structure was too high and inflexible, and on the other, overseas holdings of sterling were excessive: too much sterling was 'chasing too few dollars'. He accepted the need for complementary action in the monetary field if the pound was devalued but expressed doubts about direct action to restrict credit. By the end of July, when a decision had been all but taken, he was reported by Sir Wilfrid Eady to be very much alarmed by the absence of any proposals for a cut in government expenditure and determined to resist a tightening of monetary policy without complementary budgetary action. If there were no reduction in government expenditure, he would refuse outright to restrict credit or raise interest rates.

A few days later, on 3 August, he wrote to the Prime Minister to express his fears of a second devaluation if no action were taken to reduce inflationary pressure and deal with overseas sterling balances. These fears would lead him to recommend a larger devaluation than would be appropriate if it were undertaken as 'part of a general plan' (i.e., with the necessary accompanying measures). American pressure for devaluation was founded on the hope that it would be a step to convertibility and the relaxation of controls generally. But this was an illusion, since convertibility called for a strong pound whereas the pound would be 'convalescent' after devaluation and this would make it necessary to tighten restrictions on the use of sterling by third countries. Devaluation so soon after the Commonwealth Conference, which had just been held, was 'a hasty retreat to an unprepared line of defence'. It would cause other industrial countries to move in line with sterling so that there would be no improvement in the balance of payments with third countries. In dollar markets there was 'no reason to foresee any immediate increase in the dollar income of the sterling area'. Imports were already controlled and were unlikely to contract. The immediate effect of devaluation on net dollar earnings, in his view, was likely to be unfavourable.

This view of the effect on net dollar earnings was shared by others, including Douglas Jay, Economic Secretary of the Treasury. In a brief to the Chancellor before the meeting of the Economic Policy Committee on 8 July he argued that 'the issue [of devaluation] rests entirely on whether or not we should earn more dollars as a result and I do not feel that this has yet been established.' In June he had dismissed the 'thoroughly hypothetical economic gains' of devaluation and criticised the case submitted against it as 'altogether understated'. But by mid-July he had swung round.[31] After a meeting on 21 July at the Treasury on the possible use of tax rebates on dollar exports, he exclaimed: 'I wish to God we had done it a year ago.'

[31] In his autobiography (*Change and Fortune*) Jay (1980) says that he was much influenced by the evidence produced by Edgar Whitehead, Finance Minister of Southern Rhodesia, at the meeting in London of Commonwealth Finance Ministers at the end of June 1949 to the effect that British exports were almost all too dear in relation to competing supplies. He made up his mind after his 'usual Sunday walk around Hampstead Heath' on Sunday, 17 July, and found the next day that Gaitskell had reached the same conclusion, also on 17 July, for the same reasons. When he told Cripps that he favoured devaluation, Cripps commented, 'What, unilaterally?' (Jay, 1980, pp. 186–7).

The chances of an early expansion in dollar earnings as a result of devaluation were much debated, particularly by those who were opposed to devaluation. Even after a recommendation to devalue had gone to the Prime Minister from the ministers in charge of economic policy, Treasury officials reported that it was unlikely that devaluation would affect the loss of reserves for nine months, 'unless the devaluation was so savage, e.g. down to $2.50 as to affect the internal standard of living in the country'. Yet when a letter (drafted by Douglas Jay) was sent to Stafford Cripps at the beginning of August by the Prime Minister, it opened with a reference to 'the ever-accumulating evidence that the universal expectation of devaluation is holding back purchases of British exports day by day and discouraging the holding of sterling all over the world'. Thus, while some were concentrating on time-lags, low price elasticities and non-price elements in marketing, others focused on expectations, capital movements and short-run effects.

Official opinion changed quickly in the last week of June and the early days of July. On 22 June Robert Hall was in despair, 'surrounded by invincible ignorance and prejudice'. The main opposition at official level, he said, came from Cobbold and Wilson Smith (who regarded devaluation as 'a desperate gamble') but it was not clear to him what alternative policy other than 'old-fashioned deflation' they had in mind. There was a danger that the sharp division of opinion might continue long enough to allow the reserves to run down to a danger point at which there would be no escape from devaluation in the worst possible circumstances. Ministers were unconvinced; the Prime Minister, whom he briefed, would be more likely to echo his briefs if he left them unread. The one ray of hope was that Roger Makins (now Lord Sherfield) in the Foreign Office thought that he might carry Bevin. Max Nicholson, the Lord President's Permanent Secretary, remarked that same evening: 'We'll *have* to devalue.' Since he had Herbert Morrison's ear, he, too, might be persuaded. James Helmore, Second Secretary in the Board of Trade, was wavering and it had been got across to the President that the Economic Adviser was by no means the only protagonist of devaluation.

Treasury ministers in the meantime were adamant. The Chancellor thought devaluation wrong in principle and the expression of a policy of *laissez-faire*. He associated it in his mind with Wall Street and believed that by planning and control it was possible to achieve all that could be got by devaluation.

Yet the position was beginning to look more hopeful. Robert Hall claimed at the end of June to have converted Douglas Jay on condition that there would be no cut in food subsidies. He thought that opinion among officials was now fairly solidly in favour, with one or two conspicuous exceptions, while, of the ministers, Morrison and probably also Bevin could be counted as supporters. Harold Wilson, reacting against overstatements of the case for cuts and deflation by officials, was coming round, and his parliamentary secretary, John Edwards, was strongly in favour of devaluation, regarding it as the traditional alternative to wage cuts. Evidence of a movement in outside opinion was provided by unsolicited declarations to Cairncross, by Paul Bareau of *The Economist*, and by Richard Kahn and other economists at a Nuffield conference, that devaluation was obviously coming.

Nothing of this was apparent from the meeting of the Economic Policy Committee on 1 July, which pursued the will o' the wisp of a 'comprehensive agreement' with the United States and Canada, or from Stafford Cripps's public rejection of devaluation five days later in the House of Commons. When the Secretary of the US Treasury, John Snyder, arrived on 7 July, the Chancellor's line was that devaluation would be feasible only within the limits of a 'general settlement', the nature of which was left extremely vague. Although Cripps conducted the talks over the next two days with his usual skill, he had not slept for some days and had already made arrangements to go off to a Swiss sanatorium in less than a fortnight's time.

The talks were remarkable chiefly for the calculated absence of any reference to devaluation, which the public took to be the main subject of discussion.[32] This gave rise to a long and heated debate when the communiqué came to be prepared on the afternoon of the second day (9 July). Officials wrestled for an hour and a half, and ministers for an equal period, over what mention should be made of devaluation. Snyder wanted no reference to the subject because there had been no discussion of it. Cripps rejoined that that was all he wanted to say. Snyder, petulant and angry, felt caught in a logical trap. If they broke up without any reference to devaluation in the communiqué, the press would stick to its view that the purpose of Snyder's visit was to urge devaluation on the government; while to say that the subject had not been discussed might be taken to imply either endorsement of British views or feebleness on Snyder's part. After a 30-minute adjournment Snyder had in the end to agree, Cripps pointing out that nothing could be of more assistance in stopping the drain on reserves. The communiqué issued on 10 July said that: 'It was agreed that [a number of supplementary suggestions] should be the subject of further consideration. In this connection no suggestion was made that sterling should be devalued.'

The one concrete result of the Snyder visit was agreement that official talks should take place in Washington at the end of August on possible lines of action, with ministerial discussions following immediately.

In the course of July Hugh Gaitskell (Minister of Fuel and Power),

[32] The matter had been discussed earlier at a smaller meeting at the Treasury, when Cripps persuaded Snyder to refrain from uttering public hints about devaluation and to offer his advice in private (Jay, 1980, p. 186).

now in a key position in Cripps's absence, joined the ranks of those favouring devaluation, and he and Douglas Jay set about proselytizing their colleagues. Gaitskell's conversion is said to have been largely the work of Paul Rosenstein-Rodan in the course of a long walk on Hampstead Heath on 17 July; but others also (including Lord Kaldor, who put the case to him on 18 July) have claimed the credit. What is said to have finally convinced Gaitskell was the argument that the demand for British exports in dollar markets had an elasticity in excess of unity, an argument that he had previously doubted. His diary, however, implies a rather more sophisticated analysis.[33]

However he became convinced of the case for devaluation, it made a great deal of difference that he found Robert Hall in favour, with other Treasury officials of the same mind. Gaitskell might have taken longer to convince if officials had held a different view, and Attlee might have hesitated to override Cripps in his absence.[34]

Two days after Cripps's departure, on 21 July, Gaitskell, Jay and Wilson, the ministers who had been left in charge of economic policy, met and decided to recommend devaluation. Of the three there is no doubt that Gaitskell's was the decisive voice. Harold Wilson, when the three saw the Prime Minister later in the week argued against devaluation and at a subsequent meeting still 'took refuge in ambiguity'.[35] At the beginning of the year he had seemed the likely successor to Cripps as Chancellor, but as Douglas Jay subsequently wrote of events of July 1949, 'it was this chapter which left no doubt in the minds of those few who knew the facts that, if Cripps' health failed, Hugh Gaitskell was the only possible Chancellor.'[36]

A few days later, on 26 July, a note on the economic situation was submitted to the Prime Minister over the names of the three top officials in the Treasury, the head of the Economic Planning Staff and the director of the Economic Section of the Cabinet Office.[37] This stressed the danger that all power of manoeuvre might be lost if the reserves ran

[33] Williams, (1979, p. 199). On 20 July Gaitskell set out five reasons for devaluing the pound:

(1) Exchange control had not prevented a substantial dollar drain and would not by itself bring the money back;

(2) it was clear that the US government would offer no help in the short term and would offer long-term aid only on stiff conditions;

(3) the controls over dollar expenditure by Commonwealth countries were looser than had been supposed and were weakened when sterling prices were relatively high;

(4) since devaluation would make exports to dollar markets much more profitable, the prospects of an expansion in dollar earnings were favourable;

(5) there was a danger of a currency collapse if the reserves continued to fall.

[34] Letter from Lord Roberthall, 22 October 1981.

[35] Jay (1980), p. 197).

[36] Jay in Rodgers (1964, p. 95).

[37] PRO PREM 8/1178 Part I, 'Financial Situation in 1949–50'.

out. The measures taken had been insufficient, negotiations with the Americans were about to begin, and it was important that they should be told what further steps the government proposed to take. The inescapable fact was that British costs were out of line and that, while British costs were rising, American costs were falling. At the Commonwealth Conference it had been 'reiterated time and time again by representatives of the principal Commonwealth countries that one of their major difficulties in discriminating against dollar purchases was that so often dollar products were far cheaper than sterling'. In those circumstances a substantial readjustment of the sterling–dollar rate was necessary. The officials then went on to argue that, in order to be effective, devaluation would have to be accompanied by cuts in public expenditure and by some tempering of the cheap money policies that had been pursued since the war.[38]

This minute seems to have had some weight with the Prime Minister, although he still had difficulty in seeing any connection between the balance of payments and the Budget and noted, on an attempt by Robert Hall to explain matters, 'I don't think much of this paper.'

When the Cabinet met on 29 July the Prime Minister was given authority to take whatever action he thought necessary. A few days later he wrote to Cripps in Switzerland (in a letter drafted by Douglas Jay and delivered by Harold Wilson) telling him that 'All of us are now agreed, including the responsible officials, that [devaluation] is a necessary step (though not of course the only step) if we are to stop the present dollar drain before our reserves fall to a [dangerous] level.'[39]

The letter went on to give three reasons for this decision: that the expectation of devaluation was discouraging the holding of sterling and deterring purchases of British goods; that the United States and Canada were unlikely to take any short-term action of material assistance; and that substantial help from the Americans after the projected talks in Washington in September could not be expected sufficiently early to prevent a fall in the reserves to 'a dangerously low level.'

Next, the letter referred to official advice calling for a reduction in inflationary pressure if there was to be 'any lasting benefit from devaluation'. The Prime Minister proposed to issue 'a strongly worded directive' on government expenditure and indicated that 'supporting action in the monetary field' would be taken. It then went on to discuss the timing of a final decision and of its public announcement.

The Prime Minister stressed the importance of taking a decision before the Washington talks so as to avoid any appearance of 'trading an offer of devaluation for concessions' on the part of the Americans. The

[38] See below, p. 134.

[39] For the full text see Jay (1980, p. 188).

line to be taken was that the decision reflected the Cabinet's judgement that devaluation was the right thing to do, and that the US government was of the same opinion. This meant rejecting the position suggested at the end of June by the Chancellor, and taken up enthusiastically by the President of the Board of Trade in July, that a bargain might be struck with the Americans under which they would be required to offer further help as the price of devaluation. There was something typically British about this proposal to do the one thing that would get you out of a mess as a *quid pro quo* for a major concession by somebody else.

What form the 'further help' from the Americans was to have taken is not altogether clear, but among the ideas under discussion were American support for sterling, either directly out of Marshall Aid or through stockpiling of Commonwealth materials, an increase in the price of gold and a possible take- over by the United States of part of the sterling balances. It might be supposed that a substantial dollar loan would have figured among the proposals. But this does not seem to have been suggested at any time, no doubt because of disenchantment with previous experience of loan negotiations. The draft communiqué on 9 July said flatly that the British did not want a loan from the United States and this was cut out only at the suggestion of William McChesney Martin (at that time Assistant Secretary of the US Treasury), who was in the US delegation.

Cripps's reaction to the Prime Minister's letter, as conveyed by Harold Wilson, dwelt more on the timetable than on the issue of devaluation. Indeed, the Chancellor, who was feeling 'mouldy' from lack of sleep, had first expressed doubts as to the value of such a move but had then swung round and appeared to support it strongly. He had discussed disinflationary measures and raised the question of an autumn Budget. But it was the timetable on which he expressed himself most strongly. The timetable depended on whether there was an early election, since that would require a postponement both of devaluation and of the Washington talks. If there were no early election the matter should wait until his departure with the Foreign Secretary for Washington, when a decision might be taken either before he left or by the Cabinet while he was in Washington (he was undecided). In any event it was his understanding that there would be no question of taking a decision against his advice, and he would like to settle the matter at Chequers with the Prime Minister, the Foreign Secretary and the President of the Board of Trade. To make an announcement before the Washington talks would have the worst possible effect on the Americans and would also be contrary to the views of the Foreign Secretary, who still thought of devaluation as a bargaining counter, although Cripps did not. It would also, so Cripps was reported as saying, be 'a piece of sharp practice' and likely to undermine confidence if devaluation were announced in advance of the talks. An announcement after the

Washington talks could be made in a broadcast on 18 September once he returned from the United States.[40]

At first, devaluation had been thought of for some undefined date in September. Gaitskell in July was so perturbed by the loss of reserves that he wanted immediate action; but once it had become clear that the earliest date was 24 August he agreed that it would make little difference if action were deferred until the conclusions of talks in Washington with the Americans and Canadians. Others were less confident that the reserves would be adequate by that date to permit a controlled movement to a new exchange rate, especially in view of the exposed position of the sterling area at the junction of the dollar and non-dollar world.

Partly for this reason, it had been suggested that it would be best to devalue before the Washington talks. Other arguments in favour of this course were that it might help to get useful results from the talks and to avoid any accusation of acting under pressure from the US government. But Stafford Cripps stuck to his choice of a date (18 September) when he would be back in the United Kingdom from the IMF annual meeting in Washington and could make the announcement to the British public in person. The delay extended the rundown in reserves, which was unusually heavy in the first half of September. It was also by no means obvious that the Chancellor was the right man to explain the inevitability of devaluation, or to underline its advantages, when he had come out so strongly and repeatedly against it.

A meeting of Ministers was held at Chequers immediately after Cripps returned on 19 August. Cripps was still reluctant to agree to devaluation but ultimately agreed, subject to three conditions, all of them involving the attitude likely to be taken by the United States. He insisted that it was necessary to secure the backing of the United States in approaching the IMF, since it would not be possible to give due notice to the IMF of the government's intentions. The United States would also require reassurance that the new rate would be held. Finally, the rate selected should not be so low as to invite retaliation by the United States. Cripps went on to explain his choice of 18 September as the date for devaluation. How, he asked, could he defend such a step on the eve of his talks in Washington when nothing had changed? By waiting until after the talks he could at least link the decision with the views expressed there. This was only one of many discussions in the summer of 1949 in which the role of the United States (and, to a slightly smaller extent, Canada) absorbed the attention of ministers to the almost complete exclusion of the rest of the world.

The decisions reached at Chequers were confirmed by the Cabinet ten days later on 29 August before Cripps and Bevin left by sea for

[40] PRO PREM 8/1178, Part I. Wilson's letter to the Prime Minister is docketed with the original of the letter to Cripps.

Washington. The secret was well kept: there is very little evidence of leaks during the critical two months from the time the case was put to the Prime Minister on 21 July.[41]

The official brief for the talks in Washington describes their purpose as to work towards 'equilibrium in the balance of payments between the dollar and the sterling and non-dollar areas on a permanent basis, at a high level of trade and without the recurrence of crises'.[42] The measures for which American help was to be sought included: more favourable administration of the European Recovery Programme (i.e., more aid); a resumption of stockpiling (e.g., of tin); loans from the Export–Import Bank; drawings from the IMF; and reciprocal tariff reductions. Among the longer-term policies that the Mission should have in mind, if the progress of the talks afforded an opportunity, was an increase in the dollar price of gold. (The Treasury regarded the continuation of the pre-war price of gold as one of the most important contributing factors to the sterling area's dollar deficit.)

The Washington talks seem to have been successuful in spite of a cold reception from Mr Snyder, 'full of hostility and suspicion toward the British'.[43] The Canadians were asked to act as a go-between and materially assisted the negotiations. But what must have smoothed the way more than anything was the disclosure 'to those of ministerial rank' of the intention to devalue the pound – a disclosure not made to any other country except Australia, New Zealand and South Africa until the weekend of devaluation.[44]

Meanwhile, important issues remained to be decided: the scale and make-up of accompanying measures; what changes in government expenditure were involved or necessary; the size of the depreciation; whether the sterling area should move together; whether and how the new rate should be controlled. Some of these matters were settled very late. Cuts in government expenditure, for example, were not announced until 24 October. A few days before devaluation, on 14 September, the President of the Board of Trade still did not know the rate, which had been decided by Bevin and Cripps on 12 September at the British Embassy in Washington.

The choice of a new rate of exchange was not the subject of long

[41] There is, however, some evidence of a leak after the Americans were told on 10 September of the intention to devalue and the range within which a new rate would be fixed. On 14 September a cable from Washington (Dedip 8749) reported that the Bank of Brazil had told the British Embassy on 12 September that 'they heard that we were going to devalue to $2.80 on 18 September'.

[42] CP(49) 175, 23 August 1949.

[43] Kennan (1967, p. 458); Acheson (1970, p. 322).

[44] Plumptre (1977, p. 105). For Dedip 8749 see PRO PREM 8/973, 'Devaluation'. For the timetable of communication of the decision to devalue see PRO T229/212, 'Miscellaneous papers on devaluation'.

debate.[45] Before the Chancellor and the Foreign Secretary met to discuss the matter in Washington, their advisers (George Bolton, Hall, Plowden and Wilson Smith) had held a preliminary meeting at which they accepted Robert Hall's view that the choice lay between a rate of $2.80 and one of $3.00, and that it would be safer to be on the low side so that any pressure on the rate would be upwards rather than downwards. When the four advisers put these propositions to the ministers, Cripps turned to Bevin and asked what he thought. Bevin pursed his cheeks, hesitated and then said $2.80 and $2.80 it was.

When the Chancellor came to expound the decision to the House of Commons on 27 September he laid stress on two factors. First, there was the need to put British exporters to North American markets in 'a fairly competitive position'; this seemed to call for a rate at least as low as $3, especially as some cheap sterling transactions were taking place below this rate. There was, second, a need for finality: the rate had to be low enough to remove any danger of a second devaluation. He referred also to the possibility, which had been canvassed in the City,[46] of letting the pound float, but rejected it emphatically: if 'floating' meant that 'all our exchange and import controls should be taken off and the pound allowed to find its own level, we could not possibly think of such a course'.[47]

The possibility of letting the rate float was raised in an appendix to the memorandum circulated by the Chancellor to the Economic Policy Committee on 1 July. It was raised again at the beginning of August by the Economic Section of the Cabinet Office in a memorandum on 'The Choice of the New Exchange Rate'. After pointing out that in the end it was 'a matter of practical judgement' what rate should be fixed, the memorandum suggested that the IMF might be willing to accept a regime of variable exchange rates 'for an experimental period' before a fixed rate was settled. The Bank of England, however, was opposed to this idea on the grounds that the reserves were too low to embark on such an experiment.[48] The memorandum went on to suggest that it was 'presumably desirable to select an exchange rate which would enable the

[45] The choice had previously been explored in a number of Economic Section memoranda. On 1 June Robert Hall considered the implications of a devaluation by one-third for the United Kingdom's competitive position; later in June Marcus Fleming discussed the impact of a 25 per cent devaluation; on 2 August it was concluded that the minimum should be 20 per cent and a rate of $2.75 was favoured; by 25 August this had become 30 per cent, i.e. a rate of $2.80. Colin Clark had suggested a rate of $2.50 to $3.00 in the June issue of the *Economic Journal*, as the Economic Section noted in its memorandum of 2 August. See Clark (1949).

[46] *The Banker*, August 1949, p. 71 and September 1949, p. 159 (quoted by Dow, 1964, p. 41).

[47] House of Commons Debates, 27 September 1949, col. 12.

[48] There is no evidence of a prolonged debate with the Bank of England such as is described by Brittan (1964, pp. 160–1).

pound to be made convertible within the foreseeable future'. It would also be undesirable to have to devalue twice. These considerations pointed to a devaluation of not less than 20 per cent, i.e. to $3.20 or less; possibly to $3.00; and probably to a still lower rate.

Cobbold, as we have seen (above, p. 123), was also in favour of a large devaluation, essentially because he had no confidence that the necessary accompanying measures would be taken. He was very much afraid that one devaluation would be followed by another, and with this in mind was calling by 26 August for a rate 'midway between $2.50 and $3.00'.

Ministers do not appear originally to have contemplated so large a devaluation. At the meeting at Chequers on 19 August, Cripps was against any rate lower than $3.00. Bevin at that time favoured $3.20. Had the decision to devalue been taken earlier, before the loss of reserves reached such alarming proportions, and had it been made unanimously and deliberately with all the necessary accompanying measures, it is most unlikely that a rate below $3.00 would have been fixed, and quite possible that a rate of $3.20 would have been considered adequate.

In that event, some of the discord that resulted, especially in other parts of the sterling area, might have been avoided. There is very little mention in any of the official papers preceding the devaluation of the likely impact on other countries, even on countries holding their reserves in sterling. There are occasional references to what was seen as a dilution of the proposed devaluation if other countries – usually non-members of the sterling area – took the opportunity to devalue their currencies too. But no soundings were taken of their intentions; there was virtually no consideration of the problems presented by a 30 per cent sterling devaluation for a country like India or Australia, especially if it was given exactly two days' notice of British intentions. Although this was probably as much as such decisions allow – the IMF had less than 24 hours – and although there was plenty of speculation throughout the Commonwealth about an impending devaluation, Commonwealth countries were naturally taken aback by so large and sudden a devaluation within two months of the July Conference at which they had agreed to a 25 per cent cut in their dollar imports. Pakistan reacted by maintaining her existing parity; India expressed her displeasure at the absence of consultation; and Australia put it on record that they neither sought nor approved the devaluation.

The Treasury had, however, revealed some curious situations. Ceylon, for example, was in the unfortunate position that parity had to be maintained with the rupee as well as with sterling, so that her reserves were liable to disappear in a day as the money went round and round if Britain devalued and India did not. In Honduras the currency was convertible into dollars at a guaranteed rate while the reserves were held in sterling. Argentina was speculating in sterling because it had been given a dollar guarantee at the end of June. European central banks had absorbed large additional holdings of sterling in consequence of the precautionary movement of private funds in the expectation of devaluation.

As might be expected, the main struggle was over accompanying measures. The Prime Minister clung to the view that the external difficulties of the United Kingdom were quite unrelated to domestic policies: to suppose otherwise was 'nineteenth-century economics'. Other ministers regarded devaluation as an alternative to deflationary measures that were consequently redundant. Dalton, in particular, to judge from his diary, saw absolutely no need for any accompanying changes in the budget. No country in the world, he maintained, had carried financial austerity and rectitude so far as the United Kingdom and to suggest cuts in public expenditure was to demonstrate how politically unreliable the government's advisers really were.

According to Dalton, after the meeting of the Economic Policy Committee on 8 July, the officials were asked to leave the room. Stafford Cripps then told the Committee that he did not trust his own officials and advisers in the Treasury (and presumably also in the Bank). 'They were all really, by reason of their training and their belief in a "free economy", much more in agreement with the Americans than with British Ministers. Dalton advised him to make use of Douglas Jay and Stafford agreed. Other entries in Dalton's diary make it clear that ministers were deeply suspicious of their advisers and that the grounds for this usually lay in an almost paranoic reaction to any hint that public expenditure should be cut. 'No doubt the officials, or some of them,' wrote Dalton 'are writing minutes and papers for the record to show the Tories if they *should* win the next election.'[49] At the end of July the Prime Minister complained to Dalton that he was 'being served up from the Treasury and the Bank arguments which he thinks are fallacious on evil effects of our public expenditure'. Dalton assured him that the arguments *were* fallacious.

This reluctance of the government to accept the need for accompanying fiscal measures strengthened the suspicion of officials hostile to devaluation that it was being advocated as 'an easy way out' when the real need was to trim back government expenditure and release resources. Repeatedly, officials drew the attention of ministers to the need for accompanying measures. Bridges told the Chancellor on 6 July:

> We are all concerned that the proposals now before the Economic Policy Committee will not get us out of our difficulties. These proposals are in effect a continuation of the policy of exhortation to the people of this country to increase their productivity and to exercise restraint in their

[49] Dalton's diary, entry for 19 July.

demands for increased wages and profits, coupled with a proposal to devalue the pound while maintaining full employment.

The minimum needed was 'a definite instruction to the Bank of England to bring about some restriction of credit and a limit of Government expenditure to the estimates put forward at the time of the Budget'. Current forecasts suggested that, without any change in policy, the estimates would creep up by £140 million over the original total for 1949–50. As for credit restriction, 'the present policy of very cheap money has meant that the monetary system has put no obstacle whatever in the way of inflationary forces generally.'

The Chancellor politely took note of this point of view in red ink, without further comment, but it no doubt contributed to the distrust of his advisors which he expressed two days later. He had already told the governor of the Bank of England the previous day in categorical terms that the government – and in his view any other government – regarded a policy of deflation, including cuts in government expenditure, as out of the question. After his departure to Switzerland, Bridges tried again in a private minute to the Prime Minister, insisting on the importance of a cut in public expenditure. This was spelled out three days later in the paper referred to earlier (p. 126 above) which was submitted on 26 July over the names of five top officials. This argued that, since it was not possible to act by increasing the weight of taxation, public expenditure should at least be kept within the estimates and preferably be cut by 5 per cent as proposed by the Lord President, Herbert Morrison. There should also be a 'moderation in money rates of interest to make the present Bank rate [then 2 per cent] effective'.

Later still, when the ministerial brief for the Washington discussions was being prepared, Treasury officials insisted on including a paragraph on the need for stronger measures if only to carry conviction with the Americans. The paragraph got as far as the Economic Policy Committee but no further. In the end, no commitment to cut public expenditure was made in advance of devaluation and nothing was done to tighten monetary policy until 24 October when the expenditure cuts were at last announced. Even then it was limited to a letter from the Chancellor to the Governor calling on the banks and accepting houses to 'use every endeavour to ensure that inflationary policies are held in check'.

On the other hand, it was recognized that some form of incomes policy was highly desirable, and Bevin and Cripps eventually persuaded the Trades Union Congress to continue the standstill in wages introduced in 1948 so long as prices did not rise by more than 5 per cent. This made it necessary to work out measures conforming to this acceptance and to refrain from action that would have more than a limited impact on the cost of living.

The only deflationary measure on which Cripps and Bevin agreed before devaluation was an increase in the price of bread coupled with a reduction in the extraction ratio. Although Stafford Cripps favoured wholemeal bread and a high extraction ratio, Bevin, who was inclined to belch, thought that the working man would accept a higher price of bread more readily if offered a whiter loaf and the trade unions were thought also to regard the colour of bread as a first-class political issue. After some argument between the two, Cripps conceded the point with the unrealistic proviso that no increase in dollar expenditure should be involved.[50] Their proposal that the price of the loaf should be raised by 1½*d*. and the extraction ratio reduced to 82.5 per cent was, however, rejected. The loaf went up by 1*d*. No other measures were agreed upon until after devaluation.

Other measures were, however, discussed. These included the imposition of a tax on capital gains (since devaluation would bring stock profits); an increase in profits tax to balance the wage freeze (the rate on distributed profits was raised from 25 to 30 per cent immediately after devaluation); the possibility of a rebate of tax on profits derived from exports (dismissed as contrary to GATT); a price stop over the first month following devaluation (this was an earlier proposal of the Chancellor's). When the Chancellor at last put round a paper in mid-October he proposed a cut of £280 million, half falling on government expenditure and half on capital investment. These were cuts in programme, not from the current level of expenditure, and are correspondingly difficult to trace afterwards. The Chancellor based his total of £280 million on a calculation by Robert Hall that final demand was running at least £200 million above what had been assumed in the 1949 Budget, and that a further cut of £100 million was required to free resources for the improvements in the visible balance that devaluation would permit. The £300 million was whittled down to £280 million, and the final cuts by another £20 million. It would be broadly true to say that the cuts did little more than aim at restoring the pressure of demand to what had been contemplated in the spring before any question of devaluation arose. The proposed cut in public expenditure, by some curious logic, took credit for an increase in profits tax and a small prescription charge of a shilling under the National Health Service. It left the social services and food subsidies virtually intact, except for animal feeding stuffs and fish, and made only a very modest reduction in defence. The cut in investment was largely on paper except for housing, where it was bound to be somewhat problematic and was in fact restored early in 1950. The cuts were announced on 24 October and to the casual reader seemed to be made up largely of miscellaneous trimmings such as the Treasury might normally make in examining departmental estimates.

50 The dispute is described in Hennessy and Brown (1980b); but it took place at least a week before the meeting at the British Embassy at which the new rate for the dollar was settled.

The expenditure cuts could be the subject of an instructive case-study in their own right and have been dealt with above in very summary fashion. At the meeting of the Cabinet on 28 July, at which the Lord President's memorandum calling for a 5 per cent cut was discussed, the Economic Policy Committee was asked to 'scrutinise Government expenditure with a view to securing such economies as were consistent with the continued application of major Government policies'. Some ministers, however, insisted that the main cause of the dollar drain was not the government's internal financial policy but the fall in sales of sterling area commodities for dollars. On 4 August the Prime Minister put around a paper (CP (49)170) asking for proposals to meet the aim of a 5 per cent all-around cut in expenditure by the civil departments. The government was satisfied that measures of retrenchment must be introduced 'if only to offset the increases which must automatically follow from the expansion of policies already approved'.

Little more was heard of the 5 per cent cut until after devaluation. Then, at the request of the Chancellor, Robert Hall prepared a paper on the internal financial situation (EPC(49)102) which was circulated to the Economic Policy Committee on 5 October. This attempted to work out the size of the cut in government expenditure and investment that should accompany devaluation. Hall started from the fact that the government had spent £221 million more in the first six months of the fiscal year than in the corresponding period in 1948 and that the Budget surplus, to judge from supplementary estimates, was likely to be about £160 million less than had been hoped. There were also indications of a fall in personal savings: small savers were drawing down their deposits at a rate of about £40 million per annum. All this pointed to the need for cuts of the order of £200 million merely in order to limit the pressure of demand to what had been judged appropriate in the 1949 Budget. The changes in the foreign balance over the past six months pointed to a similar figure. As a supplementary memorandum pointed out (EPC(49)110), since the six winter months of 1948–49 when the current account was roughly in balance, the visible balance had worsened by over £20 million per month or £240 million per annum. Although exports were lower, unemployment was falling quite sharply: in the first eight months of 1949 it had come down by 115,000 compared with 30,000 in the same eight months in 1948. The home market was booming, with industrial production up by 6 or 7 per cent in spite of the fall in exports, and more imports were being absorbed. Investment, which had been consistently underestimated, was at least up to expectations. Quite apart from devaluation, a stiff dose of disinflation was called for.

But devaluation made still larger cuts necessary. To the estimate of £200 million for disinflation, Robert Hall suggested adding a further £100 million to free resources for improving the balance of payments and changing the pattern of production. It was important to act quickly or the chance of profiting from the new exchange rate would slip away. Failure to remove the inflationary tendencies at once would be irremediable, whereas if the cuts made proved to be excessive there would be no difficulty in relaxing them later, for example in or before the next Budget.

Robert Hall was obviously a little doubtful about whether he had pitched his total high enough. On 10 October he warned the Chancellor that, if he did not start with the idea that he would have to go for the whole of the £300 million, he would never get anywhere with his colleagues. Politically difficult items might, however, be knocked off the list at a later stage in the bargaining process. Three days later, in a minute to Plowden, he was querying his own total. Government expenditure was running at a level that made him suspicious that some supplementary estimates were being delayed; investment might again have been underestimated; the additional expenditure in which departments might be involved by devaluation was not fully known, and departments also had a way of circumventing restrictive policies and failing to keep within agreed limits; in addition, there could be no guarantee that wages and salaries would hold steady.

At a meeting of the Economic Policy Committee on 5 October, Robert Hall's assessment was attacked on a number of grounds. Dalton dismissed it as 'another flank attack by officials' and 'not really a proper "estimate" at all'.[51] There were those who disliked quantification in principle, although the need to quantify the cuts in expenditure was inescapable. There were others who looked to higher import prices to do the job of disinflation without assistance from cuts in government expenditure: they found it hard to accept that there would be no net disinflation once the higher cost of imports was being met from a larger volume of exports. The economies forced on consumers would be offset by a fresh demand on resources. There was also some disposition to argue that exports might be re-directed to dollar markets at the expense of sterling markets without any increase in volume, and hence without any need to cut other claims on resources. This would have been a valid argument had it been possible to disregard the low level of reserves, the commitments to sterling area countries already entered into, and the relatively modest allowance made by Robert Hall for the diversion of resources from domestic to external use. But £100 million hardly seemed excessive as an initial bid. Others argued that increased production – possibly via longer working hours – would do the trick. Finally, ministers fell back on the proposition that devaluation brought higher profits to trading departments such as the Ministry of Food and urged

[51] Dalton's diary, entry for 10 October. The suggestion by Donoughue and Jones (1973 p. 447) that the cuts proposed by the Chancellor were ever as high as £700 million seems to be unfounded.

that these profits should be brought into the budgetary reckoning. It was accepted in the end that the starting figure of £300 million might be abated by £15 million on this account.

It was assumed throughout that the budgetary change could be equated with the change in the level of final demand. The Chancellor, in asking for economies of £280 million, referred to a reduction in consumption but was clearly thinking of claims on resources since half of his total was to take the form of a cut in investment.

When Cripps defended the cuts in front of his 'openly dispirited supporters' in the House of Commons on 26 October,[52] Anthony Eden maintained that the proposals had been 'just scratched together in the last fortnight, and they represent the maximum that can be agreed without Cabinet resignation'.[53] This was fair comment. The cuts in expenditure were fought over until the very last minute. Nye Bevan contemplated resignation if they fell on the social services, Bevin and Alexander if they fell on defence and Cripps, still suffering from insomnia and nearing the end of his tether, if his proposals were not accepted.[54] Fortunately, Attlee and Gaitskell gave Cripps full support. Nye Bevan was induced to accept a small prescription charge in principle while successfully resisting a charge to hospital patients and a charge for dentures and spectacles, all three of these being designed to raise £10 million. Many of the cuts were not to come into effect at once and there were some that might never take effect. For example, the withdrawal of the feeding stuffs subsidy (put first at £30 million and later at £36 million) was to take effect only after the next Annual Review in February 1950, but how much of the cost would then fall on the farmers would depend on the outcome of the Review. The subsidy on fish was to be discontinued after decontrol at 'a convenient date' in the spring of 1950. Defence was credited with a cut of £30 million per annum, but this meant only that an intended supplementary, estimated by the Treasury at £30 million (a 'conjectural figure', accepted by the Ministry of Defence 'because they cannot think of a better') would now be limited to £17.5 million.

At the end of the day, the score board for expenditure cuts read £122.5 million instead of the target of £140 million and £79 million of the total represented feeding stuffs, defence and additional profits tax. 'Adminstrative economies' were put at £28 million, and the £10 million for the prescription charge of a shilling was the other main item. The latter, although publicly announced on 24 October, never came into effect and was killed by the Chancellor in April.

As for investment, the cuts in the programme are not visible in the

52 Donoughue and Jones (1973, p. 447).

53 *House of Commons Debates*, 26 October 1949, col. 1360.

54 Dalton's diary, entry for 12 October 1949; Donoughue and Jones (1973, p. 438).

figures for 1950, which increased by £100 million, exactly as had been expected originally. It is possible that some of the cuts (e.g. in power and transport) really did take effect, partly in 1949 and partly in 1950.[55] But it would be hard in retrospect to stigmatize them, like Douglas Jay in 1964, as 'excessively deflationary'.[56]

On the contrary, they lacked drama and appear to have fallen short of common expectations. They certainly made little impression on the City. By the end of October Dalton was commenting on 'the widespread mood in Whitehall and the City' that 'our reserves may not revive nor even hold up and that we shall have another and worse crisis in a few months time'.[57] The Bank and the Treasury began to agitate again for higher interest rates, provoking from Dalton the classic expression of postwar monetary doctrine: 'You can't allow higher interest rates while resisting higher wages rates.'[58] No fresh measures were taken. Nevertheless, by the end of the year the gold reserves had recovered strongly and the gold and dollar deficit had virtually ceased.

Lessons of the 1949 Episode

Before turning to examine how devaluation worked, there are some points in this narrative worth emphasizing.

1 Those who favoured devaluation did so for quite different reasons, and often for bad ones. Some wanted devaluation to improve the competitive position of British industry, although the current account had already reached balance in 1948. Some hoped that devaluation would improve the competitive position of British exports in dollar markets, or simply in the United States. Some saw no other way of resisting the speculative pressure against the pound. At the meeting of the Cabinet on 29 August at which the crucial decision to devalue was confirmed, Cripps himself accepted that: 'An atmosphere had . . . been created . . . in which the pound could not reach stability without devaluation.'

2 These arguments were usually advanced as if devaluation were a sufficient device for the purpose favoured, without regard to other necessary accompanying measures, or to less drastic and more effective ways of achieving the same purpose. In the end, the compelling factor in the situation was the lack of adequate reserves; but the corollary was not drawn that ways must be found of reinforcing reserves either at once or at least in time to withstand future pressure of the same kind. The rundown in reserves was attributed rather too readily to a falling-off in

[55] Dow (1964, p. 46n).
[56] Jay in Rodgers (1964, p. 95).
[57] Dalton's diary, entry for 30 October 1949.
[58] Dalton's diary, entry for 14 December 1949.

sterling area sales in the North American market, while the speculative movement of funds in anticipation of a devaluation of sterling was never analysed and the causes of it were little discussed.

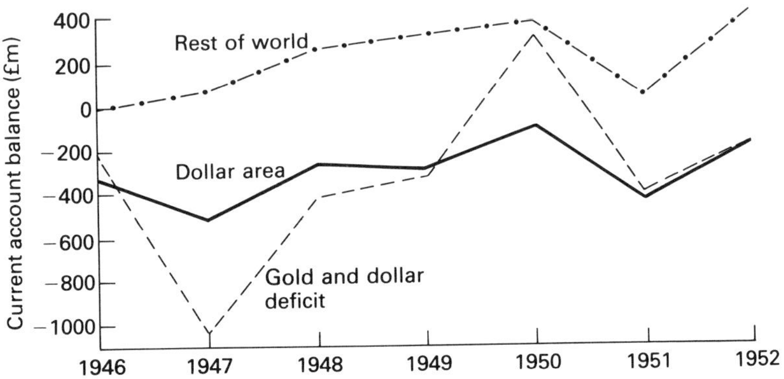

Figure 4.1 Dollar and non-dollar current accounts of the United Kingdom, 1946–52

Source: For 1946, *United Kingdom Balance of Payments, 1946 to 1950 No. 2* (Cmd 8201). For 1947–54, *Annual Abstract of Statistics for 1958.*

3 The debate in Whitehall was dominated by short-run considerations when it was arguable that the decisive factors were long-term. It should have been obvious that at some point in the postwar years it would be necessary to reconsider the sterling–dollar rate of exchange as a contribution to the solution of the so-called 'dollar problem'. That point was most likely to be reached when the first surge in British (and non-dollar) exports was beginning to lose momentum, or when exports had reached a level at which the prime requirement was not to expand the total but to effect a redistribution between dollar and non-dollar markets. In 1949 for the first time there was a margin in hand for this purpose. As will be seen from figure 4.1, the surplus on trade with non-dollar markets, which accrued in the form of a balance of 'soft', inconvertible currencies, was balanced in 1948 by a deficit in trade with dollar countries that had to be discharged in dollars. The United Kingdom was thus in danger of running out of dollars as a result of settling its deficit in 'hard' currencies and at the same time of running up equal or larger inconvertible balances in 'soft' currences through the sale of 'unrequited' exports. It was necessary to make the soft currencies harder and the hard currencies softer; there could be no more effective way of doing this than by making hard currencies dearer in terms of soft currencies. This in turn could best be brought about by devaluing sterling against the dollar and inducing other countries to devalue their currencies simultaneously.

4 From this point of view, the British balance of payments was largely irrelevant to the case for devaluation since what was in question was the value of the dollar rather than the value of the pound. The issue was not how to restore British trade to balance, since it already was in balance, but how to respond to the so-called dollar shortage. At some stage this response would have to include currency realignments. It would, however, have been premature to embark on these when exports were rising strongly but there was nothing in hand to permit a *redirection* of exports to dollar markets.

5 Except in the papers prepared for the meeting of the Economic Policy Committee of 1 July and in the memoranda by the Economic Section, there does not seem to have been a careful weighing of the pros and cons in a submission by officials, much less at a meeting of ministers. In the last resort, it was the loss of reserves that settled the matter. Although the Economic Section had given thought to the choice of rate, it was largely a matter of accident that $2.80 rather than $3.00 to the pound was the rate selected. The significance of getting other countries to move simultaneously was rarely stressed. The measures to accompany devaluation were considered separately and almost as an afterthought (although two months later the Chancellor had so far forgotten the sequence of events that he insisted that the economy cuts were decided 'side by side' with devaluation).

6 As in 1931 and 1967, devaluation took place in spite of repeated declarations by the Chancellor that he would not countenance it. This in itself hardly contributed to careful pre-planning. As in 1931, and in contrast to 1967, the Chancellor did not resign, although Cripps might have been thought more ready to do so than Callaghan.

7 In 1949 as in 1967, devaluation was delayed well beyond the point of maximum advantage: in 1949 until after a strong expectation of devaluation had developed and in 1967 until after heavy forward sales of sterling had been made. (Keynes made a similar argument about the optimal timing of devaluation in August 1931, and he too was ignored.) On each occasion ministers were unwilling to contemplate action that would have had the advantage of surprise. As Cripps pointed out in his Mansion House speech on 4 October,' Our action had been discussed, debated, and indeed almost expected, throughout the world. . . . Though the actual date and the degree of change in the sterling exchange rate may have taken people by surprise – no one can suggest that it was a matter suddenly sprung upon an unsuspecting world.' While this is substantially correct, it hardly lay with Cripps to say so, since those who *were* taken by surprise were those who took him at his word. The uncertainty that seemed to him to justify devaluation need never have been created had he taken action earlier.

8 Devaluation was seen by Cripps as an act of foreign policy quite as much as of economic policy. He was constantly insisting that 'the

relationship between the dollar and the sterling worlds is not one to which the United Kingdom alone can find a remedy. It is a problem', he told the House of Commons in July, 'in which our friends and partners in the USA and the Commonwealth are especially involved.' In this he was undoubtedly right: the problem was part of the postwar dollar problem and intimately concerned the United States and her trading partners in the Commonwealth and elsewhere. But to say this was not, as Cripps at times implied, to voice an objection to devaluation. For if that were so, it was necessary to come forward with some other equally powerful instrument for re-structuring the world economy. And the most that was ever suggested by those who preferred a 'general settlement' to outright devaluation was trivial and peripheral in comparison.

9 An important byproduct of devaluation was an improvement in USA–UK economic relations, which had become far less close than in the days of planning for the postwar world. Following the consultations by Hall and Wilson Smith in Washington, an economic minister was attached after devaluation to the British Embassy, with a member of the Economic Section on his staff. The minister was nominated alternately by the Bank of England and the Treasury; he reported to both and acted as vice deputy governor on the Boards of the IMF and IBRD. This not only allowed economic affairs to be handled more professionally by the Embassy, but also made for closer consultation and more satisfactory relations with the United States.

10 Finally, it is instructive to see who finally decided. Not Cripps, though he acquiesced. Not Bevin, though he had shown in 1931 that he had no inhibitions about devaluation. Not Morrison, though he favoured it. Not the Prime Minister, who had perhaps the oddest view of all as to what was involved. It was left to three young and relatively junior ministers – Gaitskell, Wilson and Jay – all of them economists, accidentally in a position to decide, and accidentally led by a minister (Gaitskell) of principle and determination who was not even a member of the Cabinet.

The economic background

Let us now turn to the economic background to devaluation. In the years after the war the British government continued to make use of many of the controls introduced in wartime, adapting and sometimes strengthening them for the purposes of peacetime economic management. Consumer rationing continued in force; residential, industrial and all other kinds of building were subject to a system of licensing reinforced by control over the allocation of building materials. There were residual controls over the employment of labour; over prices, particularly the prices of what were judged to be essential commodities; over bank lending, both as to quantity and direction. Imports had to conform to a programme specifying the quantity and source of the imports to be purchased by the government or to be admitted for sale if purchased privately. For exports there was also a programme, consisting more of targets at which industry was encouraged to aim than of quantities whose sale in foreign markets was assured. The government's powers over the balance of payments were further supported by exchange control over payments in foreign currencies. All the members of the sterling area operated a system of exchange control which aimed at an enforced economy in the use of foreign exchange while leaving payments by one member of the area to another free of control.

These controls were the principal instrument by which the government sought to regulate economic activity and maintain stability both in the level of prices and in the balance of payments. Many of them had been relaxed or abolished as the supply position improved, and they could not easily have been restored or intensified. But in the government's scheme of things they still occupied the centre of the stage. Fiscal policy remained important because the size of the budget surplus or deficit governed the volume of savings and so the level of capital formation that could be sustained. But monetary policy and the exchange rate played little part in the government's thinking. Hugh Dalton saw nothing inconsistent between aiming at a long term rate of 2.5 per cent on government bonds and struggling to make good wartime arrears and losses of capital assets through an appropriate expansion in fixed capital investment. Stafford Cripps could see no reason to devalue the pound when the government had power to act directly on the level of imports and exports.

There were of course protagonists of the free market who wanted to see the controls done away with: usually without much consideration of what would follow de-control. There were also sceptics, who thought that the controls leaked badly and traced the leaks to excess liquidity and over-full order books. There is no doubt that at the end of the war the money supply was greatly inflated in relation to normal requirements, and that the banks were seriously under-lent and awash with liquid funds while business was also highly liquid. It might be thought that this would quickly seep through into price inflation and into the consequences of excess liquidity with which the world has become familiar. In fact, however, the rise in prices, given what was happening elsewhere in the world and to import prices in particular, was comparatively modest. The consumer price index rose at an average rate of 5 per cent per annum over the first five postwars years (and, indeed, only half as fast as the American GNP deflator in the first three postwar years). Bank deposits grew at roughly the same rate as prices over the period, i.e. at an average rate of 5 per cent, so that there was no contraction in real money balances. But in 1949 and again in 1950 the increase in bank deposits was only 1 per cent or less, and even in 1951 it was no more than 2.5 per cent. Throughout these years, as indeed throughout the whole of the postwar period up to the end of 1951, the rate on Treasury bills remained steady at around 0.5 per cent.

The government's neglect of monetary policy may have been misguided; the weight of excess liquidity, as Hawtrey argued, may have held down exports a little and reduced the effectiveness of some of the controls. But there is nothing in the statistical record to suggest that the controls did not bite or that excess liquidity was fatal to their use for the purposes intended by the government. What the controls could not do was to redress the imbalance between the dollar and the non-dollar world. Nothing but devaluation could do that.

'Underlying the whole situation', as the ECA study of *The Sterling Area* explained later,

> was the fact that at the existing exchange rate [£1 = $4.03]., the free market demand for goods and services from the Dollar Area was greatly in excess of what could be paid for. Only by the use of controls was it possible to limit the actual size of the current deficits – there was no natural tendencey to equilibrium. Progress in the rearrangement of trade patterns and the narrowing of the dollar gap had been substantial, but the difficulties in making the necessary controls work effectively when market forces were pulling so strongly against them were great. Objections against the use of controls, too, were beginning to be strongly heard in some non-sterling countries.[59]

In this passage, the controls referred to relate to import and exchange controls operated within the sterling area, but the thesis holds true also of domestic controls designed to limit expenditure on dollar imports, and used by a much wider group of countries.

The pressures that led to devaluation are not very evident from the trade accounts for the United Kingdom or from the estimates of the current balance of payments (table 4.1). The annual figures are in no way suggestive of a crisis in 1949. Exports continued to rise, the deficit on visible trade continued to fall, and the current account remained close to balance.

Even if we concentrate exclusively on trade with the dollar area (table 4.2), there is little that makes 1949 look unusual. Clearly, there was a setback in exports, and the trend in both the visible deficit and the current account deficit was reversed. But the size of the changes was hardly enough of itself to smack of crisis.

The most the figures for the dollar deficit in table 4.3 suggest is a slight wobble in 1949 in the favourable trend between 1947 and 1950. Even the dollar deficit of the outer sterling area (table 4.3), of which so much was made at the time, was if anything less in 1949 than in 1948.

[59] Economic Cooperation Administration (1951, p. 75).

TABLE 4.1 British trade and payments, 1946–51

		(£ million)					
		1946	*1947*	*1948*	*1949*	*1950*	*1951*
Exports and	(a)	960	1180	1639	1863	2261	2735
re-exports	(b)	900	1125	1550	1790	2221	2708
Imports	(a)	1063	1541	1790	2000	2312	3424
	(b)	1100	1574	1768	1970	2374	3497
Balance on	(a)	−103	−361	−151	−137	−51	−689
visible trade	(b)	−200	−449	−218	−180	−153	789
Balance on	(a)	−127	−20	177	136	358	320
invisibles	(b)	−250	−226	98	110	382	268
Balance on	(a)	−230	−381	26	−1	307	−369
current account	(b)	−450	−675	−120	−70	−229	−521

(a) As estimated in 1980
(b) As estimated at the time
Sources: For (a), *Economic Trends Annual Supplement*, 1981 ed; for (b), *Economic Survey for 1947* (and later years to 1952)

TABLE 4.2 British trade with the dollar area, 1946–51

	(£ million)					
	1946	*1947*	*1948*	*1949*	*1950*	*1951*
Exports and re-exports	100	130	196	195	324	393
Imports	390	567	406	442	439	742
Surplus or deficit on visible trade	−290	−437	−210	−247	−115	−349
Surplus or deficit on invisibles	−11	−73	−42	−49	227	−87
Total surplus or deficit	−301	−510	−252	−296	−88	−436

Source: For 1947–52, *Abstract of Statistics for 1958*; for 1946, *UK Balance of Payments, 1946–1953* (Cmd 8976)

TABLE 4.3 UK Gold and dollar accounts, 1946–54

	(£ million)						
	1946	*1947*	*1948*	*1949*	*1950*	*1951*	*1954*
UK deficit on current account with dollar area	−301	−501	−252	−296	−88	−436	−72
Deficit of rest of sterling area with dollar area	−73	−306	−65	−54	170	102	27
Gold sales to UK by sterling area	82	84	55	68	100	78	138
Net credit or debt from transactions with non-dollar countries and organizations	46	−260	−95	−89	−12	−67	−23
Capital transactions	21	−32	−49	23	137	−84	57
Gold and dollar deficit	−225	−1024	−406	348	308	−407	127
Financed by:							
US/Canadian loans and ERP	279	812	256	345	268	63	–
Drawings on reserves	−54	152	55	3	−575	344	−87
South African gold loan/IMF dollars	–	60	95	–	–	–	−40
Gold and dollar deficit	−225	−1024	−406	−348	308	−407	127

Sources: *Annual Abstract of Statistics for 1958; UK Balance of Payments 1946 to 1953* (Cmd 8976)

There was a check to the gradual replacement of a deficit by a surplus, but it was not catastrophic. None of the main components to be financed in gold and dollars shown in table 4.3 changed very much between 1948 and 1949, nor did the total itself. The biggest single change is due to a special transaction unconnected with events in 1949: the gold loan of £80 million by South Africa in 1948. Moreover, what stands out in both years as the biggest single factor in the deficit to be financed is the

United Kingdom's own deficit on current account. And if one looks ahead to 1954 to see what sustainable pattern might emerge in the 1950s, it was in this item that the biggest change fell to be made.

But the annual figures do not tell the whole story: these were large fluctuations within the year. The gold and dollar reserves, for example, fell from £471 million at the end of March to £406 million at the end of June, to £372 million on 20 August and to £330 million by 18 September – a fall of 30 per cent within six months. The movement in the dollar deficit from quarter to quarter (figure 4.2) tells a similar story.

Figure 4.2 Gold and dollar balance of the United Kingdom, 1946–1950

Source: UK Balance of Payments, 1946–1950 Cmd 8201

How are these figures to be reconciled with the comparative stability of the annual totals? Most of the discussion at the time laid emphasis on the depressed state of the US market between the spring and autumn of 1949.[60] The recession, although short-lived, had serious repercussion on imports of materials from the sterling area, especially rubber, wool, jute and tin, reducing both the volume and the price paid for them. Taking these four commodities together, the fall in sterling area exports to the United States in 1949 was about 25 per cent, or $150 million.[61] This, though substantial, seems hardly sufficient to account for the crisis. From the annual figures we may turn to the fluctuations from quarter to

[60] Between October 1948 and June 1949 the US index of industrial production (seasonally adjusted) fell by 10 per cent. Stock-building began to decline in the autumn of 1948 and imports fell off from the third quarter onwards. The fall in the value of imports between the third quarter of 1948 and the low point a year later was $1.5 billion or over 14 per cent.

[61] Economic Commission for Europe (1950, p. 96).

quarter in the sterling area's trade with the United States (table 4.4). Estimates are given in the ECA study of the sterling area published in 1951, and although they are only approximations they indicate the magnitude of the swings during the year.[62] It will be seen that the trade deficit of the sterling area nearly doubled in the second quarter and improved thereafter quarter by quarter until, by the middle of 1950, the deficit was running $200 million per quarter below the 1948 average. The experience of the second quarter stands out as exceptional.

It is not possible to assign the deterioration in the second quarter with any precision to its various sources, but it is clear that it cannot all be attributed to the trade deficit with the United States. The rise in the dollar deficit in the second quarter was $300 million compared with the first quarter, and $200 million compared with the quarterly average for 1948. Even if we take the latter basis of comparison, the rise in the trade deficit of the sterling area with the United States (table 4.4) by $125 million per quarter does not account for much more than half the change in the total dollar deficit of $200 million.

To some extent, the higher deficit in the second quarter was foreseen. In a brief for the Chancellor before the meeting of the Economic Policy Committee on 17 June, Sam Goldman pointed out that the Treasury had been expecting the deficit to increase since early April because of heavier expenditure on food and materials (for stockpiling), the usual seasonal reduction in the dollar surplus of the colonies, bigger losses to Belgium and Switzerland, and an unfavourable turn in the working of the South African Loan Agreement. April had been in line with the target, but in May there was an overshoot of $80 million, divided in roughly equal terms between the United Kingdom, the colonial territories and the rest of the sterling area. It is rather remarkable that so small an addition to the drain on the reserves should so quickly have produced an exchange crisis, and is one more illustration of the inadequacy of the reserves in the postwar years.

In addition to the special factors mentioned in the brief, we can distinguish four different elements in the deterioration during the second quarter.

1 A large part of the increase in the dollar deficit in the second quarter – about $60 million – was due to a 38 per cent increase above the 1948 level in British import expenditures in the United States. Some of this corresponded to the stockpiling of food and raw materials already referred to. Since there was never any intention of maintaining this level of expenditure over the year, some falling back was to be expected and did occur. In addition, the alarm generated by the growing deficit led the British government to cut its import programme, and this refinforced the fall.

[62] Economic Cooperation Administration (1951, p. 76).

TABLE 4.4 Sterling area trade with the United States, 1948–50

($ million per quarter)

		Sterling area exports to USA	*Sterling area imports from USA*	*Balance of trade*	*UK imports from USA*	*Rest of sterling area exports to USA*	*Excess of RSA exports over UK imports*
1948	average	346	501	−155	161	274	113
1949	(I)	345	504	−159	170	297	127
	(II)	281	561	−280	222	217	−5
	(III) }	231	413	−182	155	162	52
	(IV) }	297	385	−88		252	
1950	(I) }	326	348	−22	122	280	158
	(II) }	361	318	43			
	(III), (IV)	457	321	136	140	352	212

Source: based on Economic Co-operation Administration (1951), table 36 and p. 77

2 The check to activity in the United States reacted on imports, particularly of raw materials, and on commodity prices, so that sales of materials such as rubber, tin and wool to the United States were depressed on both scores. Imports into the United States from the outer sterling area fell by $80 million in the second quarter and by a further $55 million in the third. When business conditions improved later in the year, inventories of materials were built up again and the movement was strengthened by a rise in the dollar price of most of the commodities supplied. Full recovery to the 1948 level did not, however, take place until the first half of 1950.

3 The expectation of devaluation led to deferments of purchases payable in sterling and of actual disbursements in sterling. It also encouraged a corresponding acceleration of imports from the dollar area and the immediate discharge of dollar obligations. This speculative element must have influenced the purchases of materials referred to above, delaying them before devaluation and accelerating them thereafter. British exports to the United States may also have suffered prior to devaluation, if only through delays in payment. American companies in London were known to be taking no chances in transferring their profits to dollar accounts as fast as possible. The fall in gold sales to the United Kingdom in the middle quarters of 1949, by 27 per cent and 20 per cent respectively below the 1948 level (see figure 4.2), reflects the same influences. Since gold sales were much the same in 1948 as in 1949, it is natural to suspect that the distortion in the pattern of sales over the year was associated with the expectation of devaluation that developed from the spring onwards.

4 Finally, one has to take account of all the governmental measures designed to reduce the drain on the reserves and of devaluation itself. The American and Canadian governments, for example, had undertaken in September to review their stockpiling programme for tin and rubber so as to enlarge the field for imports. The Commonwealth governments had agreed to cut their dollar outgoings by 25 per cent from the 1948 levels. The British government had also made various cuts in order to improve its dollar deficit. Some of these measures began to take effect well before the end of the year. They are not likely to have been much reinforced at that stage by the impact of devaluation on trade flows, but the reversal of the speculative factors referred to under point 3 must by then have been at work.

It is not easy to demonstrate the relative importance of these four factors. But the evidence suggests that the speculative element was probably at least as important as the check to domestic activity in the United States. It is significant, for example, that, although the trade deficit of the sterling area with the United States fell by $100 million in the third quarter, the loss of reserves up to 18 September was higher than in the second quarter, and in the last 30 days before devaluation amounted to £42 million (compared with £65 million in the whole of the second quarter). Although a decision to devalue had been taken before the outflow reached such proportions, the loss of reserves played a decisive part, and to that extent devaluation was a capitulation to market opinion and another of many demonstrations of the weakness of government in face of an exchange crisis.

It was the perception, not always very clearly, that devaluation was a necessary ingredient in the restoration of international equilibrium that fuelled speculative pressure; and it was the speculative pressure that in the end compelled devaluation. But if it had not been for the additional uncertainty generated by the mild depression of 1949, it is doubtful whether the pressure would have been sufficient to force devaluation in 1949, and it might have been possible to refrain from action before the outbreak of the Korean War in June 1950. Thereafter, to judge from the frequency with which revaluation was argued, the issue might not have arisen for some considerable time.

The impact of devaluation

The war in Korea began nine months after devaluation and swept through the world economy like a tornado. World prices, international trade and payments, national budgets – all were pulled into new orbits. By the time the storm died down the devaluation of sterling was a distant, almost forgotten, event and its effects hard to trace with certainty in the new pattern of trade flows.

The effects of devaluation must be judged against the expectations entertained in advance. To those who looked to devaluation primarily as a means of stopping the dollar drain, it justified itself in the increase in the gold and dollar reserves by 70 per cent in the first nine months and the still larger increase in the nine months that followed. Those who stressed the need to improve Britain's competitive position could claim that most of the advantage conferred by a 30 per cent devaluation outlasted the Korean War. Between 1949 and, say, 1954 the American GDP price deflator rose by 13.3 per cent while in Britain it rose by 16.4 per cent; as in the period following the 1931 devaluation, nearly the whole of the cost advantage remained for some time. Even those who looked to devaluation to pave the way for a surplus on the current account of the balance of payments could take satisfaction from the outcome: a surplus in all but one of the five years 1950–54 and a cumulative surplus of well over £500 million.

But what of the hope that devaluation would lay the basis for a new relationship between the sterling and the dollar worlds? Some evidence of the change after 1949 appears in table 4.3, which shows a fall in the UK deficit on current account with the dollar area in 1950 by

£200 million and a slightly larger improvement in the dollar balance of the rest of the sterling area. The first of these changes was reversed in the Korean War but reappeared when the war was over. The improvement in the dollar balance of the rest of the sterling area was not sustained, but after 1950 there remained a small and consistent surplus where in the years prior to 1950 there had been a consistent deficit.

Another way of bringing out the change that took place is to compare trade with the dollar area and trade with the sterling area (figure 4.3).

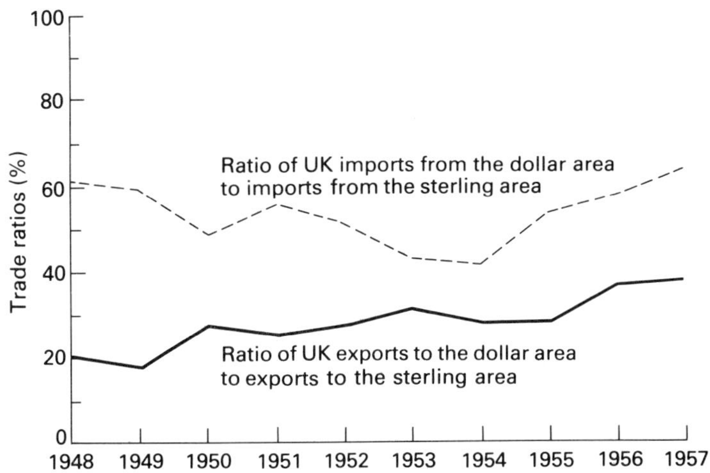

Figure 4.3 British trade with the dollar and sterling areas, 1948–57

Source: Annual Abstract of Statistics for 1958, HMSO, London

The most notable feature of this comparison is the sharp change in 1950: the proportion of British exports sold in dollar markets rose abruptly, and the proportion of imports from dollar markets fell equally abruptly. The reaction in 1951 presumably reflects the disturbance to trade and prices brought about by the Korean War. But if one takes an average of the three following years (1952-54) and compares it with the average for 1948–49, there is a striking shift in both ratios in exactly the way one would expect: up from 19.5 per cent in 1948–49 to 28.2 per cent in 1952–54 for exports, and down from 60.0 to 44.6 per cent for imports.

It is true that there were other factors in the shift quite unconnected with devaluation. Sterling area sources of supply were recovering from wartime dislocation and postwar difficulties, so that there was an upward trend in the area's trade, not only external but also internal. On the other hand, one might have expected the British authorities to take a more relaxed attitude to imports costing dollars as their reserves improved, and this may help to explain the sharp rise in the proportion of dollar imports in 1951 and the later recovery in 1954–57. However, discrimination did not extend to dollar exports, and the continuing climb in the proportion of British exports reaching dollar markets is evidence of the durability of the competitive advantage brought by devaluation.[63]

British trade, however, is only half the story: the change in parities went far beyond sterling and the sterling area. In Western Europe, for example, only Sweden and Switzerland abstained from devaluing in September, Sweden having already devalued by 30 per cent the previous year. Denmark, France, Ireland, the Netherlands and Norway all devalued by 30 per cent and Germany by 20 per cent. Belgium, Italy and Portugal made more modest devaluations while Austria, Greece and Iceland made larger ones. The rest of the world also took the opportunity to make devaluations against the dollar: even the Canadian dollar was devalued by 9 per cent. The trade-weighted devaluation of sterling may be estimated at approximately 9 per cent, too – rather larger on the import side and smaller on the export side. Thus accompanying devaluations in the first year played a larger role than in either 1931, when the ratio of effective to nominal devaluations was approximately 0.5 or 1967, when that ratio exceeded 0.95.

The net result might have been expected to be a marked check to the growth of US exports and a spurt in US imports. The record, as shown in table 4.5, bears out that this occurred in 1950.

TABLE 4.5 US Trade and national income, 1948–54

	Exports from USA (incl. services) ($b.)	*Imports into USA (incl. services) ($b.)*	*Current balance of USA ($b.)*	*US GNP at constant prices (1948 = 100)*
1948	16.88	10.37	6.51	100.0
1949	15.86	9.64	6.22	98.9
1950	13.91	12.01	1.90	105.7
1951	18.93	15.09	3.84	112.4
1954	18.00	16.01	1.99	113.6

Source: National Income and Product Accounts of the USA, 1929–74

Even if we allow for a downward trend in US exports as Europe recovered and an upward trend in US imports with the renewed growth in GNP, the size of the adjustments on both sides of the account in 1950

[63] Allowance should, however, be made for the increase in American GNP by 13 per cent between 1949 and 1951, after a growth of only 1 per cent in the previous two years.

is striking. But the very speed with which they followed devaluation makes it doubtful how far they were caused by it. In the first half of 1949 exports were running (on a seasonally adjusted basis) at $17.9 billion per annum and had already fallen to $15.5 billion in the third quarter (i.e., before devaluation). In each of the next three quarters they remained below $13.5 billion and rose above $14.0 billion only in the final quarter of 1950. Imports of goods and services fluctuated between $9 and $10 billion per annum in the five quarters between the beginning of 1949 and April 1950, but had risen from $9.5 billion in the last quarter of 1949 to $10.6 billion in the second quarter of 1950 and $13.4 billion in the third. It would seem from these quarterly movements that most of the turn-around in 1950 that can be disentangled from the effects of the Korean War came on the import side. Some of the rise in imports can be attributed to the recovery in economic activity in the United States in the winter of 1949–50. But it is not unreasonable to treat devaluation as contributing to the rise, particularly when one finds it continuing after hostilities had ceased. Making all allowances, the reduction in the current surplus of the United States after 1949 was materially assisted by the series of devaluations in 1949.

Thus whether we start from the composition of British trade or from the American current account, there is evidence of a change in the balance between the dollar and the non-dollar world that persisted into the 1950s and was an indispensable element in post-war reconstruction. From the British point of view the adjustment was by no means painless. Although in trade-weighted terms the devaluation was under 10 per cent, import prices rose between June 1949 and June 1950 by 17 per cent while export prices rose by only 5 per cent. The shift in the terms of trade represented a real cost even if it was small by comparison with the much larger shift that followed the outbreak of the Korean war.

Finally, what of the danger that costs and prices would rise so as to extinguish the competitive gains of devaluation and raise the spectre, so much feared in 1931, of a *dégringolade* of the exchanges? In spite of the rise in import prices and the relaxed stance of monetary policy, the cost of living was remarkably steady. In the year to September 1949 retail prices had risen by 3.2 per cent; in the year that followed the rise was only 2.0 per cent. Food prices, which had risen by 8.8 per cent in the year before devaluation, rose only by a further 4.5 per cent in the following year. The government kept well within its bargain with the trade unions, who had agreed to hold wages steady if the cost of living rose by under 5 per cent. The trade unions, for their part, were almost equally successful during the first post-devaluation year. Basic hourly rates for men rose by 1 per cent and although hourly earnings, measured in the biennial October survey, increased rather faster, there was no acceleration compared with the previous year, the rise being limited to 3.5 per cent.

If there was no substantial inflation of prices, this was not because of a tighter fiscal stance. Neither public expenditure nor revenue changed much in 1950, and the pressure of demand, as reflected in the level of unemployment, was also stationary. The improvement in the trade balance was at best a modest one, and the improvement over the year, as happened again in 1967, was heavily concentrated on invisibles. This may not have been quite what the advocates of devaluation would have predicted, but in other respects they had good reason to be satisfied with the way things worked out. In particular, they could point to the absence of a faster rate of inflation and the shift in exports from sterling to dollar markets. The politicians for their part could take comfort that they had largely avoided the cuts in public expenditure that their advisers kept insisting were indispensable.

5

The 1967 Devaluation of Sterling

Long before 1967, the possibility that sterling might have to be devalued was widely entertained, though not often discussed in public. It came up from time to time in the 1950s, but without any indication that it had ever been seriously considered by the government. The Tribunal inquiring into alleged leaks before the raising of Bank rate to 7 per cent in September 1957 heard evidence from financial journalists that the Chancellor had told them of his intention 'to represent most strongly' at the Annual Meeting of the IMF in Washington that 'the Government had no intention of devaluing the pound or allowing the margins of the rate to be flexible'.[1] Harold Macmillan, musing on the economic situation at the beginning of 1962, reflected that if wage inflation continued 'we might have to devalue';[2] and in writing to the Queen in March 1963 he described to her the school of thought that advocated a policy of '"Boom and do not mind busting", i.e. devalue the pound or alternatively let it float'.[3] But the only form of devaluation that he was willing to contemplate was a move to raise the price of gold, in default of action by the United States, by means of a concerted devaluation of the pound, mark and franc in the interests of increasing international liquidity.[4]

On a long view it seemed only too likely that it would become progressively more difficult to maintain the parity in the 1960s. On the one hand, the competitive position of the United Kingdom was weakening under the combined influence of rising money wages and slower growth in productivity than in other industrial countries; and on the other, the relief afforded to the balance of payments throughout the

[1] *Proceedings of the Tribunal appointed to inquire into allegations that information about the raising of Bank rate was improperly disclosed* (1958), Q 37. See also Qq 120 and 6007.

[2] Macmillan (1973, p. 49).

[3] Ibid., p. 401.

[4] Ibid., p. 381.

1950s by a steady improvement in the terms of trade could not be expected to continue for another decade.[5]

The United Kingdom's share of world trade in manufactures had fallen steadily for many years; although this was consistent with a healthy surplus on current account in the mid-1950s – and indeed with a falling deficit balance on visible trade from 1955 to 1958 – there were some signs of a weakening at the end of the decade. In 1960, for only the second time since 1951, the current account was in deficit; from then on until devaluation in 1967 deficits on current account recurred except in years of depression like 1962–63, when the most that could be achieved was a surplus of £100 million or so. (See table 5.1.) In addition, there was a substantial deficit on long-term capital account, averaging about £200 million over the four years 1963–66, the basic balance deficit on current and long-term capital account amounting over the same period to an average of £250 million per annum.[6] The reserves of gold and foreign exchange had climbed fairly steadily but slowly throughout the 1950s and were still under £1,000 million at the end of 1959 – far too low in relation to annual imports nearly four times that amount, and to liquid external liabilities that were also about four times as large.

It was not, however, a cool assessment of trends that gave force to public anxieties about the parity. Much more important in the public mind were the repeated balance of payment crises. These were identified with stop–go policies of demand management which were widely held to be injurious to economic growth. The corollary was drawn that, if the 'balance of payments constraint', as it was called, could be removed, growth would automatically accelerate. What simpler than to remove the constraint by devaluation, or still better, by letting the pound float freely?

These views did not go unchallenged. Unemployment in the 1950s had fluctuated around 1.5 per cent, so that the economy even at the worst of times was working under quite heavy pressure, with labour shortages varying between acute and very acute in most parts of the country. Any increase in demand could hardly avoid finding an escape into the international sector of the economy, sucking in additional

[5] [This at any rate was my own view at the beginning of 1961, when I was about to take over from Sir Robert Hall as Economic Adviser to Her Majesty's Government. But I saw no reason to take a fatalistic view or to devalue earlier than was necessary. It was not possible to foresee how costs would move in other countries or what success the government might have in restraining the increase in money wages. A.K.C.]

[6] The Central Statistical Office estimates in 1983 are rather different from those available at the time. In commenting on the devaluation in December 1967, the Organization for Economic Cooperation and Development pointed out that it came after the United Kingdom had run deficits on current account during six of the last eight years. See OECD (1967a, p. 3). The latest estimates, however, show surpluses in five of those eight years and a negligible deficit over the entire period.

TABLE 5.1 Elements in the balance of payments of United Kingdom, 1961–71

	Net long-term investment	Export credit less import credit	(£ million) Short-term capital movements (including balancing item)	Balance on current account	Balance for official financing
1961	68		−454	47	−339
1962	−98		135	155	192
1963	−155	−91	63	125	−58
1964	−367	−29	63	−362	−695
1965	−218	−64	−28	−43	−353
1966	−87	−196	−377[a]	113	−547
1967	−108	−189	20	−289	−671[b]
1968	−132	−281	−473	−273	−1410[c]
1969	−173	−181	570	471	687
1970	−191	−381	1078	781	1287
1971	26	−233	2277	1076	3146

[a] Including transfer of £316 million from dollar portfolio to reserves
[b] Including loss on forward transactions of £105 million
[c] Including loss on forward transactions of £251 million

Source: Economic Trends Annual Supplement, 1981

imports or checking the growth of exports. There was no reason to suppose that higher pressure would lead to additional employment, productivity or output except to a very minor degree. The much more immediate danger was inflation. It did not require much imagination to foresee the risks of creating more inflationary pressure on the heels of a devaluation. One virtue of stop–go policies was that they avoided those risks.

If the case for devaluation was to be made out, therefore, it had to be demonstrated that growth was impeded either by a fixed rate of exchange (if the case was one in favour of floating) or by an over-valuation of the pound at the current parity. The frequency of exchange crises might or might not point to the latter. Other countries suffered fluctuations not altogether dissimilar from Britain's except that, since they took place around a steeper rate of climb, they did not involve a 'stop' phase in which industrial growth ceased altogether. Moreover, there was no obvious or demonstrable connection between trend and fluctuations: most countries seemed to find that their economies stuck fairly closely, from one decade to the next, to a more or less linear upward trend in productivity, with cyclical wobbles but no apparent after-effects on the trend of cycles of varying severity. On this showing, productivity apparently suffered no lasting damage from stop–go.

These were not matters that were argued out in the literature of the early 1960s. There was a tendency to confuse two different types of growth – growth in output and growth in productivity – and to look on an expansion in capital investment as the indispensable source of both without much regard to the state of the labour market on the one hand or the conditions favouring or thwarting technical innovation on the other. There was also a tendency to explain competitive power exclusively in terms of rising productivity and to take a fatalistic view of the concomitant movement in money wages. It was widely assumed that growth should, in some sense, be export-led rather than, as more commonly happens, export-engendering. Above all, there was a curious *naïveté* about how to deal with external deficits and little realization of the difficulties of making devaluation effective. To take an example from a later analysis of the choices facing the government, two of its economic advisers start out by postulating that 'a deficit can be *corrected instantly* by either (a) floating . . . or (b) suspending convertibility by introducing exchange controls'.[7]

One of the features of these years was a kind of conspiracy of silence in relation to devaluation, much like the silence that preceded the 1931 devaluation.[8] Economists hesitated to state publicly the case for devaluation, recognizing that, the more convincingly the case for devaluation

[7] Graham and Beckerman (1972, p. 12; italics in original).
[8] For a similar comparison, see Allen (1975, p. 42).

was stated, the more difficult it would be for the government to bring it about smoothly and without speculative surges. In practice, as in time became evident, opinion formed itself without professional debate and enormous speculative positions were taken on assessments that rested on simple probabilities rather than economic diagnoses.

The first major difference between 1967 and earlier devaluations lies therefore in the character of the debate preceding it. It was far more protracted and for much of the time far less open. This was as true of the debate on the inside as of the debate among outsiders.

First difficulties

The possibility of devaluation was first raised publicly by the National Institute in January 1961, but there was no agitation for it then or in either of the next two years. Even in 1964, though much debated in private, devaluation was rarely canvassed in print.

At first the controversy turned on the rate of expansion of demand and on the possible need for measures to secure greater moderation. An external deficit was foreseen but not found 'particularly disturbing' since it could be attributed to 'a temporary burst of stockbuilding'.[9] The balance of payments on current account had remained in surplus in the second half of 1963, although unemployment had fallen below 2 per cent by the end of the year. (See table 5.2.) But at that point anxiety began to be expressed on various scores. The unemployment figures dropped sharply in February 1964 and went on falling. The trade figures for January, announced at about the same time, revealed a record deficit in the balance of trade. Forecasts of the current account extending into 1965 began to look distinctly alarming; and as time went on, they were revised progressively to show bigger and bigger deficits, as is the way of forecasts when the tide turns. It became increasingly difficult to attribute the deterioration in the payments position to stockbuilding alone.

This left open two other possibilities. The deficit might reflect excessive pressure on the economy; or it might indicate inadequate competitive power. On the first hypothesis it could be argued that, if it were possible to keep the economy in external balance with unemployment at 2 per cent, there was no particular need to worry about deficits emerging at lower levels of unemployment. The long-run advantages of running the economy at higher pressure were by no means self-evident. Alternatively, it might prove that what was to blame for the emergence of an external deficit was the unforeseen and excessive *rate* of expansion in domestic demand rather than the maintenance of a level of demand

[9] National Institute of Economic and Social Research, *Economic Review*, November 1963, p. 3.

that was excessive in relation to existing resources. The faster demand expanded, the more difficult it was bound to be to make output keep pace, and the greater would be the temptation to draw on the more elastic supply of goods available from abroad. Another kind of excessive pressure might take the form of an investment boom, which absorbed resources needed for the satisfaction of consumer demand and made it necessary to procure those resources in the form of an external deficit financed by borrowing from abroad. This particular variant was considered almost exclusively in terms of investment in stocks and short-term borrowing, either from the IMF and foreign central banks or through an accumulation of sterling balances by the countries of the sterling area. There was virtually no discussion of the possibility of long-term borrowing of the kind engaged in subsequently by the nationalized industries.

The first line of explanation, in any of its variants, pointed to deflation of demand as the appropriate remedy. But deflation was associated with 'stop–go', which was widely regarded as a discredited policy. The Federation of British Industries (FBI) in 1961 had come out against 'stop–go' and in favour of planning *à la francaise*.[10] Its members yearned for steadier and more continuous expansion in demand, and the 'Maudling experiment' of 1963–64, although hardly an example of indicative planning, was a response to their prayers. The Labour Party was even more strongly against deflation and starry-eyed about planning. Its members were inclined to regard any move to reduce the pressure of demand as *ipso facto* misconceived but seemed to have no inhibitions about borrowing, or at least not about short-term borrowing (which, as a response to the balance of payments problem, was a way of buying time but nothing more).

Given this antipathy to deflation, the alternative hypothesis of inadequate competitive power, so popular in the 1920s, was bound to find widespread support. But it was very rare for anyone who accepted this hypothesis to give it precision and to explain how inadequacy was to be measured and what degree of inadequacy the proposed measure revealed. Professor Kaldor in 1964 came close to regarding Britain's falling share of world trade in manufactures as a sufficient measure and to accepting the corollary that the pound should be allowed to fall in stages at a rate that would ensure a stable share. This rested, however, on the belief, which few observers of British industry would share, that an expanding foreign market, created by systematic under-valuation of the pound, would by itself enhance the productivity of British industry until it, too, improved at the same rate as that experienced by industry elsewhere. For if British industrial productivity showed no such

[10] It is not clear that the advocates had a proper understanding of what the French did or of the deficiencies of indicative planning.

TABLE 5.2 Balance of payments of the United Kingdom, current account, 1963–70

	Exports (f.o.b.)	*Imports (f.o.b.)*	*Balance of trade*	*Balance on invisibles*	*Balance on current account*
	(£ million seasonally adjusted)				
1963 (I)	1045	1050	−5	62	57
(II)	1073	1093	−20	51	31
(II)	1098	1131	−33	55	22
(IV)	1115	1176	−61	76	15
1964 (I)	1128	1267	−139	69	−70
(II)	1149	1252	−103	38	−54
(III)	1131	1275	−144	39	−105
(IV)	1160	1317	−157	35	−122
1965 (I)	1187	1235	−48	36	−12
(II)	1198	1289	−91	55	−36
(III)	1247	1313	−66	56	−10
(IV)	1281	1336	−55	70	15
1966 (I)	1292	1369	−77	19	−58
(II)	1256	1334	−78	65	−13
(III)	1329	1383	−54	61	7
(IV)	1399	1298	101	76	177

(Table 5.2 contd.)

	(£ million seasonally adjusted)				
	Exports (f.o.b.)	*Imports (f.o.b.)*	*Balance of trade*	*Balance on invisibles*	*Balance on current account*
1967 (I)	1395	1444	−49	84	35
(II)	1345	1442	−97	41	−56
(III)	1314	1424	−110	77	−33
(IV)	1187	1530	−343	108	−235
1968 (I)	1569	1746	−177	66	−111
(II)	1527	1758	−231	137	−94
(III)	1653	1820	−167	146	−21
(IV)	1684	1821	−137	90	−47
1969 (I)	1678	1834	−146	175	29
(II)	1800	1866	−66	166	100
(III)	1881	1861	20	159	179
(IV)	1900	1917	−17	180	163
1970 (I)	2016	1941	75	223	298
(II)	2013	2079	−66	190	124
(III)	1940	2025	−85	193	108
(IV)	2182	2138	44	207	251

Source: Economic Trends Annual Supplement, 1981

response. British exports could only maintain their share of the world market if they formed a steadily expanding proportion of manufacturing output.

It was more common to regard the trend in the trade balance, or alternatively in the current account, as a useful measure of a loss of competitive power; or to turn to comparisons of export price indices, the behaviour of unit costs in other industrial countries, indications of changes in the relative profitability of exporting and so on. None of these in 1964 can be said to have pointed to a decisive loss of competitive power. Looking back over the decade 1954–64, the OECD concluded in 1967 that, while labour costs per unit of output were rising faster in the United Kingdom than in other major industrial countries in the mid-1950s, this was no longer so between 1959 and 1964, when the United States alone among the larger countries was showing a slower rate of increase.[11] It must be remembered that the sluggishness of the British economy affected imports almost as much as exports, and that productivity and real wages kept closely in step, so that, while less was produced, less was also consumed.

What was more to the point, those who read the signs in 1964 as evidence of growing non-competitiveness were by no means unanimous in concluding that devaluation was the appropriate remedy. There were those like James Callaghan, who took a high moral line and regarded devaluation as unjust to those for whom Britain acted as international banker. There were those like Harold Wilson, who took a strong political line and were determined that the Labour Party should not come to be derided as the party that habitually devalued. But if one took a moral or political line against devaluation, one had still to propose an economic solution to the presumed over-valuation. What solutions were available? One was to brazen it out, borrow when necessary, and trust to luck that all would come right. Another was to make use of an assortment of administrative controls designed to improve industrial efficiency, tighten exchange control, subsidize import-competing industries like agriculture and so on. A third was to try to nurse the pound back to health by running the economy for a short time below capacity and trying to achieve lower wage settlements, either through reduced pressure, some form of incomes policy or a combination of both. In this way costs might be brought back into line at a pace that would depend as much on the rate of expansion in other countries as on any slowing down in Britain.

Most of this had become apparent by the end of 1964, but very little of it was appreciated at the beginning of the year. Expansion in 1963 had been very rapid, and the intention of the Chancellor (Reginald Maud-

[11] Organization for Economic Co-operation and Development (1967b, p. 17); Krause (1968, pp. 209 *et seq.*).

ling) was to allow it to continue at a more moderate pace until, in some unexplained way, the pressure generated a faster growth in productivity and expansion became self-sustaining. Initially the balance of payments would wilt and it would be necessary to draw on reserves or borrow, but with the breakthrough to higher productivity, exports would eventually respond and balance would be restored. It is hard to say how far the Chancellor really believed in this vision of things to come and how far he was the prisoner of circumstances (such as the commitment to a 4 per cent rate of growth). He took the precaution to prepare contingency plans for any balance of payments crisis that might result, and was himself willing to contemplate floating the pound if all else failed (without, of course, saying so publicly).

In the budget of 1964 the Chancellor raised taxation by £100 million (which was more than anyone seemed willing to contemplate in January but less than was generally expected by April). From then until the election in mid-October no further restrictive action was taken. The Chancellor had intended to take further measures in July on the monetary front but in the end refrained.

The index of industrial production, which remained constant from January to September, was interpreted as demonstrating that in some way the economy was stuck. But at the same time the unemployment figures told a very different story, which tallied more convincingly with the growing external deficit. What emerged later was that production had in fact been expanding quite rapidly – how rapidly depends upon which of the successive revisions of the official figures is accepted – and that by the autumn the expansion was beginning to accelerate.[12] At the

[12] The index of industrial production has been revised several times, so that it is almost as difficult now to be sure of what happened as it was at the time. The sequence of changes is illustrated below:

	Index of industrial production, 1964: quarters			
	(I)	(II)	(III)	(IV)
As published (1958 = 100)	128	128	128	130
January 1965 (1958 = 100)	127	127	127	
February 1966 (1958 = 100)	127	128	128	130
August 1966 (1958 = 100)	126	128	129	130
1980 (1975 = 100)	85.3	85.3	85.9	88.1

The picture had changed dramatically by 1966, to show a rate of increase between the first and third quarters of 5 per cent per annum, and in *Economic Trends* at the end of 1968 the index was still shown climbing throughout 1964 at a rate only a little less steep than in 1963. Later the original picture re-appeared. The most reliable guide to what really happened is probably the movement of the unemployment figures, which fell by about 30,000 between the first and third quarters while employment and vacancies both increased. It is probably that both GDP and industrial production rose in 1964 at a rate of about 5 per cent per annum. (For a different view see Boreham, 1978, pp. 140–4.)

very last minute – on the morning after the election – the Prime Minister suggested an increase in Bank rate. The suggestion was not adopted, and the Conservative government left office without any clear indication of how it would have tackled the balance of payments deficit, then estimated at £800 million of the year.[13]

The initial position of the Labour government

The Labour government, on taking office, came down firmly against devaluation. But it did so without giving much consideration to the alternative. It contented itself with ruling out devaluation as 'unmentionable' but devised no coherent strategy for avoiding it. Indeed, once it had taken this position, it neither embarked on any form of contingency planning nor sought to look beyond the various crises that seemed to succeed one another endlessly over the next few years. The focus throughout was extremely short-term.

The decisions taken in October 1964, and on all subsequent occasions when devaluation was mooted, owed little or nothing to official advice. When the Labour Government took office, ministers were presented with extensive briefs prepared in the Treasury and the Bank of England stating the case for and against devaluation. The Treasury, while less strongly opposed to devaluation than the Bank, saw it as having no compelling advantages and some considerable disadvantages. The government's incoming advisers initially were divided, with Dr Balogh opposed to devaluation and Professor Kaldor, Sir Donald MacDougall and Mr Neild in favour. But not much notice was taken of the arguments submitted by officials and advisers. The three ministers primarily concerned – Harold Wilson, George Brown and James Callaghan – had already made up their minds, and a firm decision was taken against devaluation on the first day after the election results were announced.[14]

A month later, following the Bank rate crisis of mid-November, an opportunity arose to reconsider the matter. It was uncertain whether a rescue operation of sufficient size could be mounted, and officials were asked for proposals to deal with the situation. Two papers were prepared, one by the Treasury and one by the government's new advisers, the first proposing drastic deflationary measures and the second, an

[13] The figure of £800 million, of which much was made at the time, was subsequently revised to £759 million. Of this, only £357 million represents the adverse balance on current account (less than in 1951 and substantially less in real terms). The Bank of England's estimates of the United Kingdom's assets and liabilities show that, taking into account capital appreciation, the excess of external assets over liabilities improved in 1964 *in spite of* the deficit of £400 million on capital account.

[14] Brandon, (1966, p. 43); Crosland (1982, pp. 124–6); Kellner and Hitchens (1976, pp. 46–9); Bruce-Gardyne and Lawson (1976, pp. 118–29).

immediate devaluation. As officials and advisers filed into No. 10 Downing Street on 25 November, news came through that credits amounting to $3,000 million had been arranged by the Bank of England. This was regarded by ministers as a resolution of the issue. Orders were given to destroy all copies of the papers unread, and devaluation was once again 'the unmentionable'.

From then on it was difficult for officials and advisers to know how to proceed. Within the Treasury, advice to the Chancellor that he should devalue was tantamount to an invitation to him to resign: he had made it clear that he was not prepared to devalue the pound and continue to hold office as Chancellor. George Brown was for a time the most vehement in demanding that devaluation should be excluded from further consideration; but the more it became clear that the alternative involved the government in repeated cuts, the more he, as the minister committed more than anyone else to expansionary policies, was bound to chafe at the constraints imposed by failure to devalue. Those who favoured devaluation could almost certainly count on his eventual support; but his companions on the road to Damascus could do little to bring forward the day of conversion. Others mistrusted an excess of zeal, however directed, in a matter of such complexity and uncertainty and feared a combination of expansionary measures and devaluation more than the absence of both.

In the last resort, the attitude of the Prime Minister seemed likely to be decisive; and he had committed himself so strongly to the existing parity that he was unlikely to be induced to change his views by any arguments economists could bring forward. He was very much alive to the danger that, if a Labour government devalued the pound again, as its predecessor had done in 1949, Labour would come to be regarded as the party of devaluation, too willing to run risks with sterling and take the easy way out.[15] He hoped also to accomplish a 're-structuring' of the British economy that would eventually make it more competitive and remove the pressure on the balance of payments. In bringing about this restructuring, he did not propose to rely on competition and the use of market signals working through price changes and income flows. He had never shown much faith in market mechanisms, and on the other hand had come to put increasing faith in what could be accomplished by organization and administration. There were times when he seemed to pose as a highly sophisticated computer, registering information from every nook and cranny of the economy, and producing endless printouts of instructions for the better co-ordination of activity. One such document – referred to as 'the PM's 57 varieties' – set out a long list of measures, some trivial, some less so, for improving the balance of payments through goverment action. It was as if the Prime Minister felt

[15] Wilson (1971, p. 6).

that, single-handed, he could so energize and direct the government machine that it would deliver results beyond the reach of market forces.

The keynote of government action over the next three years was largely this reliance on *ad hoc* intervention. The government would neither devalue nor deflate: it was not even interested in looking at either course of action systematically. What had to be devised was a third line of policy in the hope of nudging the economy towards balance.

Initially, the Labour government adopted a price-conscious approach. The Maudling contingency plans had concentrated on the alternatives of quota restrictions and an import surcharge, although it had never been assumed that there would be no accompanying measures of a different kind. Faced with this choice, the government opted for a surcharge of 15 per cent on imports, coupled with a rebate on exports.[16] This was greeted with indignation in Europe partly on legalistic grounds, since a surchage was contrary to the GATT and EFTA rules while import quotas were not, and partly because of the way in which the surcharge was introduced, with firm denials by British ministers at the EFTA meeting in Geneva that there were any signs of over-heating in the economy. The government was taken aback by the storm it had provoked, not least because it was slow to appreciate the growing financial strength of Western Europe and to attach importance to the views expressed by European governments at OECD meetings and elsewhere. But it was on firm ground in arguing that, for those who did not want a devaluation of the pound, a surcharge made more sense than quota restrictions and was unlikely to do more harm to the trade of Britain's European partners.[17]

To continental observers, however, the surcharge seemed a quite inadequate method of dealing with a deficit estimated at £800 million – a deficit that had caused no alarm before the election but was now trumpeted abroad with an insistence hardly calculated to give confidence in its early disappearance. Attention was inevitably focused on monetary and fiscal policy. The interim Budget introduced by the Chancellor on 11 November (which the OECD had been assured by the Treasury in October would be 'brutal') was broadly neutral: increased

[16] The decision was strongly opposed by Douglas Jay, then President of the Board of Trade, on the grounds that the surcharge was illegal, would affront the members of EFTA particularly, and would therefore have to be abandoned, whereas quotas could be retained for as long as was necessary (Jay, 1980, pp. 298–9). There is no doubt that the reactions of EFTA partners went far beyond what had been expected; but whether quotas would ultimately have caused less of a furore is by no means certain. [My own view, *after the event*, was that it might have been wiser to have had a small devaluation of 5 per cent, although I was opposed to a substantial devaluation at that stage. A.K.C.]

[17] There had been no similar outcry against the use of an import surcharge by Canada a few years before. Canada's experience had been studied carefully in the Treasury in 1963–64.

pensions and the abolition of prescription charges under the National Health Service were balanced by an extra 6*d*. on the income tax, 6*d*. a gallon on petrol and an increase in National Insurance contributions. But because of the simultaneous announcement that a new corporation tax and a capital gains tax would be included in the next (April) Budget, without any indication as to how they would operate or what rates were contemplated, any credit for financial orthodoxy was smothered in alarm. The Budget 'stunned the City, it stunned industry, it stunned foreign financial observers'.[18] The drain on the reserves began to gather speed.

The Budget had done little or nothing to check expansion, although unemployment was down to 1.5 per cent and still falling. There was a natural expectation, therefore, that if fiscal policy was to be held in abeyance, the pound might be supported by monetary policy. This expectation was heightened after a rhetorical declaration by the Prime Minister in a speech at the Guildhall on Monday 16 November: 'not only [of] our faith but our determination to keep sterling strong and to see it riding high. . . . If anyone, at home or abroad, doubts the firmness of the government's resolve and acts upon these doubts let them be prepared to pay the price.' The warning, unsupported the following Thursday by the rise in Bank rate that it appeared to presage, was unavailing: the drain continued throughout the week. It was not simply that the government found higher interest rates more repugnant than higher import duties. The Cabinet, meeting on 17 November with George Brown in the chair, had jibbed at a 2 per cent increase as panicky and thought that a smaller rise might be avoided if the United States was willing to make a loan until the exchange crisis was over. A telegram was sent by the Prime Minister the following day requesting an American loan, but no answer had come by noon on Thursday when Bank rate announcements are usually made and it was decided to leave the rate unchanged.[19] Over the week-end, however, the Governor of the Bank of England (Lord Cromer) pressed for an immediate increase, and ministers ultimately agreed to a rise in Bank rate to 7 per cent on Monday 23 November, one week after the Prime Minister's speech. A rise of 2 per cent, coming on Monday, hinted at crisis and did not prove reassuring to the market: an earlier increase of 1 per cent would have met with a different reception. Once increased, the Bank rate remained at 7 per cent until the following June.

As had happened in 1931, the delayed rise in Bank rate failed to stop the run on sterling. The rumour was that the Bank of England had already exhausted the $1,000 million short-term central bank credits put at its disposal in September as part of Maudling's contingency planning

[18] Brandon (1966, p. 53); Kellner and Hitchens (1976, p. 51).
[19] Kellner and Hitchens (1976, pp. 52–4).

and that the stand-by credit of $1,000 million secured in August from the IMF would be needed for the repayment of these credits when they fell due.[20] The Bank of England, however, was successful at very short notice in putting together credits from foreign central banks totalling $3,000 million, thanks mainly to the good offices of the Federal Reserve Bank of New York and the Bundesbank in Frankfurt. In raising those credits, the Bank of England was engaging itself to the contributing central bankers for responsible efforts by the British government to maintain the parity. It did not do so without some heartburning, since very little of the kind of action that it and its friends abroad thought indispensable for this purpose had been taken.

The banking credits helped to calm the markets but did not put a stop to the drain on the reserves. Swap arrangements with the Federal Reserve Board of New York amounting to $500 million had been arranged as far back as May 1963 and supplemented in September 1964, under the previous administration, by short-term facilities in an equal amount with other central banks. Only $200 million of these facilities had been used at the end of September and a further $215 million in October. In November the whole of the balance of $585 million was drawn as well as a further $200 million under the arrangements made on 25 November. In December use was made of $405 million more, including an $80 million three-year bilateral credit from Switzerland. The total special assistance drawn upon in the fourth quarter, apart from the loss from reserves of another £80 million, was thus $1,405 or over £500 million. Most of this had come from the Federal Reserve Bank of New York.[21]

In the meantime the stand-by of $1,000 million, negotiated in the autumn with the IMF against just such an emergency, had been drawn on 2 December and used to repay the earlier credits. Some of the facilities arranged in November were for three months only, and these were renewed in February so that the whole of the $3,000 million was available until the end of May. By that time a second drawing had been made from the IMF, this time for £500 million, repayable in five years, and once again this was used to pay off the short-term banking credits in full.

The pound remained weak and subject to periodic bouts of pressure, sometimes reaching crisis proportions. It was clear that if sterling was not to be devalued something had to be done to restore confidence in the existing parity. What was less clear was how this was to be done without resort to the traditional 'stop', which the Labour government, with its majority of four, was determined to avoid at all costs. Ministers felt trapped between their commitment to expansionist policies and the

[20] Brandon (1966, p. 65).
[21] *Bank of England Quarterly Bulletin*, March 1965, p. 5.

balance of payments constraint. They kept equating any check to their spending plans with deflation and were inclined to regard such checks as a sop to foreign speculators. But in spite of repeated cuts, of which the Prime Minister made much in his public speeches, output and employment continued to grow up to the middle of 1966 at a rate close to economic potential. Over the 18 months from the second half of 1964 to the first half of 1966, GDP increased at just over 2.5 per cent per annum and unemployment in the first half of 1966 was lower than it had been for nearly ten years. It is hardly surprising that foreigners holding sterling did not see things in quite the same light as those ministers whose struggles with the Treasury in the mid-1960s fill the pages of the first volume of Richard Crossman's *Diaries*.[22] One would hardly guess from the *Diaries* that public expenditure (in money terms) rose by over 50 per cent between 1964 and 1968, nearly twice as fast as GDP (also in money terms).

The position at the end of June 1965, as will be seen from table 5.3, was that in the three preceding quarters the government had run up debts to the IMF of £850 million, had drawn £153 million from other monetary authorities (mainly the Federal Reserve System) and on the other hand had added £90 million to its reserves.

Hardly a month went by without continuing pressure on the exchanges. The spot dollar rate, which, on a quarterly average, had remained at or above par in every quarter but one in the 1960s up to the last quarter of 1963, and was virtually at par in the next three quarters, sank to an average of 2.787 in each of the last two quarters of 1964 and did not again reach par until September 1965. It had been 'allowed to fall' to \$2.78¼ by Friday 20 November, rose to \$2.79 after the announcement of the \$3,000 million credits and was 'not allowed to fall' below that level in December.[23] A more sensitive index of confidence in sterling was the three-month forward rate for dollars, which showed a premium of under 1 per cent in September and October but averaged nearly 3 per cent in November and remained above 2.6 per cent until April 1965. Even this, however, is a poor gauge of the pressure on the exchanges, since the authorities had been supporting the forward rate from November onwards, but without disclosure of the scale of their operations. As became clear after devaluation, the diversion of pressure from the spot market greatly reduced the visible drain on the reserves but only at heavy eventual cost.

The fluctuations in the spot and forward dollar rates are shown in figure 5.1 together with the amount of official financing of the balance of payments undertaken from quarter to quarter. It would be difficult to deduce, from the movement in either the spot or the forward quota-

[22] See Crossman (1975).

[23] *Bank of England Quarterly Bulletin*, March 1965, p. 4.

TABLE 5.3 Official financing of the deficit, 1961–71

	(£ million) Official financing from			
	IMF	*Other monetary authorities*[a]	*Reserves*	*Total officially financed*[b]
1961	370	–	−31	339
1962	−375	–	183	−192
1963	5	–	53	58
1964 (I)	–	–	−1	−1
(II)	−1	5	−16	−12
(III)	1	66	59	126
(IV)	357	145	80	582
1965 (I)	−6	177	−5	166
(II)	500	−169	−165	166
(III)	–	183	13	196
(IV)	−5	−81	−89	−175
1966 (I)	35	165[a]	−203	−47[b]
(II)	−13	69	106	162
(III)	−1	448	41	488
(IV)	−6	−72	22	−56
1967 (I)	−26	−426	−57	−509
(II)	−171	30	152	11
(III)	−9	479	36	506
(IV)	−133	812[a]	−16	663
1968 (I)	–	530	−11	519
(II)	–	78	−16	521
(III)	−35	73	−14	24
(IV)	−42	265	123	346
1969	−30	−669	−44	−687[b]
1970	−134	−1161	−125	−1287[b]
1971	−554	−1263	−1536	−3147[b]

[a] Including transfers from the dollar portfolio in 1966 (I) and 1967 (IV)
[b] Excluding allocations of SDRs and gold subscriptions to the IMF 1966 (I) and 1970 (IV) and foreign currency borrowing in 1969 and 1971
Source: Economic Trends Annual Supplement, 1981

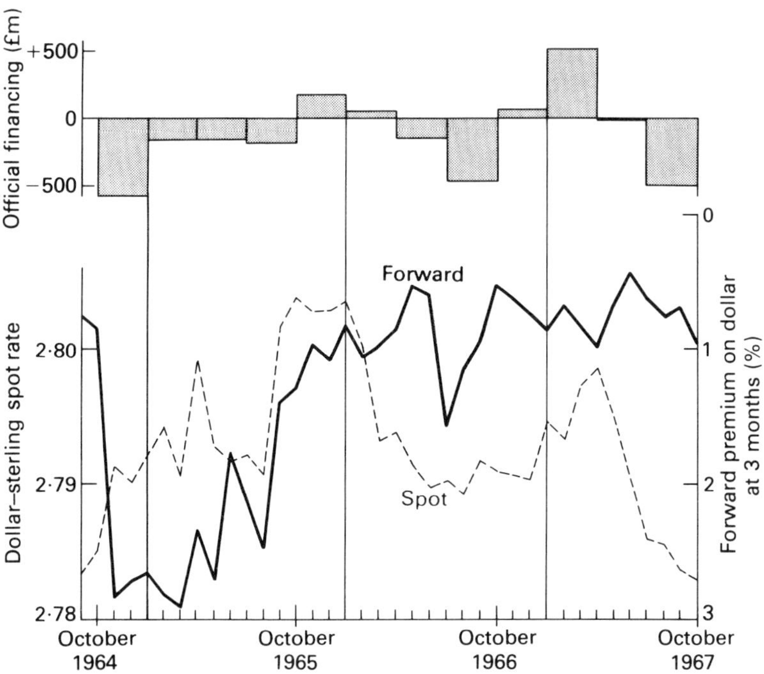

Figure 5.1 Exchange rates and the balance of payments, 1964–67

Source: Bank of England Quarterly Bulletin; Economic Trends Annual Supplement 1981

tions, what fluctuations were occurring simultaneously in pressure on the exchanges as revealed by the figures of official intervention. It is true that the spot rate rose above par in the winter of 1965–66 and recovered a little in the spring of 1967 – both of them periods in which the authorities were taking in foreign exchange. The fall in the spot rate later in 1967 also reflects increasing pressure as the year progressed. But there is otherwise no very close correspondence. Much the same can be said of movements in the forward rate, which show the influence of a consistent credit balance when it occurs but are heavily damped by official intervention. When such intervention ceased after devaluation, the volatility of the forward premium (as shown in figure 5.3, p. 196) is much more marked.

The formulation of balance of payments policy

The measures adopted by the government fell into four main groups. Of these, two affected the balance of payments indirectly and two directly. First, there were the efforts to limit the increase in money wage rates, at least as much for the sake of competitiveness as because of any concern over inflation. Second, the normal instruments of demand management were used to check excess demand or at least to reduce the level of effective demand. Third, exchange control was tightened in a number of ways, most of them designed to operate on the capital balance. Finally, a variety of measures were taken to improve the trade balance, either by promoting exports or by limiting imports.

The use of incomes policy seemed to many observers the most hopeful way to restore competitive power. It was pressed on the government by the Americans, endorsed by the IMF and the OECD, and championed with the utmost energy by George Brown. But it is doubtful whether those who insisted most strongly on the need for incomes policy appreciated its limitations. The most obvious of these was that, at the very time when the government was seeking to persuade the unions to show restraint, it was steadily increasing their bargaining power through a progressive tightening of the labour market. While George Brown negotiated with the TUC, workers were negotiating with their employers to much greater effect. Between the last quarter of 1964 and the second quarter of 1965 earnings rose at an annual rate of over 10 per cent, and over the 18 months to the middle of 1966 at an annual rate of 9 per cent. This, more perhaps than any other single circumstance, made the eventual devaluation in the following year virtually inescapable.

Apart from this, the emphasis on incomes policy paid little regard to the weakness of the TUC *vis-à-vis* dissenting unions. It also failed to take into account the mechanism by which, under payment-by-results, wage-drift (i.e. the tendency for earnings to rise faster than wage rates) set up stresses in the labour market that could not be removed and might well be intensified by incomes policy. When unemployment was already under 1.5 per cent, it was difficult to see much to be gained from incomes policy and natural to fear that it would prove a cul-de-sac for policies that should have found an outlet elsewhere.

There was also an element of self-deception about the tightening of exchange control. It is true that the net outflow of private capital was reduced from £256 million in 1964 to £39 million in 1966, but it is far from clear that this had much to do with exchange control. About half the outward investment was in the sterling area, over which no control was exercised until the introduction of the voluntary programme in May 1966. So far as the non-sterling area is concerned, outward direct investment *increased* between 1964 and 1966, from £102 to £157 million, while portfolio investment moved in the opposite direction, from a net addition of £28 million to a net realization of £44 million. But the change in portfolio investment, since it was confined to the investment currency market, had no effect on the reserves. The biggest single change over those two years was in *inward* investment in the United Kingdom, which rose from an abnormally low figure of £143 million in 1964 to a more normal total of £264 million in 1966. It would be difficult to establish any connection between this increase and a tightening of exchange control. The one change that does appear to have had an unmistakable effect on the reserves is the introduction in the 1965 budget of a 25 per cent surrender requirement, which deflected to the reserves a quarter of the investment currency premium realized on sales of foreign securities.[24] There may also have been some gain to the current account through larger remittances of profits from abroad. But one may be permitted to doubt whether the emphasis on exchange control was not, in the end, just as counterproductive as the hopes that were invested in incomes policy.

Of the measures aimed at the current account, the most important and the most controversial was the temporary import surcharge of 15 per cent on the value of imports of most kinds of manufactured goods. This, together with a lower rate of stockbuilding, had a large and immediate effect on the deficit. In spite of a reduction from 15 to 10 per cent, announced in February and operative from 27 April, the improvement in the current account continued throughout the year and into 1966. For 1965 as a whole, the deficit was a mere £50 million and in the final quarter there was an actual surplus (on a seasonally adjusted basis). It is a curious fact that, over the period from the end of 1964 until a couple of months before the devaluation of November 1967, the current account was roughly in balance.

But the import surcharge, like foreign borrowing, was primarily a means of buying time. It was never intended that it should continue for more than a limited period; as the date for its renewal approached it would be necessary to point to other factors sustaining the improvement in the current account or risk fresh speculative pressure.

Other measures, aimed at the current account, are more difficult to assess because of their heterogeneity. Some of these measures, such as the offer of extended trade credit through the Exports Credits Guarantee Department (ECGD), may have had a perverse effect in the short run since they absorbed resources, including imported materials, at some immediate opportunity cost in foreign exchange without adding for a considerable time to earnings of foreign exchange. Other measures worked in exactly the opposite direction, promising immediate relief to the reserves in exchange for a long-term cost. An example of this was the decision to build aluminium smelters by providing electricity on terms not available to other industrial users. Essentially the distortions that resulted were those normally associated with protectionism. Some could be justified on the grounds that the shadow price of foreign exchange was, say, 10 per cent higher than the market price: but to

[24] These matters are more fully discussed in Cairncross (1973, pp. 58–60); and in Tew (1978, pp. 325–37).

accept that argument was to go most of the way to accepting the case for devaluation unless the decision to apply the shadow price was temporary and reversible.

Of greater importance were the measures taken to improve the balance on invisibles. Some of these ran parallel to the protectionism just discussed: the rationing of foreign exchange to tourists is an obvious example. But the main debate concerned military expenditure overseas. This expenditure, including the cost of the British Army on the Rhine, was high in relation to the economic and financial strength of the United Kingdom in the 1960s and seemed to offer scope for substantial cuts. Such cuts, however, were not to the liking of those who wished to see Britain maintain her position as a world power, or to allies like the United States, who found British influence east of Suez a stabilizing factor.

Whatever the economies made under this head or in any other item in the list of invisibles, the net effect between 1964 and 1966 was decidedly modest. The surplus on invisibles, which had fallen quite sharply in 1964 to £153 million, had recovered only to £188 million in 1965 and was no higher in 1966. It was not until 1967 that a perceptible improvement took place to £274 million and it was then far more marked on the credit than on the debit side of the account.

These measures were scattered over the whole period up to – and, indeed, after – devaluation, but many of them were concentrated in two packages, one in the exchange crisis in July 1965 and the other in the deeper crisis a year later in July 1966.

The exchange crises of 1965 and 1966

In the first half of 1965 the economy had been expanding at a fast rate, but some slowing down was expected over the following year. In May the National Institute of Economic and Social Research put the rate of expansion in the first six months of the Labour government at 6 per cent per annum and was forecasting that this would fall to 2.5 per cent per annum in the year ahead.[25] Unemployment was down to the very low rate of 1.36 per cent and was still falling.

The April Budget had increased the taxes on drink and tobacco by £123 million and was expected to bring in an additional £94 million in a full year, mainly from motor vehicle duties. This was enough to check the growth in consumers' expenditure without arresting it. It was also in keeping with the continental view earlier in the year that nothing less than £200 million additional revenue in the Budget would justify a prolongation of the $3,000 million banking credits.

[25] National Institute of Economic and Social Research, *Economic Review*, May 1965, p. 5.

The import surcharge had been cut to 10 per cent at the end of April and monetary policy had been tightened by a 1 per cent call for special deposits on 29 April and a ceiling on clearing bank lending a week later. Meanwhile Bank rate remained at 7 per cent – for a period longer by the end of May than under any post-war administration – and the government was anxious to see it reduced for a variety of reasons: to restore its political image, to help house-building, and for tactical reasons (there were some who attached more importance to the scope for a sharp increase in Bank rate than to the level at which it was maintained). Since sterling was still weak, it was accepted that offsetting action should be taken to tighten hire purchase restrictions (i.e. restrictions on instalment buying). But these were whittled down, and when announced along with the cut in Bank rate to 6 per cent on 3 June were limited to an increase by 5 per cent in the minimum cash deposit on motor cars and electrical goods.

By this time an IMF drawing had been made on 12 May after a good deal of doubt about whether it would not be opposed by at least one of the continental countries. The Budget had left continental observers puzzled, since many of them took the simple-minded view that countries like the United Kingdom with big budget deficits ended up with balance of payments deficits too, and that the cure for the second deficit was usually a cut in the first. There was a widespread expectation that devaluation was coming – the French were said to expect one of 10 per cent – and sooner or later a run on sterling seemed inescapable. At the end of June, on a visit to the United States, the Chancellor was told by his host (William McChesney Martin) at a dinner with 36 American bankers that all of them regarded a devaluation of the pound as inevitable and that he alone took a contrary view.

There was some evidence of switching out of sterling in May and pressure increased in June. In early July, however, ministers seemed set against deflationary action of any kind. Assurances that no further measures would be taken appeared in the press and bore all the marks of non-attributable guidance from No. 10. The Chancellor, speaking off the cuff in a Third reading debate, had rashly referred to the need to resist the 'temptation' to deflate. The Cabinet seemed unaware of the seriousness of the situation and was busy discussing the National Plan to be issued in September. So far as the balance of payments was concerned, interest was concentrated on proposals for the use of import deposits.

A crisis blew up quickly after the middle of July, with heavy losses of foreign exchange in the week ending 24 July. The economic advisers brought in by the government again recommended devaluation, but without effect. George Brown, however, had been converted, and there was a long wrangle between him, the Prime Minister and the Chancellor before they finally agreed, at 1 am on 27 July, on a new package of measures, announced to the Cabinet later in the morning and to the House of Commons in the afternoon.[26]

The measures included cuts in local authority and government investment estimated at £200 million in a full year, restriction of local authority lending on mortgages, tighter exchange controls, fresh hire purchase restrictions and the introduction of building licensing of offices, shops and some other private projects costing over £100,000. They were a good deal less drastic than the Chancellor would have liked and did little to interrupt the boom: unemployment increased briefly in the third quarter before resuming its downward trend. The market reaction was at first highly unfavourable, particularly after the announcement a week later of a large fall in the reserves. The way in which the measures were introduced smacked of panic: the public was unprepared for them after earlier assurances, disconcerted by the Prime Minister's announcement a week beforehand that action would be taken without any hint that he had given thought to what was to be done, and persuaded that things must be very bad if it was impossible to wait until the reserves were announced at the end of the month or at least to quote the exchange losses at once. The result was a run on the pound in August on a scale comparable to that in November 1964.

This prompted a fresh effort to organize international support for the pound in which the United States took the lead. The US authorities were already asking themselves whether, if the pound were devalued, the dollar should follow suit, and those in favour of this course were gaining strength in Washington. The French, under instructions from General de Gaulle, declined to participate. Support was forthcoming, however, from eight other European countries, Canada and the United States, and announced on 10 September, ahead of the annual meeting of the IMF. In the meantime market sentiment had begun to change and from the beginning of September selling pressure died away.

In September and October there was also, for the first time, a sharp reduction in the authorities' outstanding forward commitments with the commercial banks. By the end of January 1966 these commitments were 'well below their level a year earlier'.[27] They continued to fall heavily in February but in the months following there was little further change.[28] The three-month forward premium on dollars, which had stood at 2.48 per cent in August, fell to 0.81 per cent in January 1966 and 0.53 per cent in May, while the spot rate rose above par in September and remained there until February.

Little further action on demand was taken before the election at the end of March, when Labour was returned with a comfortable majority.

[26] Crossman (1975, volume 1, p. 290); Bruce Gardyne and Lawson (1976, pp. 130–32).
[27] *Bank of England Quarterly Bulletin*, March 1966, p. 13.
[28] Ibid., June 1966, p. 109.

Clearing bank advances were frozen in February at 105 per cent of the level of March 1965, and in the same month still further restrictions were imposed on hire purchase transactions. At the beginning of May the Chancellor presented a Budget designed to raise nearly £400 million in additional revenue, but nearly all of this was to come from a new selective employment tax (SET), the effects of which no one could assess with much confidence, particularly in view of the large flows into and out of the Exchequer that the machinery of collection and refunds involved. The import surcharge, which had been cut to 10 per cent in April 1965, was to end on 30 November 1966, and the only fresh measure in the Budget to offset the impact on the balance of payments was the introduction of a scheme for voluntary restraint in investment in the four developed members of the sterling area.

Two months later it was clear that the country was heading for a fresh balance of payments crisis and that the government was ill-prepared to meet it. At the beginning of July the Prime Minister was still obsessed by the repeated cuts that his government had made since 1964 without regard to more obvious indications of the current pressure of demand, such as the unemployment figures. These had fallen steadily to 1.2 per cent, the lowest point reached in the entire decade, and matching the lowest annual average for any peace-time year in the twentieth century. Foreign opinion, observing the continuing tightness of the labour market, was not impressed by forecasts of an eventual improvement in the balance of payments. The general view was that the government had wasted a year; time had now run out and there was no further room for error; sterling had 'had it'.

Since the Budget, officials' time had been absorbed by the complexities of the new selective employment tax. Ministers themselves were still at odds over prices and incomes policy and the programme for public expenditure in 1967–68. No package of measures had been prepared in advance of any fresh run on sterling. There was little appreciation of the state of foreign opinion and no acceptance of the implications of the loss of confidence in sterling for domestic policy. The key decisions on economic policy continued to be taken without much reference to the Cabinet by the Prime Minister, the Chancellor and the First Secretary (George Brown).

The debate, once begun, was again confined to ministers. On this occasion, however, the issue was raised in Cabinet and made the subject of debate. George Brown was now strongly in favour of devaluation, which he wanted to combine with an application to enter the EEC and some deflationary measures less severe than those ultimately adopted.[29] Other ministers, including Jenkins, Crosland and Crossman, were in favour of floating the pound but in the end were heavily outvoted, some

[29] Brittan (1971, pp. 330–1).

of them agreeing that a moment of extreme crisis was not the right time for such a move.[30]

Sterling began to weaken in the first week of July, and the dangers in the situation were brought to the government's attention by the end of the week. The resignation of Frank Cousins, the Minister of Technology, on 3 July was widely interpreted as putting paid to an agreed incomes policy. Interest rates abroad were rising – the rate on Eurodollars had reached 6.5 per cent – the current account was back in deficit, and the trade figures for June when they appeared on the thirteenth showed a big jump in the deficit, from £27 million in May to £54 million in June (these are adjusted figures). In addition – although this was not known to the public – there was every reason to expect a very large increase in public expenditure in 1967–68. A considerable shortfall had emerged and might be made up over the next year; but apart from that, the programme showed an increase of 7 per cent in real terms and a still higher increase of 11 per cent if additional expenditures then under discussion were included. These figures, which excluded investment by the nationalized industries, were comparable with the 4.25 per cent per annum increase envisaged in the National Plan.

The first reaction of the government was to issue press guidance (apparently from No. 10) that there would be no mini-Budget. This by itself was enough to set off rumours of imminent devaluation. On 12 July the Chancellor took the opportunity to make a statement on credit ceilings and SET that appeared to imply a tightening of credit; but since he chose to make the announcement in reply to a parliamentary question the effect was unhelpful. Two days later came a belated increase in Bank rate to 7 per cent, a call for special deposits and a statement by the Prime Minister that further measures, which he did not specify, would follow. There were also rumours of Cabinet disagreement, and in the course of the following week it became known that the First Secretary had taken a stand in favour of devaluation. The Chancellor was also known in some quarters to have wavered in view of the lack of support among his colleagues for cuts in expenditure of the order required. Even what was common knowledge was enough to shake public confidence, and there were heavy losses of foreign exchange. There was therefore a danger that, whatever measures the government took before the end of the month, it might find it impossible to support the parity when the reserve figures were published on 2 August.

In the course of the second week of July a jumbo package of deflationary measures was prepared, calculated to improve the balance of payments by £250 million, partly by cuts of £150 million in overseas expenditure, partly by a reduction in domestic demand amounting to £500 million that might drive unemployment up to 2 per cent or more by

[30] Wilson (1971, pp. 256–7); Kellner and Hitchens (1976, pp. 63–4).

the end of 1967. There was also to be an immediate voluntary freeze in prices and wages.

It was these proposals, when submitted on 12 July, that had divided the Cabinet. Some ministers expressed disquiet that they should be asked to agree to such measures without any opportunity of reviewing the general economic background to them (and so raising the possibility of devaluation). The proposals to cut public expenditure met with particular opposition. Reflecting on this opposition, the Chancellor concluded that there might now be no alternative to devaluation and agreed next day to join forces with George Brown in pressing it on the Prime Minister. But when summoned that evening to a private discussion at No. 10 Downing Street with the Prime Minister he was induced to change round again on the understanding that the proposed measures would be accepted by the Cabinet and announced to the House of Commons by the Prime Minister in person.

The disagreements over devaluation were conveyed to the Cabinet on 14 July by the Prime Minister, who undertook in view of these disagreements to make a temporizing statement in Parliament that day. When he did so, he promised a further statement later, giving details of the measures that the government proposed to take in order to provide 'the restraint that is necessary'. As he was due to make a visit to Moscow two days later, on Saturday 16 July, this statement had to wait until after his return. Efforts were made in his absence to rally support for immediate devaluation by the ministers opposed to deflation. But these efforts had no great success. The Chancellor's measures were approved by the Cabinet by a large majority and were announced next day, on 20 July, by the Prime Minister. George Brown resigned, was persuaded to withdraw his resignation and three weeks later moved to the Foreign Office.[31]

The impact of deflationary measures

Superficially, the July package resembled one that ministers had been asked to consider nearly two years previously and would not so much as look at. On closer inspection it was less impressive in detail than in terms of the aggregates in the statement. The saving of £100 million in government expenditure overseas seemed highly unlikely to take full effect until 1968 or later. The official figures of military expenditure on which the cuts were to be concentrated show no such reduction: for 1965–69 they run £293, £307, £292, £294 and £298 million. Other government expenditure overseas increased year by year between 1965 and

[31] This account of ministerial attitudes is based on Kellner and Hitchens (1976, pp. 60–75). See also Bruce-Gardyne and Lawson (1976, pp. 133–38).

1969. Like so many cuts in public expenditure announced in times of crisis to assuage opinion, the saving in overseas expenditure was almost entirely imaginary. The cut in the tourist allowance, however, was real enough even if it did not effect an economy in foreign exchange quite as large as the £50 million allowed. The actual reduction between 1966 and 1967 is put in the Red Book at £23 million; but the underlying trend was upward and might have been expected to add £15 or £20 million to the total.

The deflation of domestic demand was genuine enough. There was a 10 per cent increase in indirect taxation through the use of the Regulator and a 10 per cent surcharge on surtax liabilities.[32] The biggest immediate impact on demand was expected from hire purchase restrictions and from cuts in public investment of about £100 million. Apart from the cuts in investment and some further tightening of building controls, the whole of the domestic deflation was intended to hit the consumer, and this it undoubtedly did. Consumers' expenditure in real terms fell between the second and fourth quarters of 1966 by a little over 2 per cent and did not regain the previous level until the second quarter of 1967. Much the biggest reduction was in purchases of cars, with household durable goods also depressed. Capital formation, on the other hand, mounted steadily during the 12 months following the cuts. Investment by public corporations, cuts or no cuts, showed a strong expansion (nearly 7 per cent over the 18 months from the first half of 1966 to the second half of 1967) and the figures for public housing showed an even bigger increase (more than 20 per cent over the same period). Richard Crossman had good reason to be satisfied with the government's 'priorities' in the crisis.

It could be argued that the 1966 package, had it been introduced two years previously, would have allowed the parity to be maintained. Such an argument would rest heavily on confidence factors but would gain some support from the steep rise in costs as the margin of spare capacity in the economy became progressively narrower over those two years. Whatever the size of the deficit on current account in 1964 when the Labour government took office – and it has now been written down to £362 million – the deficit over the next two, or even three, years, as is evident from table 5.1, was not such as to create difficulties in itself.

If one examines only the current account (see figure 5.2), there is little to show that the policies adopted were inadequate. Some of the improvement in 1965–66 might be discounted as a reflection of the import surcharge or other policies that could not be expected to remain

[32] In the Budget of 1961 the government took powers to raise or lower indirect taxes by 10 per cent across the board between Budgets. The use of these powers was one of two 'regulators' of demand, the other remaining inoperative.

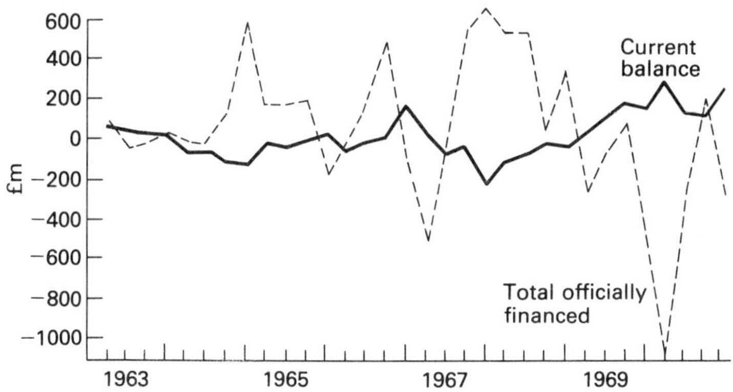

Figure 5.2 Quarterly current account and officially financed balance of payments, 1963–70

Source: Economic Trends Annual Supplement 1981

in force or produce similar results in the future. By the time the import surcharge was withdrawn in November 1966, however, the deflationary package of July 1966 had taken effect and the current account had moved into surplus. It was possible, too, as was argued strongly by the government, that some of its policies, such as the so-called 're-structuring' of industry, would eventually show up in improved competitiveness and a reduced deficit on visible trade. It was only if one started with a presumption that the current account should be in substantial surplus, or if one regarded the policies by which a deficit was held at bay as artificial, or had no confidence that the policies would be maintained or if necessary intensified, that the actual record of debits and credits could be regarded as disquieting.

But of course it was not possible to isolate the current account from the capital account, as shown in table 5.1. On long-term account, the changes were not very spectacular: from 1964 onwards there was an upward trend in the inflow of capital for investment in the United Kingdom and a slight dip in 1965–66 in the outflow, both public and private, so that the balance improved substantially over the three years, from a net outflow of £367 million in 1964 to £108 million in 1967. How far this can be attributed to changes in policy is doubtful, as has already been argued. In any event, the much bigger and crucial swings were in monetary movements.

Of the £1,490 million that required official financing over the three years from October 1964 to October 1967, £90 million represented the deficit on current account, £412 million the net outflow of long-term capital and £988 million short-term capital and monetary movements (including £43 million for the balancing item). These figures do not accurately reflect the division between capital and monetary movements since a large part of the capital outflow was to the sterling area and so brought about an immediate, offsetting short-term inflow (with what subsequent repercussions would need much further discussion) while a substantial part of the remainder involved offsetting arrangements to borrow foreign currencies. This is not a point we need pursue, since the interaction between short-term and long-term capital movements in their impact on the reserves is of subordinate interest compared with the behaviour of the reserves themselves. A steady net outflow of long-term capital of the order of £100–£150 million per annum would have been unlikely to provoke a devaluation of the currency, given confidence in the economic policy of the government. But the succession of crises left behind a growing total of short-term liabilities to central banks and the IMF as the government found itself obliged to meet large-scale movements of funds by borrowing abroad to supplement the reserves.

Allowance has also to be made for the efforts of the Bank of England to relieve the pressure on the spot market by forward dealings in sterling. No figures have been published to show the increase from quarter to quarter in outstanding forward obligations, but the total loss on forward transactions undertaken by the Exchange Equalization Account was £356 million, pointing to contracts at the time of devaluation of well over £2,000 million. That the Account engaged in forward transactions from time to time was known in the 1950s, but the scale on which it was prepared to support the forward market from 1964 onwards was a closely kept secret. This support implies forward sales on a scale substantially greater than concurrent spot sales of sterling by the Bank, and exercising a correspondingly large effect on the spot position. The magnitudes involved are shown in table 5.4.

Initially, at least, a large proportion of forward sales appear to have arisen from the hedging by overseas residents of various kinds of sterling assets to insure against a fall in their value. An increasing proportion of foreign-owned funds in London were covered by forward sales. But there was also much purely speculative pressure, chiefly by foreign operators engaging in outright forward sales unrelated to such hedging or to any commercial transaction. To that extent the Bank of England was offering foreign gamblers more advantageous terms than they would have secured at lower forward rates for sterling. On the other hand, failure to maintain an orderly forward market on reasonable terms could have led to withdrawals of funds that might have put it beyond the Bank's power to sustain the spot rate. The ultimate loss of £356 million, though very heavy, might have been substantially less but for the clumsy way in which the last stages of devaluation were handled, and has to be set against what additional reserves of £2,000 million, held over a few years, would have cost in interest sacrificed.

It can be assumed that forward sales of sterling were greatest when

TABLE 5.4 Official transactions in spot and forward exchange, October 1964–October 1967

	(£ million)
Drawings on IMF (net)	656
Other monetary authorities (incl. use of dollar portfolio)	948
Drawings on official reserves	−69
	1534[a]
Net forward sales of sterling by Bank of England, say	2100

[a] In addition to the official financing included in table 5.3, this total financed a gold subscription of £44 million to the IMF in 1966
Source: Economic Trends Annual Supplement, 1980

the pressure on the spot market was greatest. The points of pressure over the three years occur, as table 5.3 brings out, in the last quarter of 1964, the third quarter of 1966 and the second half of 1967. The points of least pressure were in the winter of 1965–66 and the spring of 1967. If these points are compared with the fluctuations in the current account shown in table 5.2, it will be apparent that there is some tendency for pressure to lag behind changes in the current account, although sometimes, as in mid-1966, the reaction in the exchange market seems altogether out of proportion.

This brings us back to the aftermath of the measures taken in July 1966. These were, for the time being, successful in relieving the pressure on sterling and the balance of payments. The current balance of payments swung into surplus, and by the end of the year there was no longer a deficit on official settlements. But by October it had become clear that public expenditure was increasing at a rate far beyond the 4.25 per cent specified in the National Plan and faster than ministers had appreciated when the July cuts were made. The increase did not, however, prevent the July measures from having their expected effect on domestic activity, and by October the first signs were evident of a sharp increase in unemployment. The uneasiness of ministers found expression in a decision to collect the figures weekly, but they resisted throughout the winter months the temptation to reflate by such time-honoured devices as relaxing hire purchase restrictions.

For a time the government meditated higher taxation to offset the rise in public expenditure. But with the continuing rise in unemployment it was decided in the end to leave taxation broadly unchanged and present the 1967 Budget as neutral. It was not in doubt, however, that if there was no change in stance the stance itself was expansionary. Later calculations suggest that on a full employment basis of comparison it was about £300 million more expansionary than the 1966 budget.[33] At the end of the financial year it transpired that the deficit of £1,827 million was not only £1,100 million more than in 1965/66, two years previously: it was also £500 million more than had been forecast. Such a relaxed fiscal stance – very different from what had been assumed in July 1966 or even in January 1967 – ran obvious risks when the external situation was so precarious. It was likely to alarm the financial markets, inflate the money supply and bring more pressure on the exchange rate. In fact the money supply (M3) did increase relatively fast: in the first nine months of 1967 the rate of increase (on a seasonally adjusted basis) was equivalent to 10.5 per cent per annum compared with 5 per cent over the previous two years. Output continued to grow at about 2 per cent in real terms and about 6 per cent per annum in monetary terms. Thus in 1967 the situation changed to one of comparative monetary ease.

This change is apparent in the behaviour of interest rates. Short-term rates had peaked at 6¾ per cent in September 1966, a month before the peak of 5.4 per cent in US rates, which had been climbing ever since 1961. By May 1967 London rates had fallen by over 1½ per cent. US rates, however, had fallen even more heavily, so that they were further below London rates than in the autumn of 1966. The spread widened still further in June to 1.8 per cent, but by July US rates had risen steeply, and from then on until devaluation in November the margin was rarely much above 1 per cent. After devaluation the money supply (M3) continued to grow at a fast pace – about 8 per cent per annum. An initial interest differential of about 2½ per cent fell through 1968 to 1 per cent at the end of the year, first under the influence of falling rates in London and then, from October onwards, as a result of a faster climb in short-term rates in New York than in London. Nothing in the behaviour of interest rates or of interest differentials suggests that purely monetary factors exercised a major influence on the movement of funds in 1967 or 1968, although they do point to a distinct easing of monetary control that can hardly have been helpful to the maintenance of the parity.

The government was not particularly conscious, however, of its dependence on monetary weapons to counter external pressure or of the risks of dispensing with them when public expenditure was rising fast. Between January and early May it reduced Bank rate in three successive steps of 0.5 per cent from 7 per cent to 5.5 per cent and removed the

[33] Price (1978, p. 187). The estimates given by Price are £810 in 1966/67 and £1,120 million in 1967/68.

lending ceilings on the clearing banks in April. At that point, however, pressure began to build up again on the exchanges and continued almost without intermission until the eventual devaluation in November.

The starting-point was a change of sentiment after the announcement by the Prime Minister on 2 May that the United Kingdom would apply formally to join the Common Market. Such an application had been in the air since November 1966, when the intention to engage in renewed discussions with the EEC was made public. Although no official estimates of the balance of payments cost of joining the Community had been issued, it was known that it was likely to be substantial, and there was also a natural suspicion that, in view of this, Britain's entry might be made the occasion for a devaluation of the pound. Ironically enough, devaluation preceded by a week or so not Britain's entry to the Common Market, but General de Gaulle's second veto.

Other factors were tending simultaneously to add to the pressure. Devaluation was increasingly the subject of public discussion, frequently in terms implying that only someone very stupid could fail to see its advantages. Out of 45 backbench speakers in the Budget debate, ten had either advocated or contemplated devaluation. The successive reductions in Bank rate, of which the last came on 4 May, had removed any interest advantage from holding sterling. In the course of the month the gilt-edged market had begun to weaken and the Bank of England had become a net buyer, so adding to market liquidity. Then at the beginning of June came the six-day Arab–Israeli War, the oil embargo and (on 7 June) the closure of the Suez Canal. These events could not fail to have a serious effect both on the balance of payments and on confidence in sterling.

In spite of these developments, the government took no steps to counteract the pressure on sterling and instead embarked on a series of reflationary measures over the summer months, starting with relaxations of the hire purchase restrictions on cars on 7 June (i.e. on the day when the Suez Canal was closed) and concluding with more extensive hire purchase relaxations at the end of August. These measures and the simultaneous expansion in public spending had their effect on domestic demand. Retail sales in the second half of the year were 3 per cent by volume above sales in the first half, and real consumer spending over the same period rose by 2.6 per cent (seasonally adjusted in both cases). Although unemployment continued to rise throughout the year and this disposed ministers to reflate, other labour market indicators and measures of capacity utilization pointed in the opposite direction. The vacancy figures, for example, which from the late 1960s onwards became a more reliable guide to the pressure of demand, ceased to fall in the third quarter and were on the increase from September onwards.

Thus as the crisis approached the government was already committed to a policy of reflation and was more than making good the drag exercised by falling exports. The drain on reserves, beginning in May, continued throughout the summer months: over £500 million went in the third quarter – almost as much as at the end of 1964. The government was warned that it was unlikely that further support would be provided in Europe and that the limits of US credit arrangements could be reached. Nevertheless, even in September there was talk in Basle of yet another operation in support of sterling, and although this fizzled out suggestions of help came spontaneously from the Swiss and the BIS. Three of the Swiss banks made deposits of £37.5 million for 12 months in London in mid-October and the BIS provided a credit of $250 million on 12 November for the re-finance of IMF debts due the following month. To some extent this help was counter-productive, since the smallness of the amounts involved was in striking contrast to the scale of assistance needed if the parity was to be maintained. The action taken to raise interest rates, first by jacking up market rates and then by raising Bank rate twice by 0.5 per cent (on 19 October and 9 November), was open to the same dismissive response: pills don't cure earthquakes.

Had the government acted in September, or even in October, it would have been spared the heavy losses of the final month and would have been seen to be less at the mercy of events and better prepared to face the tribulations ahead. But the Chancellor still hoped to get through the winter and postpone a decision until the spring. The Prime Minister was confident that the American economy would boom in an election year like 1968 and that this would be enough to rescue sterling. From mid-October onwards the foreign exchange markets showed signs of uneasiness about sterling, occasioned largely by bad trade figures and dock strikes in London and Liverpool. Later in the month the report of a Common Market Commission on the British application for entry expressed doubts about the sterling area and these were taken to imply doubts about the exchange rate.[34] Shortly afterwards, M. Couve de Murville took the opportunity to voice some of the French doubts about sterling, based on their hostility to reserve currencies, and to draw a mischievous parallel with the action taken by France in a similar situation in 1958 (when the franc was devalued twice). In this atmosphere rumours of impending devaluation spread on the Continent, and a meeting of the Committee of Finance Ministers of the Six was called for 14 November to discuss the matter. Some members of the Community felt that they would have to devalue if the United Kingdom did. Talk about the forthcoming meeting and about possible devaluation intensified the drain on the reserves.

According to Harold Wilson, who gives a circumstantial account in his memoirs of subsequent events, it was this situation that caused the Chancellor to call on him on Saturday 4 November and express doubts

[34] Blackaby (1978, p. 41).

about the parity.[35] These doubts were shared for the first time by the Prime Minister, who was prepared to agree to devaluation if the situation worsened and the Chancellor had no acceptable alternative to suggest. His preference at that stage, however, was that the pound should be allowed to float, and it was only in the course of the next week that he accepted with regret that this would not be possible.[36] He was opposed to what he called 'a major lurch into deflation', and later refused to agree to an increase in the standard rate of income tax. The Prime Minister also expressed concern that too many other countries should not follow the United Kingdom in devaluing their currencies. The main doubts related to Australia (since her example was thought likely to be followed by Malaysia, Singapore, Hong Kong and Japan) and to the EEC (the attitude of the French to a change in the parity of the franc being as obscure as their attitude to a change in the parity of sterling was crystal clear). The Chancellor was assured by Van Lennep, Chairman of the (official) Monetary Committee of the Six, whom he had asked to see him on 8 November, that he would do all in his power to ensure that the members of the Community would not devalue.

On the morning of the eighth there was a meeting of the inner circle of ministers dealing with economic policy (SEP), at which the issue of devaluation was fully discussed, and the intention of introducing import quotas, which the meeting had been called to discuss, was set aside.[37] That evening the Chancellor, who had been given depressing advice about the chances of holding the rate, called again on the Prime Minister, and by the time he left they seem to have been in agreement that devaluation was 'virtually certain'.[38] It was not until the morning of the thirteenth, however, that they finally decided, subject to the views of the Cabinet, to go ahead with devaluation plans. The main ministers concerned were summoned to a meeting the following day and met twice on 15 November, confirming at the second meeting that the pound should be devalued on 18 November to a fixed rate of $2.40 to the pound.[39] These decisions were accepted the next day by the Cabinet, which also accepted the accompanying measures proposed 'after considerable discussion'.[40] It is clear from Harold Wilson's account that the measures were accepted with some reluctance.

Running parallel with the efforts to come to a decision on devaluation were negotiations based on an entirely different strategy: the organization of fresh international support for sterling. The US Treasury was wholehearted in its attempts to put together a massive package to avert

[35] Wilson (1971, pp. 447–8).
[36] Ibid., p. 456.
[37] Ibid., p. 449.
[38] Ibid., p. 451.
[39] Ibid., p. 455.
[40] Ibid., p. 456.

devaluation of sterling, and these attempts met with at least some response in Europe. Whether any package acceptable to all parties could have been devised must be very doubtful, and whether the British government would have been wise to add still further to its short-term indebtedness must be more than doubtful. The simple truth is that without devaluation it was hard to see how an eventual surplus would emerge sufficient to allow repayment of the existing debt, much less any further debts incurred so late in the day. Nevertheless, negotiations that were to prove highly embarrassing when rumours of them appeared in the press on 16 November were still in progress on the fifteenth, a week after the Prime Minister and Chancellor had come to the conclusion that devaluation was 'virtually certain'.[41] As late as 12 November the Prime Minister saw an international package emerging which he, the Chancellor and the Foreign Secretary 'were prepared to go along with', provided the conditions attached were acceptable and it was 'sufficiently solid and lasting' to see sterling through to the New Year.[42]

The full story of the negotiations has never been published, but Harold Wilson's account makes it clear that they would have involved large-scale borrowing from the IMF ($3,000 million rather than the $1,000 million of which the rumours spoke), and that there was little if any support from the Six. It was also clear that the IMF would have laid down strict conditions – much more stringent than were accepted immediately after devaluation in the Letter of Intent, when an application was made for a stand-by of $1,400 million. The stand-by, together with other assistance from central banks, provided the $3,000 million that had been under negotiation; but since it *followed* devaluation there was a far better prospect – or so it seemed – of early repayment.

At the end of October it would still have been possible to conduct a devaluation in good order. The procedure had been carefully planned at official level and the matters for ministerial attention drawn up, awaiting decision. But by mid-November it was increasingly difficult and costly to stick to any pre-arranged timetable, and in the last few days before the announcement on Saturday 18 November, confusion mounted. The air was full of rumours, especially in Paris, where meetings of Working Party no. 3 and the Economic Policy Committee of the OECD were in progress. It was increasingly taken for granted that the pound would be devalued at the week-end, as in fact it was.

Meanwhile, no stand-by had been arranged with the IMF, which had

[41] Ibid., p. 455. The Chancellor was asked on 16 November to make a statement in the House of Commons 'on the $1,000 m. loan being negotiated with foreign banks' and declined to do so in a way that was thought to imply that the rumours were unfounded. This was taken to point to the other possibility – devaluation – and an enormous run on sterling followed.

[42] Wilson (1971, p. 452).

received little more than an hour's notice of devaluation. The acompanying measures, announced simultaneously, had been hastily put together and were generally regarded as neither coherent nor adequate. It was accepted that it would be necessary to make available £1,000 million in resources for the improvement of the balance of trade and that what was required immediately was a curtailment of demand by £500 million. But the measures announced fell well short of this. They included cuts in public spending estimated at £200 million but, as usual, difficult to pin down; the withdrawal from 31 March 1968 of export rebates costing £100 million; the withdrawal of SET premiums, saving a similar amount; a small increase in corporation tax by 2.5 per cent to be included in the 1968 Budget; hire purchase restrictions on cars; and a rise in Bank rate to 8 per cent. A week later the Chancellor resigned.

The failure of deflationary measures

Before we turn to the sequel to devaluation we must first look back on the measures of July 1966, which were intended to dispose, once and for all, of the need to devalue the pound, and ask why they were insufficient for that purpose.

One element was the continuing lack of confidence in the government's policies. After the turns and twists, delays and equivocations of the first two years, there was no full-blooded return of confidence in the market: the durability of the parity continued to be regarded with suspicion; the short-term debts remained undischarged; and the reserves were patently inadequate.

A second inheritance from the preceding two years was the mounting level of wage costs. Between the last quarter of 1964 and the second quarter of 1966, hourly earnings in manufacturing rose at an annual rate in excess of 10 per cent and hourly wage rates at a rate not much less. These rates of increase were obviously eating into the competitive position of the United Kingdom and even a temporary wage freeze might prove insufficient to restore costs to a footing comparable to 1964 in relation to costs elsewhere. In point of fact, hourly wage rates, in spite of the freeze, increased over the 16 months between July 1966 and November 1967 by 6 per cent. An initial slowing down over the first six months was followed by an accelerating rate of increase to the pre-freeze rate in the course of 1967.

This occurred in spite of an easing of the pressure in the labour market at least as great as had been expected. Unemployment rose from 1.2 per cent in July 1966 to 2.3 per cent in November 1967. Indeed, July 1966 marked the turning point not only in unemployment but even more strikingly in employment. Manufacturing employment reached a peak in the third quarter of 1966 which has never been recovered. By the time devaluation took place in November 1967, it had already fallen by over 5 per cent.

With this fall went a failure of the balance of trade to respond to the reduction in pressure; the surplus labour was not re-absorbed in exports and import-competitive industries. For a short time the visible balance improved, and by the end of 1966 it was in surplus. But 1967 was a bad year for world trade, with rising unemployment in all the leading industrial countries. Total world trade in manufactures showed little or no increase over the year, and Britain's share of it continued to decline. The volume of British exports of manufactures fell quarter by quarter throughout the year; in September it was down 18 per cent on the published figures and 12 per cent on the adjusted figures in relation to the average. The most that could be claimed was that British export prices had ceased to move up in relation to the export prices of other manufacturing countries.

Even more telling than the fall in exports, which might well reverse itself when world markets recovered, was the continued rise in imports. The figures for 1967 were subject to many abnormal influences that made analysis difficult – the withdrawal of the surcharge in November 1966, dock strikes, large imports of military aircraft, etc. – but a volume increase of 7.5 per cent when the pressure of demand had been greatly reduced gave ample grounds for reconsidering the trend in the balance of payments and pointed to a genuine disequilibrium. The figures for the first half of the year were already sufficient to raise fundamental doubts.

In the autumn months these doubts intensified. In September and October the visible balance, adjusted for seasonal factors and imports of military aircraft, was in very heavy deficit. For September the adjusted deficit was £53 million compared with a monthly average that had fallen from £45 million at its worst in 1964 to £9 million in 1966 and had been replaced by a large surplus in the final quarter of 1966. Between that quarter and the third quarter of 1967 the swing in the adjusted monthly visible balance was no less than £68 million.[43] Strong measures taken belatedly to strengthen sterling had proven much feebler than a temporary slowing down in the expansion of world markets.

In his *The Labour Government 1964–70*, Harold Wilson singles out, as the main factors behind the deterioration in the balance of payments and the weakness of sterling, the closure of the Suez Canal in early June

[43] The 'adjusted' figures used in this paragraph are taken from the *National Institute Economic Review*, February 1968, p. 85. The adjustments are for 'dock strikes and other statistical disturbances other than the dock strikes in 1967, as well as for seasonal movements and for the different number of working days'. Exports of lend-lease silver and imports of military aircraft from the United States are excluded. No account is taken in any of the figures for the under-recording of exports (Wilson, 1971, pp. 263–5) by about £65 million in 1966, £80 million in 1967 and £130 million in 1968.

and the dock strikes in September–November.[44] The first of these he estimates to have cost £20 million a month, excluding the additional cost of imported oil and presumably also any withdrawal of Arab sterling balances. As for the dock strikes, he stresses their effect on confidence in sterling and suggests that £100 million of exports were held up in London and Liverpool at the beginning of November. There is no doubt that exports in October and November were seriously affected: Higham thinks £120–£140 million a reasonable estimate of the exports held back by the dock strikes from 1967 into 1968.[45] The October figures, when they appeared in mid-November, showed a drop in exports of a full 10 per cent and an adjusted trade deficit of £110 million. It is possible to account for most of the drop in October by reference to the dock strikes. But the swing over the year of £68 million per month in the trade balance is testimony to a decline in which the dock strikes played no part, and to which even the closure of the Suez Canal could have made only a limited contribution.

The October figures were completely out of keeping with the underlying trend in more prosperous years. But they were decisive. Nobody expected the government to introduce yet another package of deflationary measures. Practically no one thought that the government could or would borrow its way out. There seemed to be only one other possibility: devaluation.

Most observers read in the figures for October a conclusive verdict against the common view that, if the pressure on the economy were reduced, the balance of payments would swing round and speculation against the currency would die away. Just as in 1931 and 1949, a quite fortuitous bout of depression abroad settled the issue through a powerful speculative run on the pound when the reserves and other finance needed to resist it were simply not available.

The aftermath of devaluation

Devaluation did not put an end to the pressure on the pound. On the contrary, throughout the next year and well into 1969 there were doubts over the government's ability to hold to the new parity. The drain on the reserves was almost as large in the first half of 1968 as in the second half of 1967 and obliged the government to engage in fresh borrowing. By the end of 1968 official liabilities to the IMF and other monetary authorities had reached a total in excess of $8 billion – over $3 billion

[44] Wilson (1971, pp. 400, 440).

[45] Higham (1980, p. 30n). The value of imports held up was probably very much lower, perhaps £25 million.

more than at the end of 1967.[46] Confidence in the pound was indeed slow in returning.

In 1969–70, however, the pressure died away, a large current surplus emerged and official short- and medium-term debts were gradually reduced until they were finally completely discharged by April 1972. For the first time since May 1964 the United Kingdom was free of all official short- and medium-term debts.[47]

At first the government was confident of an early improvement in the balance of payments. In a Letter of Intent to the IMF on 23 November, the Treasury gave as the government's target 'an improvement of at least £500 m. a year', which they coupled with a surplus in the second half of 1968 at an annual rate of at least £200 million. In fact, there was a deficit on current account which is now estimated at £135 million per annum (after seasonal adjustment) but was put at £300 million as published in 1969. It was the continuation of the deficit, and in particular the unexpected buoyancy of imports, that lay behind the persistent pressure on sterling.

It took some time for this error in forecasting to become fully apparent. But from the start there were doubts whether the measures taken by the government were adequate. The OECD took the view that a 4 per cent rate of expansion in output in 1968, on which the government based its policies, was too high and suggested that 3 per cent was enough. But expansion over the winter was well above these rates: the figures for the first quarter of 1968 are now put a full 4 per cent higher than those for the final quarter of 1967 when consumer spending was already on the increase. It is true that after the first quarter there was little further growth in GDP in 1968 and some falling off in consumer spending, so that the year-on-year increase in GDP ended up at about 4½ per cent. But this was rather more than even the government had proposed. Consumer spending in 1968, which the *Financial Statement* as late as March 1968 had expected to show a fall of over 1 per cent below the level of the second half of 1967, is estimated to have been 1.7 per cent above.[48]

With the continued pressure on sterling, the government took a series of further steps to supplement the measures of November 1967. The new Chancellor, Roy Jenkins, announced on 21 December that further

[46] See the table of outstanding foreign borrowing in Tew (1978, p. 308).

[47] *Bank of England Quarterly Bulletin*, June 1972, p. 167.

[48] Here as elsewhere, much depends on the vintage of the statistics deployed. Those given in the text are taken from *Economic Trends Annual Supplement* (1981). But the rates of expansion published in 1969–70 were appreciably lower. For example, the year-on-year increase in GDP was put in mid-1969 at 3.3 per cent on the output measure and 1.7 per cent on the expenditure measure. A few months earlier the latter figure was put at 3.2 per cent. A year later the figures read 3.8 and 3.0 per cent respectively. By 1981 they had become 4.3 and 4.4 per cent.

cuts of £600 million would be made after Christmas; these were agreed in a long series of Cabinet meetings and were announced on 16 January. Two months later, on 19 March, the Budget included tax increases designed to raise £923 million in a full year – the largest dose of deflation since the war. This ensured that the borrowing requirement remained well within the limit of £1,000 million specified in the Letter of Intent to the IMF, and the budgetary increases eventually brought the economy back into balance. But there were anxious moments before the balance of payments swung round.

Even before the Budget, sterling had been under pressure because of a large-scale move into gold by speculators fearing a devaluation of the dollar and other currencies. Throughout the latter half of March the London gold market was closed, and on the day before the Budget it was decided in Washington to end the International Gold Pool and cut off dealings between central banks from the private markets in gold. In May, monetary policy was tightened, and in November fresh hire purchase restrictions were introduced. Later in November, after a major crisis centred on the franc, the Chancellor increased indirect taxation by 10 per cent through the use of the Regulator, lowered the ceiling for bank advances fixed in May and announced an import deposit scheme under which importers of most manufactured and semi-manufactured goods were required to deposit for six months 50 per cent of the value of the goods imported. Even these measures were insufficient to restore confidence, and rumours spread of an impending break-up of the government. But in mid-December there was an unusually favourable set of trade figures for the previous month and the pressure gradually died away. Although 1969 was almost as palpitating as 1968, and as late as May some forecasters were in doubt as to whether the current account for the year would show a surplus, a powerful swing in the balance of payments was well under way.[49]

The fluctuations in sentiment in 1968–69 and the successive crises in the foreign exchange market over those two years are reflected in figure 5.3, which shows the movement from month to month in spot and forward rates and the amount of official finance provided. There are conspicuous peaks in the forward premium in March and May 1968, a sharp increase in November 1968 and further peaks in April/May 1969 and August 1969. All of these correspond to periods of pressure in the exchange market and bear witness to the absence of the large-scale intervention by the Bank of England that had characterized the pre-devaluation phase. The decline in the premium by December 1969 to its lowest level since 1964 signals the final removal of any danger of a second devaluation.

[49] National Institute of Economic and social Research, *Economic Review*, May 1969, p. 12.

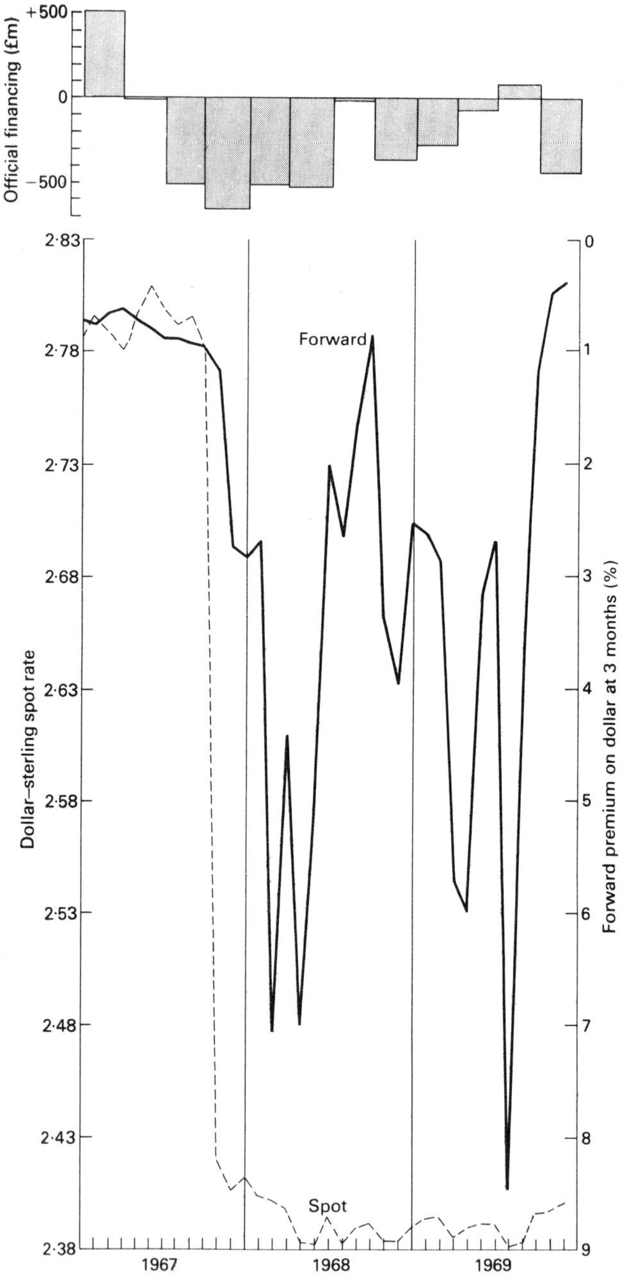

Figure 5.3 Exchange rates and the balance of payments, 1967–69

Sources: Bank of England Quarterly Bulletin; Economic Trends Annual Supplement 1981

The heaviest pressure in those two years came in the first half of 1968 when the deficit officially financed exceeded £500 million in each of the first two quarters. This was on the same scale as in the second half of 1967; but official financing was not held down, as it had been in 1967, by extensive support of the forward market. The spot rate fell steadily from January to June, through the closing of the London gold market in March and the rumours in May of devaluation of the French franc and revaluation of the Deutschmark. At the end of the year it remained close to its lower limit and continued below par in 1969. It was at its lowest in August 1969, when the French franc was finally devalued and Eurodollar rates were rising towards a peak of 11½ per cent in the first week of September.

Earlier in the year, beginning in April, there had been speculation against the franc and a large-scale transfer of funds into Deutschmarks. This brought on pressure on sterling (as well as other currencies), and when funds flowed out of Deutschmarks again they tended to be reinvested in the Eurodollar market, where US banks were bidding strongly for funds at high rates of interest.[50] The pressure continued into the autumn even after the devaluation of the French franc because of a renewed movement into the Deutschmark, which was finally allowed to float upwards in late September and formally revalued a month later. By that time the trade figures had put beyond reasonable doubt the emergence of a growing current account surplus, and the pound was recovering strongly.

The impact of devaluation

The effects of the 1967 devaluation, unlike those of the two earlier devaluations that we have discussed, have been investigated by a number of economists with the help of macroeconomic models. The London Business School, the National Institute of Economic and Social Research and the Cambridge Economic Policy Group have all applied their models to the period 1964–69 with a view to simulating policies expected to yield better results than the policies actually followed.[51] These models can equally well be applied to investigating the effects of devaluation, and both the London Business School and the National Institute have undertaken just such analyses.[52] Another, more detailed, study by J. R. Artus of the International Monetary Fund uses a small empirical model of his own construction.[53] An unpublished thesis by D.

[50] *Bank of England Quarterly Bulletin*, September 1969, p. 277.
[51] Posner (1978).
[52] For the National Institute's analysis, see NIESR (1972). For the London Business School, see Ball, Burns and Miller (1975).
[53] Artus (1975).

S. Higham of Brunel University reaches conclusions very similar to those of Artus.[54] There is also an analysis by Horne from the perspective of the monetary approach to the balance of payments.[55] A number of assessments of the likely effects were published in the months following devaluation and some of these (e.g. that of the National Institute) were subsequently updated.[56] Other studies, not specifically relating to the 1967 devaluation, have been made of the probable effects of a change in the sterling rate of exchange.[57]

The use of a model, needless to say, represents no more than the systematic framing of a series of hypotheses as to the forces controlling the behaviour of the constituent elements of the balance of payments. If we fully understood that behaviour, it is unlikely that forecasts of the balance of payments would be so consistently (and often wildly) wrong. It is true that there are fewer unknowns looking back than forward. Some of these unknowns relate to random events that are necessarily excluded from the model. In all other respects the forecaster and the model-builder are in the same boat and are seeking to isolate patterns of behaviour from the available data. It is an illusion to suppose, therefore, that those who frame their models after the event necessarily provide guidance superior to those making a forecast beforehand of the likely outcome of devaluation. This will be so only if they erect, on the basis of longer runs and more complete data, a more plausible model of the main variables, and detect trends in behaviour patterns that passed unnoticed earlier on. As we shall see, the efforts of the model-builders do throw doubt on some of the assumptions of the forecasters, particularly as to the trends governing the behaviour of imports.

The results of some of these studies are set out in table 5.5. The estimates shown in the table all relate to the year 1970, by which time most (but not all) of the effects of the devaluation can be assumed to have made themselves felt. They tell us nothing, therefore, about the time required for a positive improvement in the balance of payments to manifest itself, and pay no regard to any continuing deterioration that might have occurred in the absence of devaluation. It is, however, generally recognized that the balance of payments is likely to trace out a J curve, with the initial adverse effects offset only gradually by an improvement at a later stage. If the demand for imports is inelastic, and they have still to be paid for at world prices, the bill in foreign exchange will show little reduction. At the same time export earnings, measured in foreign exchange, will show an initial dip unless the price in sterling is adjusted upwards, and will start to increase only as the volume of

[54] Higham (1980).
[55] Horne (1979).
[56] National Institute of Economic and Social Research (1972, pp. 463–4).
[57] See for example Goldstein (1974), Ball, Burns and Laury (1977) and Odling-Smee and Hartley (1978).

TABLE 5.5 Estimates of effects of 1967 devaluation on the balance of trade and payments in 1970[a]

	Estimate by						Actual change	
	(1) Artus	*(2) Higham*	*(3) LBS1*[b]	*(4) LBS2*	*(5) NIESR1*[c]	*(6) NIESR2*	*1967–70*	*1965–67 to 1970*
Export of goods (incl. re-exports)								
Price	6.1	6.0	7.0	8.8[d]	7.6	8.5	19.0	21.5
Volume	11.9	11.8	9.0		11.5	10.0	30.0	30.6
Value	18.7	18.5	16.5	16.5	20.0	19.0	55.5	58.6
	(1243)	(1232)	(?)	(1116)	(1240)	(?)	(2910)	(3008)
Import of goods								
Price	12.9	13.0	10.0	12.6	12.5	16.5	20.6	21.2
Volume	−5.4	−5.2	0	0	0	0	17.9	25.5
Value	7.0	7.1	10.0	12.6	12.5	16.5	40.1	49.7
	(517)	(545)	(?)	(899)	(820)	(?)	(2343)	(2719)
Export of services	240			435	250		1237	1466
Property income from abroad (net)	70		89	89	80		176	154
Import of services	388			273	240		948	1067
Trade balance	726	687	419	217	420	130	567	289
Net invisibles	310	285[e]	289	251	90	295	503	564
Current balance	1036	972	708	468	510	425	1070	854

[a] Figures in upper half of the table are percentages except those in brackets which are in £ million. Figures in lower half of the table are in £ million
[b] Figures re-worked by Artus to make them subject to same constraint as other estimates, i.e. constant pressure of demand
[c] End 1969 [d] Exports of goods and services
[e] This is not an independent estimate, but an average of the estimates of columns (1),(4) and (6)
Sources: col. 1: Artus (1975, pp. 603–20); col. 2: Higham (1980, p. 326); col. 3: Artus (1975, p. 622); col. 4: Ball, Burns and Miller (1975, pp. 208–9); col. 5: Worswick (1970, pp. 86–91); col. 6: National Institute of Economic and Social Research (1972, p. 462)

exports gradually expands. The National Institute estimated over the first two years there was no net gain in export earnings, because the sacrifice through lower prices in the first year was only just offset by the gain from extra volume in the second. In that sense the devaluation 'worked' to improve the current account only after nearly two years. The London Business School model traces out a similar J curve with the visible balance showing a negative effect throughout the first year and the current account taking nearly as long to recover.[58]

The figures in table 5.5 are not entirely comparable, partly because of revisions to official statistics and partly because of differences in assumptions. The most recent official figures for imports and exports have been used in the last two columns and are rather higher than those used earlier. The LBS model allows for an increase in GNP after devaluation that works out at nearly 3 per cent by 1970 while the other calculations are on the basis of an unchanged level of activity. However, the LBS1 figures have been re-worked by Artus so as to eliminate the effects of the assumed expansion in output and this adjustment yields a substantially higher balance of payments effect. The LBS2 figures have not been re-worked and still assume an expansion in output. Another difference in assumptions is the treatment of inflation. Artus is alone in incorporating in his estimate the effects of devaluation on the rate of inflation.

The picture emerging from table 5.5 is one of general agreement between the econometricians as to the impact of devaluation on exports, but marked disagreement on imports. There is also one dissident voice on invisibles, apparently over the response on the side of exports. Artus puts the improvement in 1970 (i.e. after three years) in the current balance of payments at over £1,000 million, and no estimate is lower than £400 million. The LBS estimates, re-worked to make them comparable in assuming unchanged pressure of demand, are both likely to be around £700 million, and the first of the NIESR estimates would be of the same order of magnitude but for the low value arrived at for the effect on invisible exports. There is a very wide disagreement over the relative contribution to be expected from the visible and the invisible balances, Artus attributing 70 per cent of the total improvement to the trade balance while NIESR2 puts the proportion as low as 30 per cent.

The depreciation of sterling would have raised the price of foreign currencies uniformly by one-sixth if some of them had not been devalued simultaneously. About 20 countries devalued along with the United Kingdom, including Denmark, Eire, Finland, Hong Kong, New Zealand and Spain. Many of these countries were heavily dependent on the British market for their exports of agricultural goods and raw materials, and, as with earlier devaluations, the sterling price of the

[58] Ball, Burns and Miller (1975, p. 207).

goods they supplied rose appreciably less than the change in parity. None of the large industrial countries devalued their currencies along with sterling, so in 1967 devaluation once again raised the price of imported foodstuffs and materials less than that of imported manufactures.

If currencies are weighted in accordance with their relative importance as suppliers of imports, the average rise in the cost of foreign exchange was not 16.7 per cent but 13.9 per cent.[59] It seems reasonable to assume, with Artus, that virtually the whole effect of devaluation on import prices was passed through within the first year. Comparing import prices in the third quarters of 1967 and 1968, the actual increase was around 7 to 8 per cent for foodstuffs and fuel, 12.5 per cent for raw materials and 17.5 per cent for manufactures, averaging 13 per cent for all items.[60] Over the same period, world market prices fell slightly, a rise of 1.5 per cent in the price of manufactures being more than offset by falls in the prices of other imports, especially fuels. The change in sterling import prices, adjusted for the simultaneous movement in world market prices, accords closely with the average appreciation of the currencies of the supplying countries, weighted by their share in UK imports of the commodities concerned. Thus, for example, the import-weighted cost of foreign exchange for the purchase of foodstuffs for the British market rose by 10.4 per cent, the world price of foodstuffs in foreign exchange fell by 2 per cent, and the sterling price of UK imports of foodstuffs rose by 8 per cent, i.e. in very close accord with the difference between the two.

The movement in world market prices, expressed in foreign exchange, makes it clear that they could not have been greatly affected by devaluation. The impact on UK import prices, therefore, cannot have been much less than the increased cost of foreign exchange, weighted by the shares of the supplying countries. Making a small allowance for the abatement of world market prices, Artus puts the average increase in sterling import prices caused by devaluation at 12.7 per cent. For manufactures the increase works out at 15 per cent, for raw materials at 13 per cent and for foodstuffs at 9 per cent. These results seem plausible and, as will be seen from table 5.5, they are very close to the estimates reached independently by LBS and NIESR. The fact that import prices had risen a good deal more by 1970 reflects the movement in world market prices after 1968 rather than a belated pass-through effect of devaluation.

What is more difficult to assess is the effect on the volume of imports.

[59] Artus (1975, p. 599).

[60] Ibid. A similar result can be obtained by comparing import until values over the first three quarters of 1967 with the average for 1968. The National Institute's index of current import prices for food, materials and fuels shows an increase of 13.8 per cent on this basis and one of 11.5 per cent on a comparison between third quarters only.

It is normal to expect some falling-off in import volume when import prices are raised by devaluation, but in 1968 there was actually a steep rise with no falling back in the course of that year or in 1969. The increase in the import volume in 1968 in comparison with the first half of 1967 (after adjustment for abnormal factors) was 8 per cent, about twice the normal increase from year to year. This was, to say the least, disconcerting, and it still disconcerts those who would expect to find some early check to the growth of imports after devaluation. Moreover the marked increase, although most pronounced in manufactured goods, where it reached over 20 per cent by volume between the third quarter of 1967 and the first quarter of 1968, was common to the whole range of imports with the exception (after the first quarter) of foodstuffs. The Board of Trade was reported to have experimented with over 30 different equations in a vain attempt to explain the rise. The National Institute came to accept that the rise in import prices had exercised no check on the growth of imports. The London Business School would appear to have taken an equally pessimistic view.

Closer scrutiny suggests that an acceleration was already in progress in 1967 which was concealed by the comparative stability of the volume of imports between 1964 and 1966 and the subsequent halt in 1967 in the upward movement in import prices. In 1967 there were a number of abnormal influences at work pushing up imports in the early months and holding them down during the dock strikes towards the end of the year. But for the year as a whole there was an unmistakable quickening in the rate of increase in the unadjusted figures for the volume of imports, from about 2.5 per cent in 1966 to 7.5 per cent in 1967, in spite of a very perceptible slackening in economic activity (unemployment had risen from an average of 1.4 per cent in 1966 to an average of 2.2 per cent in 1967).[61] If we confine the comparison to finished manufactures, where the continued expansion in imports in 1968 was thought particularly surprising, the rise by volume of 16 per cent in 1967 was substantially larger than the increase by 9 per cent the following year (see figure 5.4).[62] It is in fact just as difficult to account for the rise in imports in 1967 as in 1968. Some of the rise in 1967 – 2 per cent or so – can be attributed to the absence of the surcharge in 1967, and some imports may have been delayed until January in order to take advantage of the

[61] Higham (1980) puts the increase in the volume of imports, excluding special factors but not taking account of the dock strikes, at 6.8 per cent in 1967 and 8.1 per cent in 1968. If we make a modest allowance for the dock strikes (Higham suggests £20 million in 1963 prices), it would seem that the acceleration in the growth of imports in 1968 must have been quite small and less than was to be expected, given the transition from contraction in 1967 to expansion in 1968.

[62] Based on the (adjusted) figures in Higham (1980). Finished manufactures (SITC 7 and 8) have been adjusted to exclude aircraft, engines, ships and boats and semi-finished manufactures. SITC 5 and 6 have been adjusted to exclude silver and precious stones.

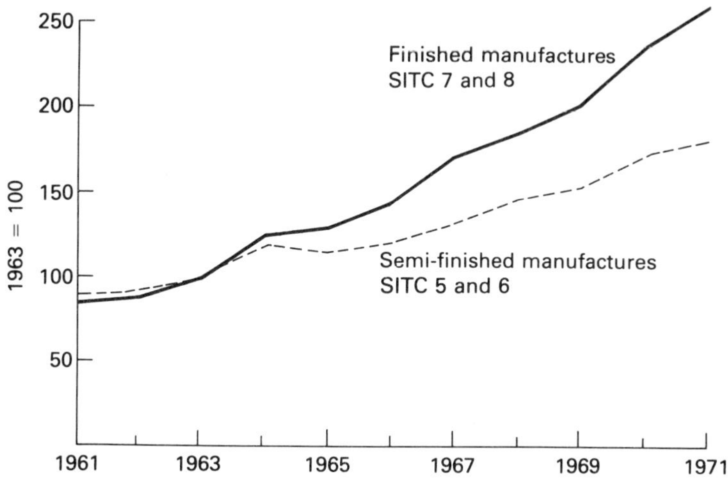

Figure 5.4 Volume of UK imports of manufactures, 1961–71

Source: Higham (1980)

ending of the surcharge on 30 November 1966. But it is hard to resist the conclusion that the propensity to import manufactures was on an upward trend, independently of any price advantage they enjoyed, and that, as the National Institute put it, 'the reason why the original expectations of devaluation have been disappointed is because they were entertained in ignorance of a sharp worsening in the underlying situation, which had been occurring during 1967'.[63] The National Institute itself had failed to foresee the worsening when it forecast in February 1967 an increase in imports during the year of only £50 million.[64] Allowing for the withdrawal of the surcharge, this was equivalent to an actual fall and compares with a recorded increase of £400 million. It is true that the National Institute expected GDP to be a mere 0.3 per cent higher in 1967 instead of the 2.6 per cent now shown in official statistics. But even if the level of GDP had been known in advance, no one would have predicted so large an increase in imports.

For semi-finished manufactures, which share some of the characteristics of raw materials, the increases in 1967 and 1968 corresponding to those in finished manufactures were 9 and 13 respectively, the bigger increase in 1968 largely offsetting the smaller increase in finished manufactures.

[63] National Institute of Economic and Social Research, *Economic Review*, February 1969, p. 17.

[64] National Institute of Economic and Social Research, *Economic Review*, February 1967, p. 13. The *London and Cambridge Economic Bulletin* reached much the same conclusions, putting the increase in imports at £100 million with a rise in GDP of 0.3 per cent (*The Times*, 13 March 1967, p. 17).

It is not therefore just a failure to disaggregate, as Artus suggests, that has made economists hesitate to attribute a reduction in the volume of imports to devaluation, but rather a failure to take account of a change in the trend of imports of manufactures, of which the evidence was already to hand by the end of 1967.

Artus's own estimates make use of elasticities of demand for manufactures of -1.0 for finished manufactures and -3.4 for semi-finished manufactures derived from observations covering the period 1960–72. These relatively high elasticities reflect his insistence on a comparison between import prices and the prices of *comparable* domestic products, where relative price changes tend to be quite small and exercise correspondingly large effects on demand, particularly if the products are fairly homogeneous. For food, raw materials and fuels Artus uses elasticities taken from the Cambridge Growth Project of 0.3, 0.1 and 0.6 respectively. For total imports this implies an average elasticity somewhat higher than unity.

Artus found no significant differences between price elasticities in the pre-devaluation period (1960–67) and the post-devaluation period (1968–72). He also found that the changes in relative prices took effect within a year for finished manufactures and within two years for semi-finished manufactures.[65]

The upshot of Artus's calculations is a drop of 5.4 per cent in the volume of imports. It must be said that this is a great deal more plausible than the assumption in the other estimates of a nil effect. As Artus points out, one must take account of other policy measures affecting the actual behaviour of imports and exports in the later 1960s; some of these were likely to exercise a very material influence. The abolition of the import surcharge and of export rebates, the Import Deposit Scheme, changes in taxation (including the imposition and withdrawal of the selective employment tax), the Kennedy Round of tariff reductions, payments for US military aircraft and so on all took place in the period under discussion. There was also an important cyclical swing between 1966 and 1968 which depressed activity in 1967 and was followed by a recovery in 1968. This was reflected in the slow growth of world trade in manufactures in the first, and the much faster growth in the second, of those years.[66] It is only after taking stock of all these influences on the post-devaluation growth of imports that one can reconcile a perceptible check caused by devaluation with the observed rapid growth that actually occurred.

The impact of devaluation on exports was slow to make itself felt.

[65] This result seems hard to reconcile with the large increase in imports of manufactures in 1968 and the large negative residuals for that year in his reconciliation between estimated and actual developments (Artus, 1975, table 12, p. 624).

[66] World trade in manufactures grew from \$23.2 billion in 1966 to \$24.9 billion in 1967 and \$28.6 billion in 1968, i.e. by 7.3 per cent in 1967 and 14.9 per cent in 1968.

Except for textiles, the changes in 1968 were disappointingly small and the United Kingdom's share of world trade in manufactures continued to decline. But in 1969 there was a spurt, with a growth in volume of over 13 per cent.[67] As table 5.1 brings out, there is little disagreement about the total effect by 1970. The various estimates shown there agree on an increase in the value of exports by between 16.5 and 20 per cent, on price increases of between 6 and 9 per cent and on volume increases of between 9 and 12 per cent. Artus obtains the lowest price increase, the highest volume increase and, by implication, uses the highest estimate of price elasticity. For semi-finished and finished manufactures, which together made up 85 per cent of UK exports in 1967, he puts the elasticity of demand at 2.5 and 1.4 respectively on the basis of observations covering the period 1960–72. His results are derived from estimates of the movement of prices for foreign products competing with UK imports obtained by weighting disaggregated foreign price series by the shares of the exporting countries in the world market; the series for each product have then been weighted in accordance with their share in UK exports. The assumptions underlying the estimates of UK export prices are discussed below in connection with the behaviour of wages and other costs after devaluation.

Estimates of the effects on invisibles are usually much more sketchy and rely largely on extrapolation of trends. The main effect is generally taken to be on travel services (tourism and transportation services), which show a comparatively high elasticity, but there are also increases, measured in sterling, in property income from abroad and other items. Worswick's (1971) estimates for net invisibles of £90 million by the end of 1969 is the only one to differ from the general consensus on a figure of £250–£300 million. Since it is based on the export side on inspection of trends and on the import side on the assumption that the volume of services imported was unaffected, we need not discuss it further, especially when the actual improvement from all causes in the invisibles balance was as large as £500 million. Indeed, the fact that the improvement was so large in comparison with the improvement in the trade balance makes one wonder whether the effect of devaluation on invisibles may not have been underestimated.

Apart from the effects so far considered, there are a number of others that need to be taken into account. The figures in table 5.2 relate exclusively to the current balance, and yet, as we shall argue, there were inevitably important repercussions on the capital balance, not all of them temporary. There were also changes in relative prices affecting demand in ways not analysed above: changes causing a switch to expenditure on non-traded goods such as housing and services for final consumption. Although some theorists lay great stress on this effect,

[67] Higham (1980, p. 181).

and assume that for traded goods domestic prices are quickly brought into line with world prices so that elasticities have little chance to operate, there is not much evidence that this channel of influence on the trade balance was of great significance in the 1967 devaluation.[68] Similarly, the changed pattern of demand necessarily implied a changed pattern of production, including an expansion in manufacturing output for the home market and for exports, and this in turn reacted on requirements for raw materials and semi-finished manufactures and so on total imports.[69] However, devaluation's supply effect must have been small in relation to the much larger direct effects on demand, since the import content of UK manufactures was not much above 20 per cent. Finally, one has to take account of capacity constraints that may have delayed or thwarted the response in output permitted by the elasticities of demand. These limitations would also enhance the danger of more rapid inflation and hence of the extinction of the price disparities produced by devaluation.

This brings us to the critical issues of timing on the one hand and the movement of costs on the other. The *modus operandi* of devaluation is essentially to lower the cost of labour in terms of the devalued currency by comparison with its cost abroad and to facilitate changes in the pattern of demand and output over the limited period during which this disparity in labour costs can be sustained. The speed with which demand and output respond, and with which the cost advantage is eroded, is as important as the magnitude of the short-run elasticities of response. The rise in import prices brought about by devaluation is bound to set in motion other price adjustments including wage adjustments, and a wage–price spiral may ensue that rapidly wipes out most or all of the disparity that devaluation created.[70]

In the case of the 1967 devaluation the government sought to hold back the rise in wages by various forms of incomes policy. After the freeze introduced in July 1966 there had been a period of severe restraint; in March 1968 the government took powers to postpone wage settlements and announced a norm for wage increases of zero with a maximum of 3.5 per cent in exceptional circumstances. The effects of this policy are not easy to establish and so far as they were appreciable are best treated as part of the devaluation package and inseparable from the effects of that package.

Economists have not been very successful in modelling the behaviour of money wages under inflationary conditions. There is also a sharp division of view between those who regard money wages as responding primarily to price changes and those who regard the line of causation as

68 Artus (1975, pp. 614–15).
69 Ibid., p. 617; Worswick (1970, p. 91).
70 For an approach along these lines, see Aukrust (1977) and the references cited therein.

running more frequently from wages to prices. On the first view, the running is made by the movement of prices on world markets to which the movement in prices for traded goods in the United Kingdom must conform, and this in turn governs the scope for wage increases in the industries making traded goods, i.e. in manufacturing industry. Other wages follow and the rise continues across the whole field of employment until money wages have come back into line with prices. On this view of the matter there is no need to investigate elasticities in order to establish the eventual effect of devaluation. The effects on the balance of payments are evanescent; any deficit reflects an excess addition to the money supply and will disappear once the money supply has been reduced to the necessary extent.

On the second view, there is no reason why wages should rise to the point at which the cost advantage opened up by devaluation disappears entirely. Apart from any influence on world market prices exerted by devaluation itself, there need be no automatic conformity between the movement of prices on world markets and domestic prices for traded goods even in an open economy like the United Kingdom. This is so because of the heterogeneity of competing products, market imperfections and impediments, the time required for competition to become effective, and the influence that the movement of costs in Britain itself exercises on world prices. The cost of living need not rise, therefore, to the full extent of the devaluation unless other independent inflationary forces are at work. Nor is the pace of wage increases set by the rise in the cost of living in any determinate way. The wage structure is not fixed, and a somewhat larger increase in wages in the traded goods sector is only to be expected if this sector expands relatively to the rest of the economy. What happens to real wages depends on profit margins and on the movement in the terms of trade which, in the British case, is unlikely to be very substantial. If, as was probably true in 1967, the most that was needed to offset such a movement was a 1 per cent check to the secular improvement in real wages, it is hard to see how this can be dismissed as unrealistic by *a priori* reasoning. Without question, devaluation usually requires accompanying measures, which may be either fiscal or monetary or both. But to regard monetary factors as the *exclusive* cause of balance of payments disequilibrium or the *only* means by which deficits can be removed is going much too far.

With this dispute in mind let us look at the actual record. The annual rate of increase in hourly earnings had reached a peak of nearly 10 per cent in the winter of 1965–66 and had then fallen to about 4 per cent in 1967. Throughout 1968 and 1969 the rate remained around 7.5 per cent, and although there was a sharp increase in 1970 when wage restraint ended, the increase in 1968–69 was no higher than it had been in 1963, a comparatively depressed year unaffected by devaluation. The increase over the three years 1968–70 was about 33 per cent; this compares with an increase of over 25 per cent in the years 1964–66. Artus reckons on the basis of his model that the increase up to 1971 attributable to devaluation alone was no more than 6.8 per cent for hourly earnings and 5.6 per cent for consumer prices. Real earnings improved in each successive year, but until 1970 at a markedly slower rate than output per head. There is no evidence that the rate of increase in 1968–69 was less than in previous years: the increase in the two years before 1967 averaged 2.0 per cent and in the two years after, 3.0 per cent, while in 1967 itself the increase was a mere 1.0 per cent.[71]

One reason why the wage reaction was so limited over the first two critical years was that, as explained above, food import prices rose by much less than other import prices after devaluation. Between the third quarter of 1967 and the third quarter of 1968 retail prices for foodstuffs increased by only 3 per cent. For drink and tobacco the rise was 4 per cent and for housing it was also 4 per cent. Thus for a large proportion of consumer goods the rise was well within the 5 per cent that the government had indicated as the likely effect at the time of devaluation; indeed, the rise in the consumer price index was a little below 5 per cent. By the autumn of 1968 most of the increases directly resulting from devaluation had been passed through into consumer prices. As wage-earners had obtained increase in pay sufficient to allow their real earnings to improve, there was no obvious reason why the secondary effects of devaluation through wage adjustments need be large or need thwart a continuing improvement in the balance of payments. No doubt devaluation operated to widen profit margins in manufacturing; but since these had previously been depressed by the over-valuation of sterling, such a widening need not have set off a wage explosion.

The final change in the balance of payments depended not only on the movement of wages but on the balance of the economy and in particular on the fiscal policy of the government. It was open to the government to exploit the possibilities of a substantial favourable balance by making a corresponding addition to the budget surplus, removing obstacles to investment abroad, and aiming at the prolongation of the cost advantages initiated by devaluation. In the early 1960s the government had felt itself obliged to stimulate consumer demand by tax cuts until a balance of payments crisis forced a reversal of policy. Devaluation held out the opposite prospect that, by taking fiscal measures to check or limit consumer demand, the way might be left open for a larger growth in exports offset by the repayment of foreign debt or, subsequently, increased investment abroad.

This was in fact the path followed from the March Budget of 1968 onwards. The initial measures earlier taken were shaped by no such ambition; although nominally designed to remove £500 million in

[71] For a fuller analysis, see Dennis (1977, pp. 46–8).

purchasing power to 'make room' for an improvement in the balance of payments, they were widely and rightly judged insufficient for that purpose. Indeed, it has been common in later years to accuse the government of taking expansionary measures before devaluation and failing to take resolute action in November 1967 to check the expansion. The unexpected rise in the volume of imports in 1968 is attributed to this failure and is explained in terms of the excess demand generated by government policy.

No doubt the November measures were inadequate. But it must be remembered that unemployment had doubled in the previous 18 months, and that there was very little evidence of pressure on capacity. Over the winter of 1967–68 unemployment continued to increase, and in the first quarter of 1969 it was as high as a year previously and higher than at the time of devaluation. It is true that there was a slight dip in unemployment in the middle of 1968, but it was very slight. The pressure of demand as measured by unemployment remained throughout 1968 and 1969 very close to the level to which it had fallen in 1967. If this still seems too high it must be pointed out that it proved to be consistent with a much larger improvement in the balance of payments than the government announced as its objective in November 1967. It is only if one uses some index of demand pressure other than unemployment that one can argue that the pressure increased after devaluation.

Other indices do, however, tell a different story from the unemployment figures. Vacancies, which have since proved a more reliable guide, increased quite sharply in the second quarter of 1968 and remained higher than in 1967, though well below the level of 1964–66. Capacity utilization in *manufacturing*, as measured by a variety of indices prepared by Dr Higham (using the methods of the Wharton School), the Bank of England and the IMF, shows an unmistakable rise, and a higher proportion of industrial firms told the Confederation of British Industries that they were working at capacity limits.[72] It is fair to conclude that devaluation, as was intended, put particular pressure on manufacturing industry while the measures accompanying it were not specifically designed to limit the pressure on manufacturing capacity. But even in manufacturing the pressure remained appreciably below what had been experienced in 1964–65.

What was more disturbing was the consumer buying spree that stretched from devaluation to the budget of March 1968. This spree was brought on by public statements that prices were likely to rise by 5 per cent and by expectations of higher taxes or hire purchase restrictions. It is unlikely that it did much to inflate consumer expenditure over the whole year, since most of the additional spending was anticipatory and was offset by diminished spending later on. If one looks at the behaviour

[72] Higham (1980, p. 65).

of the savings ratio, it fluctuated between 8.1 and 9.3 per cent in the first three quarters of 1967 (after seasonal adjustment of consumers' expenditure and personal disposable income), fell to 7.8 and 6.9 per cent in the next two quarters and rose to 10.2 per cent in the following quarter after the March Budget. The average for thc first three quarters comes to 8.6 per cent and for the next three to 8.3 per cent, so it is not likely that the flow of expenditure over the whole period was much affected.

Nevertheless, the spending spree did have a genuine effect. It combined with the rise in imports in the early months of 1968 (to which it contributed) to create a state of uneasiness and doubt that the devaluation had failed. The danger of a second devaluation, or of an uncontrolled fall in the value of the pound, was ever present; market opinion was not encouraged by the apparent acquiescence of the government in the wave of consumer buying.

That the government took no action was due to a number of circumstances. First of all, it would have been difficult to raise indirect taxes soon after the devaluation when deflationary measures had just been taken and the shops were already stocked up for Christmas. By January ministers were preoccupied with drastic cuts in public expenditure, and by the end of the month the Budget was little more than six weeks away. Ministers also felt that there was enough slack in the economy without adding to it in advance of the response to devaluation; that extra spending in January would relieve the pressure come July. But whatever the arguments in favour of waiting, the alarm that waiting produced made it that much easier for ministers to settle on a programme both for public expenditure in January and for taxation in March that put it beyond doubt that demand would be reined back so as to allow devaluation to take full effect. If doubts persisted all through 1968 and well into 1969 they were not over ministerial resolution, but about the magnitude of the adjustments called for and the apparent ineffectiveness of devaluation as an instrument in making them.

The fact that the United Kingdom's balance of payments position remained precarious for so long had little to do with devaluation or the measures by which it was accompanied. Far more important was the fact that the United Kingdom delayed devaluation until her credit had been exhausted in more senses than one. At the time of devaluation the government had contracted heavy foreign debts, amounting to nearly $5,000 million, all of them short-term.[73] The Bank of England had given equally lavish support to the forward market and had now to accept heavy losses. The reserves at the government's disposal, encumbered by these liabilities, were totally inadequate to the contingencies that lay ahead. Market opinion was also short of confidence and was unwilling

[73] Tew (1978, p. 308).

to give the government the benefit of the doubt. The gap in the balance of payments that opened up in the world recession of 1967, and widened with the dock strikes in the autumn, was deeper than suspected and the acceleration in imports was more powerful. It took a long time, therefore, for devaluation to exercise a visible effect: even in mid-1969 the National Institute did not expect the current account to be in surplus until the autumn and put the surplus for the year at £25 million (as contrasted with the £470 million now officially recorded). Yet it ought to have been apparent at the end of 1968 that the danger was over and the swing in progress.[74]

How was it possible for the United Kingdom to finance the deficit of 1968 after the heavy deficits that had gone before and the absence of market support? It is too easily taken for granted that the only thing that matters after devaluation is what happens to the current account. A deficit on current account has still to be financed: the capital account needs equal attention.

TABLE 5.6 Finance of the deficit, 1964–69

	(£ million)	
	Deficit officially financed	*Borrowings from other monetary authorities*
1964	695	573
1965	353	599
1966	591	625
1967	671	556
1968	1410	1296
	3720	3649

In each of the five years 1964–68 the United Kingdom had to provide large sums for the finance of its deficits. How was this done? The answer is shown in table 5.6. Put briefly, the deficits were financed by recourse to other monetary authorties, including the IMF, and by the sale in 1966–67 of the dollar portfolio of securities accumulated earlier. The rough equivalence in the totals shows that it was possible to balance the accounts without drawing more than marginally on reserves. By far the largest deficit and the largest borrowings were in 1968: it was only strong support by the monetary authorities in the United States and elsewhere that enabled the United Kingdom to withstand market pressure in that

[74] [This was my own view when I left the Treasury at the end of 1968. A.K.C.]

year. But over the next three years, as devaluation took effect, the situation was completely transformed. A surplus of £5,378 million officially financed more than offset the officially financed deficits of 1964–68, and monetary authorities abroad were more than repaid the £3,649 million that had been borrowed.

TABLE 5.7 Make-up of the deficit, 1968 and 1969

		(£ million)	
	1968	*1969*	*Swing between 1968 and 1969*
Current balance	−273	471	744
EEA loss on forward transactions	−250	—	250
Net overseas investment less bank borrowing to finance it	23	−101	−124
Export credit *less* import credit	−281	−181	100
All other transactions	−502	105	607
Balancing item	−126	393	519
	−1410	687	2097

Why was it necessary to borrow nearly £1,300 million in 1968 when the current account deficit was only £273 million? The balance for official financing was made up as shown in table 5.7. Leaving aside the loss on the pre-devaluation forward purchases of sterling, we are left with two items: net overseas investment and net export/import credit, which together accounted for less of the deficit than they did the following year, and a miscellany of items, nearly all of which reflect the movements, open or disguised, of short-term funds. The last two items shown in table 5.7 accounted for nearly half the deficit and were more than twice the size of the current account deficit. If one looks at the enormous swing between 1968 and 1969, these short-term flows accounted for more than half the total and were substantially larger than the big swing in the current balance. Thus what mattered was not just the improvement in the current balance but market recognition of that improvement, as registered in confidence in the new parity and the flow of funds springing from that confidence. The ability of the British authorities to hold on until that confidence was restored rested in turn on the attitude of other monetary authorities, either individually or in the IMF.

Why did they enjoy such support? Here we touch the nub of the whole matter. Sterling was not just this or that currency, but a currency of particular interest to other industrial countries, the outer defences, so to speak, of the dollar. If sterling were devalued, still more if the devaluation failed, the whole Bretton Woods system might be jeopardized and the power of the United States to sustain a dollar standard greatly weakened. In all the negotiations in Paris, Washington, Basle and elsewhere that preceded and followed the devaluation of sterling – negotiations that would need a chapter to themselves – the support that was offered reflected a common interest in the international monetary system and the attitudes of the leading countries to that system. Had it been otherwise the United Kingdom, freed from the obligations of its reserve currency status, would probably have devalued much earlier and without scruple; it would probably have been obliged to do so in any case for lack of the support that in fact it was given.

Conclusion

The devaluation of 1967 was a more long-drawn-out, complex and controversial affair than either of the earlier devaluations of 1931 and 1949.

There is first an issue of diagnosis. Was there in some sense an underlying disequilibrium in the balance of payments for which devaluation was an appropriate remedy? At what point was the evidence of such a disequilibrium sufficient to warrant concern, when did it become compelling and how large an adjustment did the evidence suggest?

Next there is an issue of prescription. Disequilibrium in the balance of payments can be handled in various ways. What alternatives were there to devaluation? Could they be relied on to effect a continuing improvement, or were they likely to afford only temporary relief? Was it reasonable to expect that the forces operating on the balance of pay -ments could be held in equilibrium indefinitely at some lower parity, or would they assert themselves again and renew the need for an adjustment in the exchange rate? If so, was the right solution to allow the pound to float? On the other hand, were there perhaps dangers in devaluation that made it an uncertain cure for disequilibrium? Once rates of exchange ceased to be fixed, did that not introduce fresh elements of instability, nationally and internationally, that would make it *more* difficult to restore equilibrium?

What made prescription particularly difficult was that international opinion was hostile to the kind of remedies that would at one time have suggested themselves: quantitative import controls such as had been used before, during and after the war; and a floating rate on the model of the 1930s. Once borrowing started, it was inevitable that regard was paid to the international reactions such measures might provoke. Floating rates, for example, would have been incompatible with a loan or stand-by from the IMF.

The three key ministers adopted policies that they judged sufficient to make devaluation unnecessary: *ad hoc* devices for improving the current account, from the surcharge to limitations on tourist expenditure abroad and reductions in overseas military commitments; operations on the capital account; 're-structuring' of industry; incomes policy; credit restriction and eventually undisguised deflation. These policies proved insufficient; and those who backed their judgement that that would happen cannot be dismissed as speculators when some of the government's own specially chosen advisers were known to share that view. There was a certain lack of proportion in the measures adopted. The competitive position of a country is not transformed by a few mergers; there are severe limits to what controls over long-term capital movements will do; an incomes policy is rarely of use in limiting wage increases in the face of an increasing shortage of labour; credit restriction is not very effective when the money supply is increasing rapidly, as in 1967; measures of deflation may be offset by rising pressure elsewhere, and may leave the budget in increasing deficit. The market had some reason to be sceptical that the succession of measures would work and for viewing ministers in the same light as ministers viewed *them* – as speculators.

There is a further issue as to the interplay of political and economic judgement. It lay within the competence of ministers to decide whether to devalue or not, and it was open to them also to disregard any advice offered to them. They could, therefore, allow their judgement to be dominated if they chose by political considerations, which were not likely to favour a deliberate devaluation. A decision by its very nature had to be taken in conditions of great secrecy by a small number of ministers. In 1967, from start to finish, the views of three ministers only were of account, and in the last resort it was the judgement of the Prime Minister that was decisive. But, like Stafford Cripps in 1949, he had ruled out the possibility of devaluation without taking stock of the economic arguments for and against. From October 1964 onwards no position paper setting out these arguments was ever asked for by ministers. It is one of the major drawbacks of a fixed rate system that changes in parity are part of the political process; they put at stake the political career of the key figures involved; and they can rarely be timed and co-ordinated with other actions because of the strong resistances they inevitably encounter.

So far as diagnosis is concerned, the experience of 1964 at the very least suggested a weak competitive position that was tending to become weaker. But 1964 was exceptional in a number of respects affecting both the current and capital accounts. The disequilibrium might prove quite modest when the stock-building phase was over and the pressure on capacity less extreme. It did not appear so large at that stage that it was incapable of remedy without devaluation, provided the competitive position could be improved over time by other means. The government could reasonably claim that the surcharge might offer the necessary breathing space and that there was too much at stake politically to justify immediate devaluation. The market had, after all, swallowed almost without a qualm a current account deficit of £240 million over the first nine months of 1964, before the Labour government took office, and as things turned out, this was more than the cumulative deficit over the next three years. Where was the compelling evidence of a fundamental disequilibrium?

But the future of the parity did not rest solely on Britain's competitive power. It depended also on confidence and market opinion; and the market had an eye on a number of things not closely connected with competitive strength. It paid regard to the outlook of the government on public expenditure, the size of the Budget deficit, the pressure on the economy and the state of the labour market, and to Britain's trading relations with other countries, especially the Common Market. It was aware also of the limited reserves on which Britain could draw and the much larger foreign holdings of liquid funds in London. Once the future of the parity was put in doubt, there was every reason why foreigners should seek to hedge their sterling assets if this was possible at reasonable cost. Even at favourable times over the years before devaluation there were very large spot and forward obligations to foreigners. The foreign exchange obtained from the IMF and from other monetary authorities was in excess of $3,000 million by June 1965, and the figures for June and December remained above $3,000 million from then until June 1967 when the total was $2,500 million.[75] To this must be added a large (but unpublished) figure for forward obligations. (See Table 5.4.) This constant overhang made the pound vulnerable to shifts in opinion that might or might not be well-grounded.

No doubt the market was out of sympathy with the government, resented the new taxes introduced and dismissed its various remedies as palliatives. But there were genuine grounds for concern, particularly if one took the view (which Conservative governments had accepted) that the balance of payments was not likely to swing round or the competitive position to improve when the pressure on the economy was so high. Labour in 1964 was clearly determined to maintain or even increase the pressure; the frequency with which the Prime Minister, right up to July 1966, listed the various cuts the government had made conveyed an unintended message that enough had already been done to limit government spending and effective demand when the employment figures for the past and the forecasts for the future told a completely different story. There seemed no chance that a government dedicated to growth

[75] Tew (1980, p. 308).

and planning would turn its back on both and introduce the kind of measures that the balance of payments deficit, which was advertised with such gusto, seemed to require. In any event, a socialist government could hardly be expected to relish cuts or introduce them with the drama necessary to impress and reassure financial markets.

By the same token, it was doubtful whether devaluation in October 1964 would have done what its proponents hoped. A major boom is rarely the best time to devalue, and 1965 was a year of unmistakable boom. There is no reason to suppose that the government would have taken stronger action to check the boom if it had devalued. It did, after all, introduce the surcharge without accompanying action. True, the surcharge is reckoned to have improved the balance of payments by some £250 million over two years, so devaluation in 1964–65 would not have been completely ineffective.[76] But without strong supplementary action it is doubtful whether it would have done much to change the course of events for the better.

Whatever the initial diagnosis, the events of 1967–68 provided much more convincing evidence of disequilibrium than the data available in 1964. In the three years after 1964 wages and costs had risen more steeply, not less; there was no sign that productivity was rising faster; and the country's appetite for imported manufactures was clearly growing. The experience of those years also made it difficult to look for much help to the expedients introduced by the government in order to narrow the gap in the balance of payments. How large the disequilibrium had become is difficult to say, but there can be little doubt that a devaluation by 10–15 per cent was not excessive in the circumstances.

There is, however, another way of judging the matter. Given the strength of market fears and expectations and the large bear position that had been built up, the government had to ask itself, almost independently of the merits of the case, how long it was prepared to go on borrowing in order to hold the parity. This meant viewing the matter in terms of psychological warfare rather than economic analysis. It was in fact because the government was not prepared to engage in further borrowing that it threw in its hand. But of course the market would not have held so strong a view if there had not been a powerful group convinced of the need to devalue in order to restore balance in the exchange market; the government would not have yielded if it had not felt that its case for maintaining the parity was losing credibility.

By November there was no choice but to devalue. When, ideally, should action have been taken? One answer would be: any time from July 1966 onwards. By that time the government had become reconciled to leaving a little slack in the economy and some ministers were willing to accept, as part of the strategy of avoiding devaluation, a level of

[76] Artis (1978, p. 347).

unemployment of around 2 per cent. While July 1966 might have been the wisest date to choose, there was something to be said for waiting to see how the measures worked and whether the balance of payments *would* swing round as the pressure was reduced. In that event, the best choice would have been early May 1967, when the devaluation might have been coupled with the application to enter the Common Market. At that point the bad news was yet to come and the external indebtedness to other monetary authorities was at its lowest point, so that any resulting exchange losses would have been minimized. It would also have been possible to take reinforcing action to check domestic demand without all the complications attending a devaluation so near to Christmas.

When should it have been recognized that there was no alternative to devaluation? The answer must depend on the risks it was reasonable to run, and these risks were different for different participants in the decision-taking process. By October it was virtually certain that it would be necessary to devalue – even by mid-September it was beginning to look indefensible to refrain from acting. The government could not simply sit out the winter doing nothing and waiting for an election-year boom in America to rescue the pound in 1968. There was no longer any real prospect of a surplus at the existing parity in 1968, and little chance of regaining the volume of exports necessary for equilibrium. British producers had lost share in their own market and in foreign markets under conditions that should have helped them to become more competitive. It needed only another month's bad figures for the reserves to fall below the safety margin. The choice before the government, since it could not then justify inaction, was between import controls and devaluation. Import controls held out no hope of ultimate balance at an unchanged exchange rate. So devaluation it would have to be.

6

Concluding Reflections

It is scarcely possible to exaggerate the extent to which our three devaluations of sterling differed from one another. Indeed, the differences are so striking that it sometimes seems as if the only thing these three devaluations had in common was their coincidence on each occasion with an eclipse of the moon.[1] None the less, a comparison of the three episodes reveals a surprising number of similarities – significant enough, in any case, to encourage us to attempt to generalize regarding the causes and effects of the three devaluations.

The international economic situation

The international economic situation was radically transformed between 1931 and 1949 and again by 1967. In 1931 the world was entering a depression of unprecedented severity and long duration. Unemployment, already high both in Britain and in a number of other countries, was mounting rapidly. Capital flows, indispensable to continued expansion outside of industrialized Europe and North America, already showed signs of stagnation, while the problem of reparations and war debts remained unresolved. Behind the depression, the unemployment and the suspension of capital flows lay the contraction of world markets. Behind the contraction of markets lay in turn the absence of effective management of the world economy. That responsibility was beyond the capabilities of the United Kingdom; and the United States, far from accepting the responsibility, was preoccupied with the task of restoring stability to its domestic economy. The deflationary impulses created by the depression were all the more difficult to accommodate because of the imbalance between the United States and other countries – later christened 'the dollar shortage'.

In such a situation the United Kingdom could not fail to feel the

[1] Voyant (1971–72, p. 229).

weight of the international slump in a loss of exports of goods and services. As an international banker she was also at risk from unwelcome changes in financial flows, and her large liquid obligations and heavy debts laid her peculiarly open to those risks. To these difficulties were added the effects of an over valued pound, which had the further disadvantage that it stood in the way of an expansionist policy. But the UK was not only acted upon by the world economy: it could itself affect conditions in the rest of the world. The United Kingdom could still deploy market power such as no other country apart from the United States possessed. It constituted the largest market to which primary producing countries had free access and was the largest supplier of manufactures to these countries. It was also, after the United States, the major source of long-term capital for investment abroad. Its political influence was felt throughout the independent Dominions and, more directly, in the colonies. Thus, when devaluation was forced upon the UK, it was possible to rally, in mutual support, a large group of countries trading comparatively freely with one another, and settling accounts in sterling without restriction on payments within the sterling area.

By 1949 some of these circumstances had changed completely. Unemployment had virtually disappeared while world markets were expanding rapidly. Capital flows in the form of American aid and, to a lesser extent, American investment were nourishing recovery in Europe and helping to alleviate the dollar problem – the problem of balancing trade and payments between the United States and the rest of the world at current levels of income and employment and at current rates of exchange. This problem was rendered more difficult by the persistence of serious imbalance in the world economy. That imbalance was visible in the form of inconvertible currencies and in the difficulty of settling a surplus in 'soft' currencies against a deficit in 'hard' currencies. By 1949 this was perceived in the current account forecasts for 1953 (at the end of the Marshall Plan) of the deficits of the members of the OEEC, which amounted, on a realistic assessment, to some $3 billion per annum and were thought likely to persist for many years. The restoration of balance between the dollar and non-dollar worlds remained a preoccupation even when a major slump had given way to a major boom.

In 1967 the situation was again completely different. The international boom was still in full swing, but the United States had moved from chronic surplus to what seemed to be chronic deficit. Where in 1949 the underlying trend in the British balance of payments, interrupted by the recession in the United States, was strongly upwards, in 1967 it was gently downwards. But the development of greatest moment was the decline in Britain's position in the world economy. Her share of world trade in manufactures had fallen from about 25 per cent in 1949 to 12 per cent in 1967. Nowhere was the decline in her international position so evident as in the response overseas to the devaluation of sterling. When Britain left the gold standard in 1931, all the members of the Commonwealth and many countries outside it had followed her. Nearly without exception they pegged their exchange rates to sterling, and a solid currency bloc under the leadership of the United Kingdom was formed. In 1949 the devaluation of sterling had been accompanied by an equally extensive set of devaluations involving all the members of the Commonwealth except Pakistan and all the members of the OEEC except Austria, Greece and Turkey. But in 1967, the only countries of any consequence to move with Britain were New Zealand, Ceylon, Denmark, Iceland and Spain.

The three devaluations of sterling were superimposed upon different secular trends in the international terms of trade. There is a striking contrast between the rapid improvement in the terms of trade in the two years preceding the devaluation of 1931 and their deterioration in the four years leading up to the devaluation of 1949. The gradual improvement between 1964 and 1967 is in contrast to both of these experiences. The movement in the terms of trade *after* devaluation was itself affected by the change in the exchange rate but was also influenced, like the movement before devaluation, by conditions in world markets. These other factors had a powerful influence over the response to devaluation both externally, on the balance of payments, and internally, on the behaviour of wages and prices.

Even before devaluation, the depression of 1929–31 had moved the terms of trade a long way – approximately 20 per cent – in favour of the United Kingdom. Import prices fell by nearly 30 per cent in two years. After the gold standard was abandoned, most of Britain's principal suppliers of foodstuffs and raw materials pegged their currencies to sterling, which meant that sterling import prices were relatively little affected. Indeed, import prices continued to fall after devaluation, although more gradually than before, and the terms of trade moved still further in favour of the United Kingdom over the next two years. These changes contributed in no small way both to the absence of significant inflationary pressures in the early 1930s and to the recovery in economic activity that set in from 1932 onwards.

The 1949 devaluation took place against a very different background. Between 1945 and 1951 there was an adverse shift in the terms of trade of nearly 25 per cent and a rise in import prices of 125 per cent. To a great extent, these developments were concentrated in the period after the outbreak of the Korean War and were related only peripherally to devaluation. The shift in relative prices had begun earlier: in the three years after the war, the terms of trade had slid down by about 10 per cent, and although they improved slightly in 1949 they were still, by the standards of the previous two decades, highly unfavourable.[2] The

[2] Feinstein (1972, table 64).

further adverse shift of 8 per cent between 1949 and 1950 undoubtedly overstates the change in the terms of trade that was due to devaluation, since import prices were depressed in 1949 by the American recession and inflated in 1950 by the Korean boom. But the important point is that the devaluation in 1949 took place against an unpropitious background of deteriorating terms of trade and – once recovery began in the United States – rapidly rising import prices.

In 1967 conditions in international markets were again somewhat different. The terms of trade had been relatively steady in the early 1960s, and there was a favourable shift of roughly 6 per cent between 1964 and 1967. In the two years following devaluation, this improvement in the terms of trade was partially reversed by a swing of nearly 4 per cent against the United Kingdom. Thereafter, the terms of trade swung back to their pre-devaluation level. Thus the international situation in 1967 was relatively favourable, at least in comparison with 1949. The change in the terms of trade was a modest one. World markets were not thrown into confusion by a military confrontation as in 1950. The only serious threat to the success of devaluation from abroad came from the 'events of May' 1968 in Paris and the repercussions of these events on the attitude of workers in subsequent wage negotiations in the United Kingdom.

The domestic economic situation

The differences in the state of the domestic economy paralleled those in the international situation. In 1931 production was clearly far below full capacity levels, and unemployment was nearing a record high. In 1949, in contrast, there was little, if any, slack in the economy: unemployment, already extremely low, was continuing to fall. In 1967 the economy was running slightly below capacity because of a decline in exports and the deflationary measures taken in July 1966. But the margin of spare capacity was narrow, and the economy remained close to full employment. Corresponding to these differences, inflationary pressure was strong in 1949 and 1967 but completely absent in 1931, when prices, but not wages, had been falling intermittently for a decade.

Another important difference lay in the instruments of control at the command of the authorities. In 1931 the government had to rely on monetary and fiscal devices, on the use of foreign exchange reserves and on foreign borrowing when it wished to intervene in international markets. There were virtually no administrative controls that could be imposed on the balance of payments, and controls over capital movements were negligible. By 1949 all this had changed, and the government possessed a formidable array of weapons for limiting imports, encouraging exports and controlling capital flows. It had relied on these weapons for managing the nation's international accounts over the postwar period, a task facilitated from 1946 by the US and Canadian booms and, from 1947 onwards, by Marshall Aid, prospective or actual. The government's reluctance to devalue in 1949 was, in large measure, attributable to its faith in the power of administrative controls and its unwillingness to accept that market forces might reduce or even destroy their effectiveness.

In 1967 many of these controls had been laid aside, but other methods had been devised, such as the import surcharge and import deposits, to influence the current account. Controls over capital movements were more fully developed and articulated. The government was still far from accepting that changing the price of foreign exchange was preferable to direct controls as a way of operating on the balance of payments.

The fiscal situation also differed greatly from one devaluation to another. In 1931 the struggle was to balance the budget without reducing unemployment benefit. The idea of deliberately running a deficit in order to stimulate the economy would have been repudiated both by the outgoing Labour Government and by the National Government that succeeded it shortly before the gold standard was abandoned. In 1949 the budget was already in handsome surplus, although the surplus was not as large as had been envisaged earlier in the year. What was difficult for ministers to accept was that, even in circumstances of financial rectitude, further cuts in public expenditure might be required in order to keep the economy in balance. In 1967 the budgetary situation was equally complex. Ministers felt that they had already made a succession of cuts, culminating in the measures taken in July 1966, and that to make further cuts would merely increase unemployment. But the public sector borrowing requirement virtually doubled over the course of 1967, and its increase played a major role in the difficulties of the government in restoring external balance.

There were differences too in the monetary situation, although they were given little emphasis in contemporary assessments. In 1931 the money supply had been contracting slowly, but as prices were falling because of the world depression, the value of real money balances was higher than in 1929 – perhaps by as much as 8 per cent, judging from the figures for the London clearing banks. Early in 1932, when funds began to move into sterling at the lower rate of exchange, the money supply was allowed to expand at a remarkably rapid rate (6 per cent between February and June), and it was this expansion that laid the basis, through massive purchases of government bonds by the banks, for the conversion operation announcement at the end of June. The conversion of over one-quarter of the national debt from a 5 per cent to a 3.5 per cent basis within ten months of devaluation was the true starting point of the era of cheap money. The effects on interest rates were among the most important consequences of the abandonment of the gold standard.

In 1949 the money supply was swollen by wartime borrowing, and the government was attempting to prolong the low interest rates of the past two decades in conditions of scarce capital and rising prices. It relied for this purpose largely on administrative controls over capital formation and bank lending and kept short-term interest rates at around 0.5 per cent throughout the years 1946–51. Given the effects of these and other controls and their continued use well into the period following devaluation, there is no reason to suppose that there existed any simple relationship between exchange market pressure and the money supply before devaluation or between the balance of payments and the money supply afterwards.

The monetary situation was equally complicated in 1967. The money supply, as measured by sterling M3, had been growing at about 5 per cent per annum over the previous three years, compared with output growth at less than half that rate. In 1967 the growth in the money supply accelerated with little change in the growth of output. Thus devaluation took place at a time of monetary ease. This persisted in 1968 so far as the money supply was concerned, the growth in sterling M3 over the year being just under 8 per cent, but not in terms of the availability of bank credit, which contracted in the second half of the year. Long-term interest rates rose steeply at the end of the year, and in 1969 Eurodollar rates shot up in the spring, compelling a sympathetic but much smaller increase in British rates. These developments, and the severe fiscal regime introduced by the 1968 budget, help to account for the deceleration in the growth of the money supply to 2 per cent in 1969.

Nothing in all this suggests that monetary conditions exercised a decisive influence either in precipitating devaluation or in prolonging the exchange crisis that followed. The expansion in the money supply in 1967–68 certainly contributed to the difficulties of those years, and monetary conditions abroad might have proved disastrous in 1969 had the balance of payments not begun to swing so strongly into surplus. But the Budget was much the more important element in both periods.

Common elements in the three devaluations

In spite of these important differences in domestic and international conditions, the three devaluations had many features in common. The first point of similarity lies in the part played on each occasion by recession in the United States and its impact on world markets. In 1931 the recession was deep and prolonged, whereas in 1949 and 1967 it was shallow and transitory. But deep or shallow, the effect on sterling was decisive. On the two later occasions, but not in the 1930s, recovery in the United States greatly assisted the subsequent improvement in Britain's balance of payments.

On each occasion also, devaluation of sterling was a matter of international concern and diplomacy. In 1931 the sterling crisis was precipitated by events in central Europe and involved support from France and the United States. In 1949 there were negotiations with the United States and Canada for assistance in relieving the pressure on sterling, not in the form of a loan but as part of a 'general settlement'. However, the Americans took a somewhat sceptical and unenthusiastic view of the United Kingdom's attempts to maintain the existing parity, regarding devaluation of sterling as a way of limiting the amount of Marshall Aid required and as a step towards a world of convertible currencies and free, multilateral trade. By 1967 the International Monetary Fund had come on the scene, a system of swaps between central banks had grown up, and international support operations in the interest of a system of fixed parities had been developed. The pound sterling occupied a strategic position, particularly in relation to the dollar, since the United States was also in chronic deficit. Failure to avoid devaluation undermined the stability of the dollar, which took sterling's place as the weakest of the major currencies, and pulled the plug on the Bretton Woods system of fixed parities.

In seeking to maintain the parity, the United Kingdom had at its disposal very limited reserves of gold and foreign exchange. Its reserves were quite inadequate in times of crisis, even when supplemented by foreign borrowing. Sometimes the resources obtained in this manner proved sufficient for the crisis to be surmounted, as in 1961, but in 1931 and 1967 this was not the case. While it is rare for explicit conditions to be attached to such borrowing, there are parallels between the kind of fiscal action that Morgans would have liked to see in 1931 and that were promised in the Letter of Intent to the IMF in 1967.

When we turn from the international aspects to the attitude of successive governments to the option of devaluation, the first and most obvious lesson of all three episodes is the reluctance of governments to devalue at all. Their prestige becomes involved, then their credit, and the economic aspects that may in the end prove decisive are submerged. In 1931 and again in 1967 there was little if any room for deliberate choice in the final crisis; 1949 differed in that a decision to devalue was made well in advance, but again largely in the belief that there was little choice.

The fact is that decisions of this kind are never likely to be the outcome of a careful analysis of the facts (including facts that cannot possibly be known until after the event). Those who take them are not necessarily moved wholly or largely by economic considerations. The peculiar interest of devaluation as a case study in government decision-taking is precisely that it reveals so clearly the nakedness in the face of uncertainty of ministers who of necessity have only an imperfect understanding of the economics of trade and payments.

But perhaps 'decisions' is too strong a word. There is no record of a

British government deliberately deciding to devalue the pound as an act of policy in the absence of strong – perhaps irresistible – pressure from the market. The nearest approach to such a decision would be the pegging of the pound at $4.03 to the pound in September 1939; and there is no evidence that this was a decision submitted for Cabinet approval or even for approval by the Prime Minister. In 1931 the pound simply was allowed to float when reserves were insufficient to continue support for the parity. In 1949 it was the rundown in reserves that finally induced Cripps to acquiesce. In 1967 devaluation again virtually was forced on a reluctant Chancellor. What is interesting, therefore, is not so much the decision to devalue as the earlier, more deliberate, decisions, in 1930–31, in the spring of 1949 and in 1964–67, *not* to devalue.

Once the issue of devaluation is raised publicly, it becomes increasingly difficult to resist the pressures that caused the possibility to be considered in the first place. The incentive for speculators to gamble on devaluation often proves irresistible, and only the most dramatic and decisive steps at an early stage will suffice to stem the run on the currency. The sort of decisive action that is required can in most instances be taken only by a relatively small group of ministers in a position of authority.

The same is true of the decision not to take such steps but to devalue instead. The actual decision is often made by a small group of individuals who may neither seek nor accept official advice, who may have firm convictions in which narrowly economic considerations play little part, and who are unlikely to engage in a careful analysis of the measures that would either provide a convincing alternative to devaluation or be an indispensable accompaniment to it.

On all three occasion discussed in this volume, what governments found hardest to swallow was the bitter pill of expenditure cuts. Labour governments regarded the kind of cuts that might have put a stop to the run on the pound as a flouting of the deepest convictions of the Party. In 1931 the cuts on which the Labour Cabinet could not agree might not have prevented devaluation, but they almost certainly would have delayed it. In 1949 the cuts that officials thought indispensable either were not accepted or, if accepted, were not fully implemented; but at that time the underlying movement in the balance of payments – as distinct from the dollar balance – was still strongly upwards. In 1964–67 the cuts came too late and failed to stem the rising trend; the biggest cuts, in 1966, were followed by the steepest rise of the deficit. On all three occasions additional expenditure cuts had to be made *after* devaluation, and on all three occasions there is reason to doubt whether things would have gone better in the long run if the cuts had been so much larger that devaluation had been delayed or avoided altogether.

Finally, it is clear that ministers have great difficulty in accepting market verdicts on their performance. They overestimate their ability to employ political power to suppress or override market forces and too readily dismiss unwelcome trends in financial markets as the work of speculators. While it is not true that governments are necessarily worse judges of appropriate changes in exchange rates than are market operators, they are liable to take too firm a position in face of uncertainties and to be more limited in the resources on which they can draw than financial markets reflecting international opinion. While market opinion is often divided and always conscious of the determination with which governments can intervene to enforce their views, short of draconian controls it is the market that in the end has the last word.

The development of thought on devaluation

Before we address ourselves directly to the effects of devaluation, let us review briefly how thinking about exchange rates has changed over the past 50 years. In the 1920s, arguments about exchange rates ran mainly in terms of what stable rate was appropriate, and purchasing power parity was the criterion to which it became customary to turn in order to calculate the appropriate rate. When the effects of exchange rate changes were discussed, these discussions were framed, often implicitly, in terms of price elasticities of import demand at home and abroad. But price indices, however constructed, were a very imperfect guide to a nation's competitive position, and changes in the competitiveness of home and foreign goods were but one of many influences on the balance of payments. At no time was the trade balance the dominant component in Britain's overall balance of payments. In times of crisis, the factor of greatest importance was the state of confidence and sentiment, or the state of expectations. It was these expectations that dominated the capital account of the balance of payments. An expanding volume of speculative capital, which moved from one financial centre to another largely on the basis of such expectations, was an increasing preoccupation of the late 1920s and the 1930s. It was the movement of funds in reaction to the continued erosion of confidence that precipitated devaluation in 1931.

Thus, even 50 years ago there was already a question how far official views as to the appropriate exchange rate could be made to prevail over market sentiment. The reserves held by any one central bank were small – in the case of the Bank of England, very small – in relation to the funds in private hands that might move once confidence was disturbed.

All this had special relevance to sterling because of its role as an international currency. The importance of London as a financial centre meant that there was normally a large outstanding volume of commercial credit denominated in sterling that was sensitive to prospective changes in the exchange rate. Many countries – including those that came to be included in the sterling area after 1931 – held their reserves in sterling but not all of them were committed to holding reserves exclusively in this form. Any large–scale movement out of sterling by foreign commercial banks or governments could endanger the parity or, if devaluation had already become inevitable, enforce a larger depreciation than the authorities would have contemplated.

These considerations presumably were dominant factors in the move back towards a fixed rate of exchange during the 1930s. From 1932 onwards until the dollar rate was pegged at $4.03 to the pound in September 1939, fluctuations in the rate of exchange were held within a narrower range in successive years. The authorities were unwilling to delegate to the market the responsibility for exchange rate determination. Later, when the Bretton Woods Agreement was under negotiation, it was taken for granted that the international monetary system should be based on fixed rates. Recollections of the role of hot money in the 1930s were reflected in the provision for indefinite control over capital movements.

By the time of the 1949 devaluation, the illusion had developed that exchange control could prevent destabilizing movements of funds and that a country's international accounts could be balanced by administrative action (e.g., through import control) without disturbing the rate of exchange. But the limitations of exchange control had already been demonstrated in the convertibility crisis of 1947, when leads and lags in international credit were first detected. In 1949 it was abundantly clear that even comprehensive exchange control was powerless to prevent large shifts of funds out of sterling. These shifts were a decisive factor in the devaluation that followed. But, as in 1931, there was also a need to improve Britain's competitive position, in hard currency markets at least.

The devaluation of 1949 is interesting as the first occasion on which the 'absorption approach' to the balance of payments was employed in an analysis of the measures required to make the devaluation effective. The government's economic adviser, Robert Hall, calculated the amount of purchasing power that should be withdrawn from the economy in order to restore the pressure of demand intended in the 1949 Budget (and so eliminate the additional and unintended pressure that made itself felt between April and September). To this he added a further £100 million to allow for the improvement required in the balance of payments. Similar calculations were made in 1967 when the government announced its intention to reduce absorption by £500 million in order to strengthen the balance of payments.

Calculations of this kind help to explain why each successive devaluation was coupled with a bitter struggle over cuts in public expenditure. On each occasion there was a school of thought that saw a reduction in final demand accomplished through expenditure cuts as indispensable for avoiding devaluation. Curiously enough, this was equally true whether the economy was fully employed, as in 1949, or suffering from heavy unemployment, as in 1931.

In 1931 it would have been difficult to argue that raising taxes and cutting government spending was necessary to reduce levels of employment and capacity utilization further in order to defend the exchange rate. In that instance the argument for balancing the budget clearly rested on market sentiment: demonstrations of the government's resoluteness and orthodoxy were needed to reassure the market of the authorities' commitment to the existing parity.

In 1949 the situation was very different. Inflationary pressure had been mounting throughout the year and had contributed to the weakening in the balance of payments. At the official level both the proponents and the opponents of devaluation agreed that some cuts in public expenditure were required. It was only ministers who thought otherwise; their unwillingness to contemplate cuts of any kind confirmed the doubts of officials who saw no value in devaluation unaccompanied by cuts. When measures to reduce public expenditure finally were introduced, they had the hallmark of afterthoughts and fell short in their impact of the total accepted by the Cabinet as the basis for action.

In 1967 events followed a similar course. There was a division of opinion at the official level between those who pressed for devaluation and those who thought that the deflationary measures that would have to accompany devaluation might well dispense with any need for it. As in 1949, the ministers who resisted devaluation were self-righteous about the 'everlasting cuts' they had already made, and neither they nor their opponents in the Cabinet showed any interest in 'accompanying measures' until the very last minute. Not only did public expenditure rise extremely rapidly in 1967, but the cuts made at the time of devaluation did not add up to the required reduction in final demand and had to be supplemented, after devaluation, by much larger reductions than anyone had contemplated before devaluation.

The interconnection between fiscal policy, the balance of payments and the exchange rate may be evident enough. But ministers untrained in economics – and some like Hugh Dalton who were professional economists – did not readily make the connection. It was all too easy to debate the pros and cons of devaluation without explicit recognition that the true alternatives under debate were packages of measures of which a change in the rate of exchange was only a part.

The effectiveness of devaluation

We come finally to the nub of the matter. Does devaluation work? What light do the three episodes throw on how it works and whether it had any useful effects on the balance of payments?

There is little evidence in any of these three episodes that the immediate gain in competitiveness – either in world markets or, more important, in non-sterling markets – was quickly extinguished by an inflation of wages and prices. Ironically enough, thc danger that devaluation would do no more than feed inflation was most widely feared in 1931, when recollections of the currency collapses of the 1920s were still vivid but the risks of inflation were least. As it happened, sterling import prices continued to fall after devaluation so that the real wages of the employed continued to rise. Money wages were held down by the large and growing volume of unemployment and began to increase only after 1934. Contrary to the fears of many contemporaries, there was therefore no threat to the effectivenesss of the devaluation from the side of wage rates. In 1949 it was the Bank of England that insisted that one devaluation was likely to produce another and was sceptical that devaluation was capable of curing sterling's fundamental weakness. However, Ernest Bevin and Stafford Cripps obtained assurances from the TUC that kept wages steady for the critical first year after devaluation. By 1967, when the fears of 1931 would have been more appropriate, the danger that a reduction in the external value of the pound would serve merely to produce a reduction in its internal value received comparatively little attention. What has been described as 'real wage resistance' was already in evidence, and it was at least conceivable that, as prices responded to devaluation, an inflation of wages would ensue. In any case, there was no perceptible acceleration in the movement of wage rates after devaluation: in the year before devaluation and in each of the two years succeeding it, the increase in wage rates lay between 5 and 6 per cent. There was thus in fact no immediate dilution of the effects of devaluation on any of the three occasions studied because of the response of money wage rates.

This preoccupation with relative prices and costs reflects the concern typically vested in trends in the current account. But what emerges from earlier chapters is that the capital account is far more volatile and that, even when the trend in the current account provides the motive force, it is short-term capital flows that bring pressure on the exchange rate. These flows are most powerful when, for good or bad reasons, devaluation is anticipated. They operate much less powerfully after devaluation unless a fresh devaluation is expected. In 1931 it took some months and a heavy fall in the exchange rate before funds began to flow back into sterling; in 1949 the interval was shorter because the US economy had resumed its expansion in the final quarter of the year; but in 1967 even a resumption of growth in world markets was insufficient to restore strength to sterling. The initial deterioration in the trade balance – called for the first time the 'J curve', although well-known previously in less graphic terms – was accompanied by capital outflows that dwarfed even those that had taken place before devaluation, and capital movements were not reversed until well after the current account had started to improve. In 1967–69 it was not the impact of devaluation on wages but destabilizing capital flows that threatened to bring on a second devaluation.

Let us return to the question whether devaluation did any good. There would be general agreement that going off the gold standard in 1931 helped to lay the basis for economic recovery in Britain. Perhaps the most important contribution came not from any change in the external accounts but from the greater freedom that a floating rate lent the monetary authorities: a floating rate, be it observed, that was combined with stable money wages. The fall in interest rates and the fillip this gave to investment would have been unlikely if not impossible at the old parity. It is arguable that balancing the budget (or seeking to do so) was a further prerequisite, and hence that recovery of the private sector rested on a contraction in public spending; but these hypotheses remain to be tested.

In 1949 the effects of devaluation are less clear-cut. They certainly did not include an easing of monetary policy and an expansionary thrust on the economy. Nor is it clear that there was any substantial improvement in the balance of payments. The contribution of the 1949 devaluation was of a different kind, as had been foreseen by those who pressed for it first. It consisted of an easing of the dollar shortage by making hard currency markets more attractive and hard currency supplies more expensive. It was a first indispensable step on the road back to convertibility.

Devaluation in 1967 is even more difficult to assess. It was not an isolated event that can be disentangled from what went before and what came after. Once the rate for sterling had fallen, other rates also became vulnerable: recognition of this fact had been a source of support for sterling before 1967 and gave strength to speculative attacks on other currencies in 1968 and later years. Thus we must take account not only of the impact on the British economy but also of the blow that was struck at the whole system of fixed exchange rates. An earlier, deliberate and smaller devaluation might have avoided some of these repercussions.

So far as the British economy is concerned, devaluation in 1967 did, to all appearances, extinguish the external deficit and replace it by a surplus. The swing in the balance of payments paralleled a corresponding swing in the government budget, throwing into relief the significance of the strong measures taken in the 1968 Budget. For three years following devaluation, unemployment remained steady at 2.25–2.5 per cent, so the whole of the change in the balance of payments represented expenditure-switching unsupported by any reduction in the pressure of demand.

But devaluation in 1967 worked slowly and doubtfully compared with earlier experience. It left behind growing doubts as to the power of exchange rate changes to eliminate balance of payments deficits. The paradoxical conclusion was drawn that, if exchange rate changes had little effect, it was likely that the benefits of stable rates had been exaggerated. It might be better to let the rate float. The stage was set for a world of floating exchange rates, and the play was to commence sooner than most expected.

References

Acheson, Dean (1970), *Present at the Creation*, Hamish Hamilton, London.

Aldcroft, Derek H. (1967), 'Economic Growth in Britain in the Inter-war Years: A Reassessment', *Economic History Review*, 311–26.

—— (1970), *The Inter-war Economy: Britain 1919–1939*, Columbia University Press, New York.

Alexander, Sidney (1952), 'Effects of a Devaluation on a Trade Balance', *IMF Staff Papers*, 263–78.

Aliber, Robert Z. (1962), 'Speculation in the Foreign Exchanges: The European Experience', *Yale Economic Essays*, 171–245.

Allen, G.C. (1975), 'Advice from Economists – Forty-Five Years Ago', *Three Banks Review*, 35–50.

Amery, L.S. (1955), *My Political Life*, Hutchinson, London.

Argy, Victor and Joanne Salop (1979), 'Price and Output Effects of Monetary and Fiscal Policy Under Flexible Exchange Rates', *IMF Staff Papers*, 224–55.

Artis, M.J. (1978), 'Monetary Policy II', in F. Blackaby (ed.), *British Economic Policy 1960–74*, Cambridge University Press, Cambridge, 258–302.

Artus, J.R. (1975), 'The 1967 Devaluation of the Pound Sterling', *IMF Staff Papers*, 595–640.

Aukrust, O. (1977), 'Inflation in the Open Economy: A Norwegian Model', in L.B. Krause and W.S. Salant (eds), *Worldwide Inflation*, Brookings Institution, Washington, D.C.

Bakke, E. Wight (1935), *Insurance or Dole? The Adjustment of Unemployment Insurance to Economic and Social Facts in Great Britain*, Yale University Press, New Haven, Connecticut.

Baldwin, Robert E. (1958), 'The Commodity Composition of Trade: Selected Industrial Countries, 1900–1954', *Review of Economics and Statistics*, supplement, 50–71.

Ball, R.J., T. Burns and G. Miller (1975), 'Preliminary Simulations with the London Business School Macro-economic Model', in G.A. Renton (ed.), *Modelling the Economy*, Heinemann, London, 181–212.

——, T. Burns and J.S.E. Laury (1977), 'The Role of Exchange Rate Changes in Balance of Payments Adjustment', *Economic Journal*, 1–29.

Balogh, T. (1947), *Studies in Financial Organization*, National Institute of Economic and Social Research, Cambridge.

Bank for International Settlements (1931), *First Annual Report*, BIS, Basle.

—— (1953), *The Sterling Area*, BIS, Basle.

Bank of England (1968), 'The Exchange Equalisation Account: Its Origins and Development', *Bank of England Quarterly Bulletin*, 377–390.

Bassett, R. (1958), *Nineteen Thirty-One: Political Crisis*, Macmillan, London.

Bell, Philip W. (1956), *The Sterling Area in the Postwar World*, Clarendon Press, Oxford.

Benjamin, Daniel and Levis Kochin (1979), 'Searching for an Explanation of Unemployment in Interwar Britain', *Journal of Political Economy*, 441–78.

Bennett, Edward W. (1962), *Germany and the Diplomacy of the Financial Crisis, 1931*, Harvard University Press, Cambridge, Massachusetts.

Bilson, John F.O. (1978), 'A Dynamic Model of Devaluation', *Canadian Journal of Economics*, 194–209.

Blackaby, F. (1978), 'Narrative, 1960–74', in F. Blackaby (ed.), *British Economic Policy 1960–74*, Cambridge University Press, Cambridge, 11–76.

Bloomfield, Arthur I. (1959), *Monetary Policy Under the International Gold Standard, 1880–1914*, Federal Reserve Bank of New York, New York.

—— (1963), 'Short-Term Capital Movements Under the Pre–1914 Gold Standard', *Princeton Studies in International Finance*, no. 11.

Boreham, A.J. (1978), 'A Statistician's View', in Michael Posner (ed.), *Demand Management*, Heinemann, London, 139–50.

Bouvier, Jean (1981), 'The French Banks, Inflation and the Economic Crisis, 1919–1939', prepared for the Banco di Roma Conference on Banks and Industry in the Interwar Period, Cambridge, Massachusetts.

Boyce, R.W.D. (1982), 'Montagu Norman and the Financial Crisis', prepared for the SSRC Conference on the 1931 Financial Crisis and its Aftermath, Clare College, Cambridge, England.

Boyer, Russell (1977), 'Devaluation and Portfolio Balance', *American Economic Review*, 54–63.

Brandon, H. (1966), *In the Red*, André Deutsch, London.

Brittan, Samuel (1964), *The Treasury under the Tories*, Pelican Books, Harmondsworth; revised and re-issued as (1971), *Steering the Economy*.

Brown, A.J. (1938), 'The Liquidity Preference Schedules of the London Clearing Banks', *Oxford Economic Papers*, 49–82.

Brown, W.A. (1940), *The International Gold Standard Reinterpreted 1914–1934*, National Bureau of Economic Research, New York.

Bruce Gardyne, J. and Lawson, N. (1976), *The Power Game*, Macmillan, London.

Burns, Arthur F. and Wesley C. Mitchell (1946), *Measuring Business Cycles*, National Bureau of Economic Research, New York.

Cagan, Phillip (1956), 'The Monetary Dynamics of Hyperinflation', in Milton Friedman (ed.), *Studies in the Quantity Theory of Money*, University of Chicago Press, Chicago.

Cairncross, A.K. (1953), *Home and Foreign Investment 1870–1913,* Cambridge University Press, Cambridge.

—— (1973), *Control of Long-Term International Capital Movements*, Brookings Institution, Washington, DC.

—— (1982), 'The Rate of Exchange as an Instrument of Policy', Brooman Memorial Lecture Delivered to the Open University.

Calmfors, Lars (1982), 'Employment Policies, Wage Formation, and Trade Union Behavior in a Small Open Economy', *Scandinavian Journal of Economics*, 345–73.

Capie, Forrest (1980), 'The Pressure for Tariff Protection in Britain, 1917–31', *Journal of European Economic History*, 431–48.

Casas, F.R. (1975), 'Efficient Macroeconomic Stabilization Policies Under Floating Exchange Rates', *International Economic Review*, 682–98.

Cassel, Gustav (1920), *Memorandum on the World's Monetary Problems*, International Financial Conference, Brussels.

—— (1936), *The Downfall of the Gold Standard*, Oxford University Press, London.

Chang, T.C. (1951), *Cyclical Movements in the Balance of Payments*, Cambridge University Press, Cambridge.

Cheng, H.S. (1959), 'Statistical Estimates of Elasticities and Propensities in International Trade: A Survey of Published Studies', *IMF Staff Papers*, 107–58.

Clark, Colin (1949), 'The Value of the Pound', *Economic Journal*, 198–207.

Clarke, Sir R.W.B. (1982), *Anglo-American Collaboration in War and Peace*, Oxford University Press, Oxford.

Clarke, S.V.O. (1967), *Central Bank Cooperation, 1924–1931*, Federal Reserve Bank ofNew York, New York.

Clauson, G.M. (1939), 'The Colonial Empire', no. 4 in Institute of Bankers, *Lectures on the Sterling Area*.

Clay, H. (1957), *Lord Norman*, Macmillan, London.

Committee on Currency and Foreign Exchanges After the War (1918), *First Interim Report*, Cd 9182, HMSO, London,

Committee on the Currency and Bank of England Note Issues (1925), *Report*, Cmd 2393, HMSO, London.

Committee on Finance and Industry (1931), *Report*, Cmd 3897, HMSO, London.

Committee on National Expenditure (1931), *Report*, Cmd 3920, HMSO, London.

Condliffe, J.B. (1940), *The Reconstruction of World Trade*, W.W. Norton, New York.

Cooper, Richard (1968), 'The Balance of Payments', in Richard E. Caves (ed.) *Britain's Economic Prospects*, Brookings Institution and George Allen & Unwin, Washington DC and London.

—— (1971), 'Currency Devaluation in Developing Countries', *Princeton Essays in International Finance*, no. 86.

Cottrell, P.L. (1975), *British Overseas Investment in the 19th Century*, Macmillan, London.

Courakis, A.S. (1981), 'Aspects of Bank Behavior in the United Kingdom of the Interwar Years', prepared for the Banco di Roma Conference on Banks and Industry in the Inter-War Period, Cambridge, Massachusetts.

Crosland, Susan (1982), *Tony Crosland*, Jonathan Cape, London.

Crossman, Richard (1975), *The Diaries of a Cabinet Minister* (ed. Janet Morgan), Hamish Hamilton and Jonathan Cape, London.

Dacey, W. Manning (1958), *The British Banking Mechanism*, Hutchinson, London.

Dalton, Hugh (1962), *High Tide and After*, Frederick Muller, London.

—— (1983), *Diaries*, (ed. J.A.R. Pimlott), Jonathan Cape, London.

Dalton, R.W. (1931), *Economic and Trade Conditions in Australia to December 1930*, HMSO, London.

Davis, W (1968), *Three Years Hard Labour: The Road to Devaluation*, André Deutsch, London.

Dennis, G.E.J. (1977), 'The Devaluation of Sterling in 1967', in P. Maunder (ed.), *Case Studies in International Economics,* Heinemann (for the Economics Association), London.

Devons, Ely (1970), 'Planning by Economic Survey', in *Planning and Economic Management*, Manchester University Press, Manchester.

Dimsdale, N.H. (1981), 'British Monetary Policy and the Exchange Rate', in W.A. Eltis and P.J.N. Sinclair (eds), *The Money Supply and the Exchange Rate*, Clarendon Press, Oxford, 306–49.

Donoughue, B. and G.W. Jones (1973), *Herbert Morrison: Portrait of a Politician*, Weidenfeld and Nicholson, London.

Dornbusch, Rudiger (1973) 'Devaluation, Money and Nontraded Goods', *American Economic Review*, 871–80.

—— (1974), 'Real and Monetary Aspects of the Effects of Exchange Rate Changes', in R.Z. Aliber (ed.), *National Monetary Policies and the International Financial System*, University of Chicago Press, Chicago.

Dow, J.C.R. (1964), *The Management of the British Economy, 1945–60*, Cambridge University Press, Cambridge.

Dowie, J. (1968), 'Growth in the Interwar Period: Some More Arithmetic', *Economic History Review*, 93–112.

—— (1975), '1919–20 is in Need of Attention', *Economic History Review*, 429–50.

Drummond, Ian M. (1974), *Imperial Economic Policy 1917–1939*, Allen and Unwin, London.

Eatwell, Roger (1979), *The 1945–51 Labour Government*, Batsford, London.

Economic Commission for Europe (1949), *Economic Survey of Europe in 1949*, United Nations, New York.

—— (1950), *Economic Survey of Europe in 1950*, United Nations, New York.

Economic Cooperation Administration (1951), *The Sterling Area: An American Analysis*, ECA, London.

Eichengreen, Barry J. (1979), 'Tariffs and Flexible Exchange Rates: The Case of the British General Tariff of 1932', PhD dissertation, Yale University.

—— (1981a), 'Sterling and the Tariff, 1929–32', *Princeton Studies in International Finance*, no. 48.

—— (1981b), 'A Dynamic Model of Tariffs, Output and Employment under Flexible Exchange Rates', *Journal of International Economics*, 341–59.

—— (1982), 'Did Speculation Destabilize the French Franc in the 1920s?' *Explorations in Economic History*, 70–99.

—— (1983a), 'Effective Protection and Exchange Rate Determination', *Journal of International Money and Finance*, 1–15.

—— (1983b), 'Protection, Real Wage Resistance and Employment' (International Finance Discussion Paper no. 150, Board of Governors, Federal Reserve System, Washington, DC), *Weltwirtschaftliches Archiv*.

Einzig, Paul (1931), *International Gold Movements*, Macmillan, London.

—— (1932), *Montagu Norman: A Study in Financial Statesmanship*, Macmillan, London.

—— (1935), *World Finance Since 1914*, Kegan Paul, Trench, Trubner, London.

—— (1937), *The Theory of Forward Exchange*, Macmillan, London.

Eltis, W.A. and P.J.N. Sinclair (eds) (1981), *The Money Supply and the Exchange Rate*, Clarendon Press, Oxford.
Ethier, Wilfred (1976), 'Exchange Depreciation in the Adjustment Process', *Economic Record*, 443–61.
Feinstein, Charles (1972), *National Income, Expenditure and Output of the United Kingdom, 1855–1965*, Cambridge University Press, Cambridge.
Feis, Herbert (1930), *Europe: The World's Banker, 1870–1914*, Yale University Press, New Haven, Connecticut.
Financial Secretary to the Treasury (1932), *Return Relating to the National Debt*, HMSO, London.
Flanders, M. June (1963), 'The Effects of Devaluation on Exports: A Case Study, United Kingdom 1949–1954', *Bulletin of the Oxford Institute of Economics and Statistics*, 165–198.
Ford, A.G. (1962), *The Gold Standard, 1880–1914: Britain and Argentina*, Clarendon Press, Oxford.
Francis, E.V. (1939), *Britain's Economic Strategy*, Jonathan Cape, London.
Frenkel, Jacob A. (1978), 'Purchasing Power Parity: Doctrinal Perspective and Evidence from the 1920s', *Journal of International Economics*, 169–91.
—— and Harry G. Johnson (1976), *The Monetary Approach to the Balance of Payments*, George Allen and Unwin, Boston.
—— and C. Rodriguez (1975), 'Portfolio Equilibrium and the Balance of Payments: A Monetary Approach', *American Economic Review*, 674–88.
Friedman, Milton and Anna Schwartz (1963), *A Monetary History of the United States, 1867–1960*, Princeton University Press, Princeton, New Jersey.
Friedman, Phillip (1974), *The Impact of Trade Destruction on National Incomes*, University of Florida Press, Gainesville.
Goldstein, M. (1974), 'The Effect of Exchange Rate Changes on Wages and Prices in the United Kingdom: An Empirical Study', *IMF Staff Papers*, 694–739.
Graham, Andrew and Wilfred Beckerman (1972), 'Introduction: Economic Performance and the Foreign Balance', in W. Beckerman (ed.), *The Labour Government's Economic Record, 1964–70*, Duckworth, London.
Haberler, Gottfried (1949), 'The Market for Foreign Exchange and the Stability of the Balance of Payments: A Theoretical Analysis', *Kyklos*, 193–218.
Hall, N.F. (1935), *The Exchange Equalisation Account*, Macmillan, London.
Hancock, K.J. (1962), 'The Reduction of Unemployment as a Problem of Public Policy, 1920–29', *Economic History Review*, 328–43.
Hancock, W.K. and M.M. Gowing (1949), *British War Economy*, HMSO, London.
Harberger, Arnold (1950), 'Currency Depreciation, Income, and the Balance of Trade', *Journal of Political Economy*, 47–60.
Harris, S.E. (1931), *Monetary Problems of the British Empire*, Macmillan, New York.
—— (1936), *Exchange Depreciation*, Harvard University Press, Cambridge, Massachusetts.
Harrod, Roy F. (1952), 'The Pound Sterling', *Princeton Essays in International Finance*, no. 13.
—— (1963), *The British Economy*, McGraw-Hill, Maidenhead.
Hatry, Clarence (1938), *The Hatry Case – Eight Current Misperceptions*, privately printed, London.

Hawtrey, R.G. (1925), 'Public Expenditure and the Demand for Labour', *Economica*, 38–48.
—— (1933), 'Public Expenditure and Trade Depression', *Journal of the Royal Statistical Society*, 438–77.
—— (1938), *A Century of Bank Rate*, Longmans, Green, London.
—— (1954), *Towards the Rescue of Sterling*, Longmans, Green, London.
Hemming, M.F.W., C.M. Miles and G.F. Ray (1959), 'A Statistical Summary of the Extent of Import Control in the United Kingdom Since the War', *Review of Economic Studies*, 75–109.
Hennessy, P. and M. Brown (1980a), 'Deciphering the "Rose" Code', *The Times* (3 January).
—— (1980b), 'Cripps and the Search for a Whiter Loaf', *The Times* (4 January).
—— (1980c), '19-month Progress to Devaluation', *The Times* (8 January).
Higham, D.S. (1980), 'The Effects of Exchange Rate Changes on the UK Balance of Payments, with Special Reference to the Devaluation of 1967', D. Phil. thesis, University of Oxford.
Hodson, H.V. (1938), *Slump and Recovery 1929–37*, Royal Institute, London.
Horne, Jocelyn (1979), 'The Effect of Devaluation on the Balance of Payments and the Labour Market: United Kingdom, 1967', *Economica*, 11–26.
Howson, Susan (1974), 'The Origins of Dear Money, 1919–1920', *Economic History Review*, 88–107.
—— (1975), *Domestic Monetary Management in Britain, 1919–1938*, Cambridge University Press, New York.
—— (1976), 'The Managed Floating Pound 1932–1939', *The Banker*, 249–55.
—— (1980a), 'The Management of Sterling 1932–1939', *Journal of Economic History*, 53–60.
—— (1980b), 'Sterling's Managed Float: The Operations of the Exchange Equalisation Account', *Princeton Studies in International Finance*, no. 46.
—— and Donald Winch (1977), *The Economic Advisory Council, 1930–1939*, Cambridge University Press, New York.
Hume, L.J. (1970), 'The Gold Standard and Deflation', in S. Pollard (ed.), *The Gold Standard and Employment Policies between the Wars*, Methuen, London.
Hurst, W. (1932), 'Holland, Switzerland and Belgium and the English Gold Crisis of 1931', *Journal of Political Economy*, 638–60.
Imlah, A.J. (1958), *Economic Elements in the Pax Britannica*, Harvard University Press, Cambridge, Massachusetts.
International Monetary Fund (1972), *IMF Balance of Payments Yearbook*, vol. 23, IMF, Washington, DC.
—— (1977), *The Monetary Approach to the Balance of Payments*, IMF, Washington, DC.
—— (1979), *Direction of Trade Yearbook*, IMF, Washington, DC.
Jack, D.T. (1927), *The Restoration of European Currencies*, P.S. King and Sons, London.
Jay, D. (1980) *Change and Fortune*, Hutchinson, London.
Jenks, L.H. (1927), *The Migration of British Capital to 1875*, Knopf, New York.
Jewkes, J. (1948), *Ordeal by Planning*, Macmillan, London.
Johnson, Harry G. (1958), 'Towards a General Theory of the Balance of Payments', in H.G. Johnson, *International Trade and Economic Growth*,

Harvard University Press, Cambridge, Massachusetts, 153–68.
—— (1972), *Further Essays in Monetary Economics*, Allen & Unwin, London.
—— (1977), 'The Monetary Approach to the Balance of Payments: A Nontechnical Guide', *Journal of International Economics*, 231–50.
Johnson, P.B. (1968), *Land Fit For Heroes: The Planning of British Reconstruction 1916–1919*, University of Chicago Press, Chicago.
Jones, J.H. (ed.) (1935), *Britain in Depression*, Pitman and Sons, London.
Kahn, Alfred E. (1946), *Great Britain in the World Economy*, Columbia University Press, New York.
Kahn, Richard (forthcoming), *The Making of Keynes' General Theory*, Banca Commerciale Italiana, Rome.
Kaliski, S.F. (1961), 'Some Recent Estimates of "The" Elasticity of Demand for British Exports: An Appraisal and Reconciliation', *Manchester School*, 23–42.
Keleher, Robert (1975), 'Urban Unemployment and Real Wages: A Comparative Study: The United Kingdom and United States 1925–1938', PhD dissertation, Indiana University.
Kellner, Peter and Christopher Hitchens (1976), *Callaghan: the Road to Number Ten,* Cassell, London.
Kemp, M. (1970), 'The Balance of Payments and the Terms of Trade in Relation to Financial Controls', *Review of Economic Studies*, 25–31.
Kennan, George F. (1967), *Memoirs 1925–1950*, Hutchinson, London.
Keynes, J.M. (1930), *A Treatise on Money*, 1st edn, Macmillan, London; Vols V and VI of *The Collected Writings of John Maynard Keynes*, Macmillan and St Martin's Press for the Royal Economic Society, London.
—— (1931), *Essays in Persuasion*, 1st edn, Macmillan, London; Volume IX of *The Collected Writings of John Maynard Keynes*, Macmillan and Cambridge University Press for the Royal Economic Society, London.
—— (1932), 'Reflections on the Sterling Exchange', *Lloyds Bank Limited Monthly Review*, 3, 148–9.
—— (1936), *The General Theory of Employment, Interest and Money*, 1st edn, Macmillan, London; Volume VII of *The Collected Writings of John Maynard Keynes*, Macmillan and St Martin's Press for the Royal Economic Society, London.
—— (1971), *Activities 1914–1919: The Treasury and Versailles*, Volume XVI of *The Collected Writings of John Maynard Keynes*, Macmillan and St. Martin's Press for the Royal Economic Society, London.
—— (1977), *Activities 1920–22: Treaty Revision and Reconstruction*, Volume XVII of *The Collected Writings of John Maynard Keynes*, Macmillan and Cambridge University Press for the Royal Economic Society, Cambridge.
—— (1979), *Activities 1944–46: The Transition to Peace,* Volume XXIV of *The Collected Writings of John Maynard Keynes*, Macmillan and Cambridge University Press, London.
—— (1981), *Activities 1929–31: Rethinking Employment and Unemployment Policies*, Volume XX of *The Collected Writings of John Maynard Keynes*, Macmillan and Cambridge University Press, London.
—— (1982), *Activities 1931–39: World Crises and Policies in Britain and America*, Volume XXI of *The Collected Writings of John Maynard Keynes*, Macmillan and Cambridge University Press for the Royal Economic Society, London.

—— and Hubert Henderson (1929), *Can Lloyd George Do It?* The Nation and Athenaeum, London.

Kindleberger, C.P. (1937), *International Short-Term Capital Movements*, Columbia University Press, New York.

—— (1973), *The World in Depression, 1929–1939*, University of California Press, Berkeley, California.

Kindersley, Sir Robert (1932), 'British Foreign Investments in 1930', *Economic Journal*, 177–95.

—— (1933), 'British Overseas Investments in 1931', *Economic Journal*, 187–204.

—— (1934), 'British Overseas Investments in 1932 and 1933', *Economic Journal*, 365–79.

—— (1935), 'British Overseas Investments in 1933 and 1934', *Economic Journal*, 439–55.

—— (1936), 'British Overseas Investments in 1934 and 1935', *Economic Journal*, 645–61.

Kirby, M.W. (1977), *The British Coalmining Industry 1870–1946: A Political and Economic History*, Anchor, Hamden.

—— (1981), *The Decline of British Economic Power Since 1870*, George Allen and Unwin, London.

Kooker, J.L. (1976), 'French Financial Diplomacy: The Interwar Years', in Benjamin M. Rowland (ed.), *Balance of Power or Hegemony: The Interwar Monetary System*, New York University Press, New York.

Krause, L.B. (1968), 'British Trade Performance', in R.E. Caves (ed.), *Britain's Economic Prospects*, Brookings Institution, Washington, DC, 198–228.

Krueger, Anne O. (1969), 'Balance-of-Payments Theory', *Journal of Economic Literature*, 1–26.

Krugman, Paul (1978), 'Purchasing Power Parity and Exchange Rates: Another Look at the Evidence', *Journal of International Economics*, 397–408.

League of Nations (1927), *Memorandum on International Trade and Balances of Payments, 1912–1926*, League of Nations, Geneva.

—— (1931a), *Course and Phases of the World Economic Depression*, League of Nations, Geneva.

—— (1931b), *Review of World Trade 1930*, League of Nations, Geneva.

—— (1932), *Review of World Trade 1931 and 1932 (First Half)*, League of Nations, Geneva.

—— (1938), *Review of World Trade 1937*, League of Nations, Geneva.

—— (1945), *Economic Instability in the Postwar World*, League of Nations, Geneva.

Lewis, W. Arthur (1949), *Economic Survey, 1919–1939*, George Allen and Unwin, London.

—— (1980), 'Rising Prices: 1899–1913 and 1950–1979', *Scandinavian Journal of Economics*, 425–36.

Lindert, Peter (1969), 'Key Currencies and Gold, 1900–1913', *Princeton Studies in International Finance*, no. 24.

Lipsey, R.E. (1963), *Price and Quantity Trends in the Foreign Trade of the United States*, National Bureau of Economic Research, New York.

Lloyd, T.O. (1970), *Empire to Welfare State*, Oxford University Press, New York.

Lloyd George, D. (1929), *We Can Conquer Unemployment*, Cassell and Company, London.
Lucas, R.E. (1982), 'Interest Rates and Currency Prices in a Two-Country World', *Journal of Monetary Economics*, 335–60.
Lundberg, Erik (1968), *Instability and Economic Growth*, Yale University Press, New Haven.
Machlup, Fritz (1939), 'The Theory of the Foreign Exchanges', *Economica*, 375–97.
—— (1955), 'Relative Prices and Aggregate Spending in the Analysis of Devaluation', *American Economic Review*, 255–78.
McKibban, Ross (1975), 'The Economic Policy of the Second Labour Government 1929–31', *Past and Present*, 95–123.
McKie, David and Chris Cook (1972), *The Decade of Disillusion: British Politics in the Sixties*, Macmillan, London.
McKinnon, Ronald I. (1981), 'The Exchange Rate and Macroeconomic Policy: Changing Postwar Perceptions', *Journal of Economic Literature*, 531–57.
Macmillan, H. (1973), *At the End of the Day*, Macmillan, London.
Mallalieu, William C. (1956), *British Reconstruction and American Policy 1945–1955*, Scarecrow Press, New York.
Marquand, David (1977), *Ramsay MacDonald*, Jonathan Cape, London.
Meade, J.E. (1948), 'Financial Policy and the Balance of Payments', *Economica*, 1–15.
—— (1951), *The Theory of International Economic Policy, Volume 1, The Balance of Payments*, Oxford University Press, Oxford.
Methorst, H.W. (1938), *Recueil international de statistiques economiques 1931–1936,* Office Permanent de L'institut International de Statistique, La Haye.
Metzler, L.A. (1947), 'Exchange Rates and The International Monetary Fund', in L.A. Metzler, Robert Triffin, and Gottfried Haberler, *International Monetary Policies*, Postwar Economic Studies, no. 7, Board of Governors of the Federal Reserve System, Washington DC.
—— (1948), 'The Theory of International Trade', in H.S. Ellis (ed.), *A Survey of Contemporary Economics*, Blakiston, Philadelphia, 210–54.
Michaely, M. (1960), 'Relative Prices and Income-Absorption Approaches to Devaluation: A Partial Reconciliation', *American Economic Review*, 144–7.
Middleton, Roger (1981), 'The Constant Employment Budget Balance and British Budgetary Policy, 1929–1939', *Economic History Review*, 266–86.
—— (1982), 'The Treasury in the 1930s: Political and Administrative Constraints to the Acceptance of the "New" Economics', *Oxford Economic Papers*, 48–77.
Ministry of Labour (1934), *Twenty-First Abstract of Labour Statistics of the United Kingdom*, HMSO, London.
Mitchell, Joan (1963), *Crisis in Britain, 1951*, Secker and Warburg, London.
Moggridge, D.E. (1969), *The Return to Gold, 1925*, Cambridge University Press, Cambridge.
—— (1970), 'The 1931 Financial Crisis – A New View', *The Banker*, 832–39.
—— (1971), 'British Controls on Long Term Capital Movements, 1924–31', in D.N. McCloskey (ed.), *Essays on a Mature Economy: Britain Since 1840*, Princeton University Press, Princeton, 113–38.

—— (1972), *British Monetary Policy 1924–1931*, Cambridge University Press, New York.

—— (1980), *Keynes*, 2nd edn, Macmillan, London (1st edn 1975).

Moreau, E. (1954), *Souvenirs d'un Gouverneur de la Banque de France; histoire de la stabilisation du franc, 1926–1928*, Genin, Paris.

Morgan, A.D. (1978), 'Commercial Policy', in Frank Blackaby (ed.), *British Economic Policy 1960–1974*, Cambridge University Press, Cambridge.

Morgan, E.V. (1952), *Studies in British Financial Policy*, Macmillan, London.

Morton, W.A. (1943), *British Finance, 1930–1940*, University of Wisconsin Press, Madison, Wisconsin.

Mosley, Oswald (1968), *My Life*, Nelson, London.

Moulton, Harold G. and Leo Pasvolsky (1932), *War Debts and World Prosperity*, Brookings Institution, Washington, DC.

Mowat, Charles Loch (1955), *Britain Between the Wars 1918–1940*, Methuen, London.

Mundell, Robert (1968), *International Economics*, Macmillan, New York.

National Economic Development Office (1976), *Cyclical Fluctuations in the British Economy*, Discussion Paper no. 3, NEDO, London.

National Institute of Economic and Social Research (1943), *Trade Regulations and Commercial Policy of the United Kingdom*, Cambridge University Press, Cambridge.

—— (1972), 'The Effects of the Devaluation of 1967 on the Current Balance of Payments', *Economic Journal*, supplement, 442–64.

National Monetary Commission (1910), *Interviews on the Banking and Currency Systems of England, Scotland, France, Germany, Switzerland and Italy*, Senate Document no. 405, Washington, DC.

Nevin, Edward (1953), 'The Origins of Cheap Money, 1931–1932', *Economica*, 24–37.

Nurkse, Ragnar (1944), *International Currency Experience*, Geneva, League of Nations.

Obstfeld, M. (1980), 'Sterilization and Offsetting Capital Movements: Evidence from West Germany, 1960–1970', National Bureau of Economic Research Working Paper, no. 494.

—— (1981), 'Capital Mobility and Devaluation in an Optimizing Model with Rational Expectations', *American Economic Review*, 217–21.

Odling-Smee, J. and N. Hartley (1978), 'Some Effects of Exchange Rate Changes', *Treasury Working Paper*, no. 2, H.M. Treasury, London.

Oppenheimer, P.M. (1966), 'Monetary Movements and the International Position of Sterling', *Scottish Journal of Economics*, 89–135.

Orcutt, Guy H. (1950), 'Measurement of Price Elasticities in International Trade', *Review of Economics and Statistics*, 117–32.

Organization for Economic Cooperation and Development (1967a), *Economic Outlook*, December, OECD, Paris.

—— (1967b), *Economic Surveys: United Kingdom*, OECD, Paris.

Organization of the European Economic Commission (1950), *Internal Financial Stability in Member Countries*, OEEC, London.

Paish, F.W. (1937), 'The British Exchange Equalisation Fund, 1935–1937', *Economica*, 343–49.

Peacock, A. and J. Wiseman (1967), *The Growth of Public Expenditure in the United Kingdom*, Allen and Unwin, London.

Pick, Franz (1955), *Black Market Yearbook 1955* (Pick's World Currency Report).

Plummer, Alfred (1937), *New British Industries in the 20th Century*, Pitman and Sons, London.

Plumptre, A.F.W. (1977), *Three Decades of Decision*, McClelland and Stewart, Toronto.

Polak, J.J. (1957), 'Monetary Analysis of Income Formation and Payments Problems', *IMF Staff Papers*, 1–50.

Pollard, Sidney (1969), *The Development of the British Economy, 1914–1967*, Edward Arnold, London.

—— (1970), *The Gold Standard and Employment Policies Between the Wars*, Methuen, London.

Posner, Michael (ed.) (1978), *Demand Management*, Heinemann, London.

Pressnell, L.S. (1978), '1925: The Burden of Sterling', *Economic History Review*, 67–88.

Price, R.W.R. (1978), 'Budgetary Policy', in F. Blackaby (ed.), *British Economic Policy, 1960–74*, Cambridge University Press for the National Institute of Economic and Social Research, London, 77–134.

Proceedings of the Tribunal Appointed to Inquire into Allegations that Information about the Raising of Bank Rate was Improperly Disclosed (1958), HMSO, London.

Redmond, John (1980), 'An Indicator of the Effective Exchange Rate of the Pound in the Nineteen-Thirties', *Economic History Review*, 83–91.

Richardson, J.H. (1936), *British Economic Foreign Policy*, Allen and Unwin, London.

Richardson, H.W. (1961), 'The New Industries Between the Wars', *Oxford Economic Papers*, 360–84.

—— (1967), *Economic Recovery in Britain, 1932–1939*, Weidenfeld and Nicholson, London.

Robbins, Lionel (1933), *The Great Depression*, Macmillan, London.

Robertson, D.H. (1928), *Money*, University of Chicago Press, Chicago.

—— (1954), *Britain in the World Economy*, Allen and Unwin, London.

Robinson, Joan (1937), 'The Foreign Exchanges', in *Essays in the Theory of Employment*, Macmillan, New York.

Rodgers, W.T. (ed.) (1964), *Hugh Gaitskell 1906–1963*, Thames and Hudson, London.

Routh, G. (1960), *Occupation and Pay in Britain, 1906–1960*, Cambridge University Press, Cambridge.

Royal Commission on Unemployment Insurance (1931), *Report*, Cmd 3872, HMSO, London.

Royal Institute of International Affairs (1937), *The Problem of International Investment*, RIIA, London.

Sachs, Jeffrey (1980), 'Wages, Flexible Exchange Rates and Macroeconomic Policy', *Quarterly Journal of Economics*, 731–48.

Salop, J. (1974), 'Devaluation and the Balance of Trade Under Flexible Wages', in G. Horwich and P. Samuelson (eds), *Trade, Stability and Growth*, Academic Press, New York.

Sargent, J.R. (1952), 'Britain and the Sterling Area', in G.D.N. Worswick and P.H. Ady (eds), *The British Economy 1945–1950*, Clarendon Press, Oxford, 531–49.

Sauvy, Alfred (1965), *Histoire économique de la France entre les deux guerres*, Volume I, Fayard, Paris.

Sayers, R.S. (1957), *Central Banking after Bagehot*, Clarendon Press, Oxford.

—— (1960), 'The Return to Gold 1925', in L.S. Pressnell (ed.), *Studies in the Industrial Revolution*, University of London, London.

—— (1976), *The Bank of England, 1891–1944*, Cambridge University Press, London.

—— (1979), 'Bank Rate in Keynes's Century', *Proceedings of the British Academy*, 191–206.

Scammell, W.M. (1957), *International Monetary Policy*, Macmillan, London.

Siegfried, André (1931), *England's Crisis*, Jonathan Cape, London.

Skidelsky, Robert (1967), *Politicians and the Slump*, Macmillan, London.

—— (1975), *Oswald Mosley*, Macmillan, London.

Snowden, Philip (1934), *An Autobiography*, Volume I, Nicholson and Watson, London.

Snyder, Rixford Kinney (1944), *The Tariff Problem in Great Britain, 1918–1923*, Stanford University Press, Stanford, California.

Stewart, R.B. (1938), 'Great Britain's Foreign Loan Policy', *Economica*, 45–60.

Stolper, W. (1941), 'British Monetary Policy and the Housing Boom', *Quarterly Journal of Economics*, supplement, 1–165.

Strange, Susan (1971), *Sterling and British Policy*, Oxford University Press, New York.

Svennilson, I. (1954), *Growth and Stagnation in the European Economy*, United Nations, Geneva.

Taylor, A.J.P. (1965), *English History 1914–1945*, Atheneum, New York.

Tew, J.H.B. (1952), *International Monetary Co-operation 1945–52*, Hutchinson, London.

—— (1978), 'Policies Aimed at Improving the Balance of Payments', in F. Blackaby (ed.), *British Economic Policy, 1960–74*, Cambridge University Press, Cambridge, 304–59.

Thomas, T.J. (1975), 'Aspects of UK Macroeconomic Policy During the Inter-war Period', PhD dissertation, Cambridge University.

Thorbecke, Erik (1960), *The Tendency towards Regionalization in Trade, 1928–1956*, Martinus Nijhoff, The Hague.

Tinbergen, Jan (1934), *International Abstract of Economic Statistics 1919–1930*, International Conference of Economic Services, London.

Tomlinson, Jim (1981), *Problems of British Economic Policy*, Methuen, London.

Triffin, Robert (1964), 'The Evolution of the International Monetary System: Historical Re-Appraisal and Future Perspectives', *Princeton Studies in International Finance*, no. 12.

—— (1968), *Our International Monetary System: Yesterday, Today and Tomorrow,* Random House, New York.

Tsiang, S.C. (1961), 'The Role of Money in Trade Balance Stability: Synthesis of the Elasticity and Absorption Approaches', *American Economic Review*, 912–36.

Van der Wee, H., and K. Tavernier (1975), *La Banque Nationale de Belgique et l'histoire monetaire entre le deux guerres mondiales*, Banque Nationale de Belgique, Brussels.

Viner, J. (1932), 'International Aspects of the Gold Standard', in Q. Wright (ed.), *Gold and Monetary Stabilization*, University of Chicago Press, Chicago.

Voyant, Claire (1971–72), 'Clio Sells Sterling Short', *Explorations in Economic History*, 228.

Waight, L. (1939), *The History and Mechanism of the Exchange Equalisation Account*, Cambridge University Press, Cambridge.

Whitaker, J.K. and M.W. Hudgins, Jr (1977), 'The Floating Pound Sterling of the Nineteen-thirties: An Econometric Study', *Southern Economic Journal*, 1478–85.

Williams, D. (1959), 'Montagu Norman and Banking Policy in the 1920s', *Yorkshire Bulletin of Economic and Social Research*, 38–55.

—— (1963), 'The 1931 Financial Crisis', *Yorkshire Bulletin of Economic and Social Research*, 92–110.

Williams, Philip (1979), *Hugh Gaitskell*, Jonathan Cape, London.

Wilson, Sir Harold (1971), *The Labour Government, 1964–70,* Weidenfeld & Nicolson and Michael Joseph, London.

Wilson, Thomas (1966), 'Instability and the Rate of Economic Growth', *Lloyds Bank Review,* 16–32.

Winch, Donald (1969), *Economics and Policy*, Walker, New York.

Worswick, G.D.N. (1970), 'Trade and Payments', in Sir Alec Cairncross (ed.), *Britain's Economic Prospects Reconsidered*, George Allen and Unwin, London, 61–100.

Wright, J.F. (1981), 'Britain's Inter-war Experience', in W.A. Eltis and P.J.N. Sinclair (eds), *The Money Supply and the Exchange Rate*, Clarendon Press, Oxford, 282–305.

Wright, K.M. (1954), 'Dollar Pooling in the Sterling Area, 1939–1952', *American Economic Review*, 559–76.

Yeager, Leland B. (1966), *International Monetary Relations*, Harper and Row, New York.

Zecher, J. Richard (1976), 'Monetary Equilibrium and International Reserve Flows in Australia', in J.A. Frenkel and H.G. Johnson (eds), *The Monetary Approach to the Balance of Payments*, George Allen and Unwin, London.

Zupnick, E. (1957), *Britain's Post-war Dollar Problem*, Columbia University Press, New York.

Dramatis Personae

Alexander, A.V. (later Lord) Secretary of Parliamentary Committee of Co-operative Congress; First Lord of the Admiralty 1929–31, 1940–45, 1945–46; Minister of Defence 1947–50; Chancellor of the Duchy of Lancaster 1950–51; Leader of the Labour Peers 1955–65.

Allen, Professor G.C. Professor of Economics, University College, Hull 1929–33; University of Liverpool 1933–47; University of London 1947–67.

Allen, Sir Thomas Member, Committee on Finance and Industry 1929–31; President, Co-operative Congress; Vice-Chairman, Co-operative Wholesale Society and International Co-operative Congress.

Attlee, Clement R. (later Lord) Deputy Leader (1931–35) and Leader (1935–40) of the Labour Party; Lord Privy Seal 1940–42; Deputy Prime Minister 1942–45; Minister of Defence 1945–46; Prime Minister 1945–51.

Balogh, Thomas (later Lord) Economist; member, Economic and Financial Committee of the Labour Party 1943–64; Fellow of Balliol College, Oxford, 1945–73; economic adviser to the Cabinet 1964–67; consultant to the Prime Minister 1968; Minister of State, Department of Energy 1974–75.

Bareau, Paul Financial journalist, in postwar years on the staff of *The Economist*; later editor of *The Statist*.

Beaverbrook, Lord Canadian newspaper proprietor (Daily Express); Minister of Information 1918; member of War Cabinet 1940–45.

Bevan, Aneurin ('Nye') Minister of Health 1945–51; Minister of Labour and National Service 1951.

Bevin, Ernest British trade union leader; member, Committee on Finance and Industry 1929–31; General Secretary, Transport and General Workers Union 1921–40; Chairman of Trades Union Congress 1937; member of War Cabinet 1940–45; Secretary of State for Foreign Affairs 1945–51.

Bolton, George (later Sir) British Executive Director (1945–52) and alternate Governor (1952–67), IMF; adviser to Bank of England 1941–48; Director of Bank of England 1948–68; Director, Bank for International Settlements 1949–57.

Bradbury, Lord Member, Committee on Finance and Industry 1929–31; Joint Permanent Secretary, HM Treasury 1913–19; President, British Bankers' Association 1929–30, 1935–36.

Bridges, Sir Edward (later Lord) HM Treasury 1919–38; Secretary of Cabinet 1938–46; Permanent Secretary, HM Treasury 1945–56.

Brown, George (later Lord George Brown) Labour MP 1945–70; Minister of Works 1951; First Secretary and Secretary of State for Economic Affairs 1964–66; Secretary of State for Foreign Affairs 1966–68.

Callaghan, James Entered civil service as tax officer 1929; Parliamentary Secretary to the Ministry of Transport 1947–50; Admiralty 1950–51; Chancellor of the Exchequer 1964–67; Home Secretary 1967–70; Secretary of State for Foreign Affairs 1974–76; Prime Minister 1976–79.

Cassel, Professor Gustav Swedish economist; delegate to World Monetary and Economic Conference 1933; Professor, University of Stockholm from 1904.

Chamberlain, Neville Minister of Health 1923, 1924–29 and 1931; Chancellor of the Exchequer 1923–24 and 1931–37; Prime Minister 1937–40.

Churchill, Winston (later Sir) First Lord of the Admiralty 1911–15, 1939–40; Chancellor of the Exchequer 1924–29; Prime Minister 1940–45, 1951–55; Leader of the Opposition 1945–51.

Citrine, Walter (later Lord) Member, Economic Advisory Council 1930; member, Committee on Economic Information 1931–33; General Secretary, Trades Union Congress 1926–46.

Clarke, R.W.B. (later Sir Richard) Assistant Secretary, HM Treasury 1945; Under-Secretary 1947; Third Secretary 1955; Second Secretary 1962; Permanent Secretary, Ministry of Aviation 1966; Ministry of Technology 1966–70.

Clay, Sir Henry Professor of Economics, University of Manchester 1922–30; Economic Adviser to Bank of England 1930–44, Warden of Nuffield College, Oxford 1944–49.

Cobbold, Cameron F. (later Lord) Executive Director (1938), Deputy Governor (1945) and Governor (1949–61), Bank of England.

Cole, G.D.H. Economist, University Reader and Fellow of University College, Oxford 1925–44; Fellow of Nuffield College 1939–59; member, Economic Advisory Council 1930; member, Committee on Economic Information 1931–39.

Cousins, Frank Trade union leader; General Secretary, Transport and General Workers Union 1956–69; Minister of Technology 1964–66.

Cripps, Sir Stafford Lord Privy Seal and Leader of the House of Commons 1942; Minister of Aircraft Production 1942–45; President, Board of Trade 1945–47; Minister of Economic Affairs 1947; Chancellor of the Exchequer 1947–50.

Cromer, Earl of Managing Director, Baring Brothers & Co. 1948–61, 1967–70; UK Executive Director, IMF 1959–61; Governor, Bank of England 1961–66; British Ambassador, Washington 1971–74.

Crosland, Anthony Fellow of Trinity College, Oxford 1947–50; Minister of State for Economic Affairs 1964–65; Secretary of State for Education and Science 1965–67; President, Board of Trade 1967–69; Secretary of State for Local Government 1969–70; Secretary of State for Environment 1974–76.

Crossman, Richard Fellow of New College, Oxford 1930–37; Labour MP 1945–74; Minister of Housing and Local Government 1964–66; Lord President and Leader of the House of Commons 1966–68; Secretary of State for Social Services 1968–70.

Cunliffe, Lord Director (1895), Deputy Governor (1911) and Governor (1913–19), Bank of England.

Dalton, Hugh (later Lord) Reader in Economics, London School of Economics 1925–36; Minister of Economic Warfare 1940–42; President of the Board of Trade 1942–45; Chancellor of the Exchequer 1945–47; Chancellor of the Duchy of Lancaster 1948–50.

Douglas, Lewis President, Mutual Life Insurance Co. of New York 1940–47; US Ambassador to the United Kingdom 1947–50.

Eady, Sir Wilfrid Civil servant 1913–52; Deputy Chairman (1940–41) and Chairman (1941–42), Board of Customs and Excise; Joint Second Secretary, HM Treasury 1942–52.

Eden, Sir Anthony (later Lord Avon) Secretary of State for Foreign Affairs 1935–38, 1940–45 and 1951–55; Leader of the House of Commons 1942–45; Deputy Prime Minister 1951–55; Prime Minister 1955–57.

Edwards, John Labour MP; Parliamentary Secretary to Board of Trade 1947–50; Economic Secretary to HM Treasury 1950–51.

Fleming, J. Marcus Economist; Deputy Director, Economic Section of Cabinet Office 1947–51; Visiting Professor, Columbia University, New York, 1951–54; IMF 1954–76.

Franks, Sir Oliver (later Lord) Fellow (1927–37) and Provost (1946–48), Queen's College, Oxford; Permanent Secretary, Ministry of Supply 1945–46; British Ambassador, Washington 1948–52; Chairman, Lloyds Bank 1954–62; Provost of Worcester College, Oxford 1962–76.

Gaitskell, Hugh Reader in Political Economy, University of London 1938; Minister of Fuel and Power 1947–50; Chancellor of the Exchequer 1950–51; Leader of the Labour Party 1955–63.

Gregory, Sir Theodore Economist; member, Committee on Finance and Industry 1929–31; Professor of Economics, London School of Economics 1927–37; Economic Adviser to Government of India 1939–46.

Hall, Robert (later Lord Roberthall) Economist; Fellow, Trinity College, Oxford 1927–50; Ministry of Supply 1939–46; Director, Economic Section of Cabinet Office 1947–53; Economic Adviser to HM Government 1953–61.

Harriman, W. Averill US Ambassador to USSR 1943–46; Ambassador to United Kingdom 1946; US Secretary of Commerce 1946–48; US Special Representative in Europe under Economic Co-operation Act 1948–49.

Harrison, George L. Assistant General Counsel, then Deputy Governor, Federal Reserve Board 1914–28; President of the Federal Reserve Bank of New York 1928–40.

Harrod, Sir Roy Economist; Student of Christ Church, Oxford 1924–67; Nuffield Reader in Economics 1952–67; President, Royal Economic Society 1962–64.

Harvey, Sir Ernest Comptroller (1925–28), Director (1928–29) and Deputy Governor (1929–36), Bank of England.

Hatry, Clarence British financier, arrested on charges of fraud on 19 September 1929 and sentenced to 14 years' imprisonment. Hatry's company, Austin Friars Trust, controlled United Steel, the second biggest company in the British steel industry.

Hawtrey, Sir Ralph British economist and civil servant; Director of Financial Inquiries, HM Treasury 1919–45; Professor of Economics, Royal Institute of International Affairs 1947–52.

Helmore, Sir James Board of Trade 1929–52; Second Secretary 1946–52; Permanent Secretary, Ministry of Supply 1953–56.

Henderson, Sir Hubert Economist; editor, *Nation and Athenaeum* 1923–30; Joint Secretary, Economic Advisory Council 1930–34; member, Committee on Economic Information 1931–39; Economic Adviser, HM Treasury 1939–44; Drummond Professor of Political Economy, University of Oxford 1945–51.

Hopkins, Sir Richard Chairman, Board of Inland Revenue 1922–27; Controller of Finance and Supply Services (1927–32), Second Secretary (1932–42), and Permanent Secretary (1942–45), HM Treasury.

Jay, Douglas Financial journalist and politician; Fellow of All Souls

College, Oxford 1930–37, 1968–; city editor, *Daily Herald* 1937–41; Economic Secretary to HM Treasury 1947–50; President, Board of Trade 1964–67.

Jenkins, Roy Minister of Aviation 1964–65; Home Secretary 1965–67; Chancellor of the Exchequer 1967–70; Deputy Leader of Labour Party 1970–72.

Kahn, Richard (later Lord) Economist; Assistant Secretary, Economic Advisory Council Committee of Economists 1930; Fellow of King's College, Cambridge 1931– and Professor of Economics, University of Cambridge 1951–72.

Kaldor, Nicholas (later Lord) Fellow of King's College, Cambridge 1949– and Professor of Economics, University of Cambridge 1966–75; Special Adviser to the Chancellor of the Exchequer 1964–68.

Keynes, John Maynard (later Lord) Fellow of King's College, Cambridge 1909–46; member, Committee on Finance and Industry 1929–31; member, Economic Advisory Council (EAC) 1930; Chairman, EAC Committee of Economists 1930; HM Treasury 1914–19, 1940–46; editor, *Economic Journal* 1911–44.

Kindersley, Lord Robert Director, Bank of England 1914–46.

Lewis, Sir Alfred Director and Chief General Manager, National Provincial Bank; member, Economic Advisory Council 1930; member, Committee on Economic Information 1931–39.

MacDonald, J. Ramsay Prime Minister 1924 and 1929–35, Lord President of the Council 1935–37.

McDougall, Sir Donald Economist; Fellow of Nuffield College 1947–64; Director-General, Department of Economic Affairs 1964–68; Head of Government Economic Service 1969–73; President, Royal Economic Society 1972–74.

McKenna, Reginald Chancellor of the Exchequer 1915–16; Chairman, Midland Bank 1919–43; member, Committee on Finance and Industry 1929–31; member, Advisory Council on Financial Questions 1931–32.

Macmillan, Sir Harold Minister of Housing and Local Government 1951–54; Minister of Defence 1954–55; Secretary of State for Foreign Affairs 1955; Chancellor of the Exchequer 1955–57; Prime Minister 1957–63.

Macmillan, Lord H.P. British Lawyer; Chairman, Committee on Finance and Industry 1929–31; member, Advisory Council on Financial Questions 1931–32.

Makins, Roger (later Lord Sherfield) Assistant Under-Secretary of State, Foreign Office 1947–48; Deputy Under-Secretary of State, Foreign Office 1948–52; British Ambassador to the United States

1953–56; Joint Permanent Secretary of HM Treasury 1956–59.

Martin, William McChesney Chairman and President, Export–Import Bank 1946–49; Assistant Secretary, US Treasury 1949–51; Chairman, Board of Governors, Federal Reserve System 1951–70.

Maudling, Reginald Economic Secretary to HM Treasury 1953–55; President of the Board of Trade 1959–61; Secretary of State for the Colonies 1961–62; Chancellor of the Exchequer 1962–64; Home Secretary 1970–72.

May, Sir George (later Lord) Secretary, Prudential Assurance Co. 1915–31; Chairman, Committee on National Expenditure 1931; Chairman, Import Duties Advisory Council 1932–39.

Meade, James Economist and Nobel Laureate; Economic Assistant (1940–45), Economic Section of the Cabinet Office; Professor of Economics at London School of Economics 1947–57; Professor of Economics at University of Cambridge 1957–68.

Moreau, Emile Director-General, Banque de l'Algerie 1906–26; Governor of Bank of France 1926–30; President, Banque de Paris et des Pays Bas 1930.

Morrison, Herbert (later Lord) Minister of Transport 1929–31; Home Secretary 1940–45; Lord President of the Council and Deputy Prime Minister 1945–51; Foreign Secretary 1951.

Mosley, Sir Oswald Chancellor of the Duchy of Lancaster 1929–30; founder of British Union of Fascists 1932.

Neild, Robert Economist; Deputy Director, National Institute of Economic and Social Research 1958–64; Economic Advisor to HM Treasury 1964–67; Professor of Economics, University of Cambridge 1971–.

Nicholson, Max Permanent Secretary, Office of Lord President of Council 1945–52, Director-General, Nature Conservancy 1952–66.

Niemeyer, Sir Otto HM Treasury 1906–27; Controller of Finance 1922–27; Director, Bank of England 1938–52; Chairman of the Board (1937–40) and Vice-Chairman (1941–64), Bank for International Settlements.

Norman, Montagu (later Lord) Director (1907–44), Deputy Governor (1918–20) and Governor (1920–44), Bank of England.

Pigou, Arthur Cecil Economist; member, EAC Committee of Economists 1930; Professor of Political Economy, University of Cambridge 1908–44.

Plowden, Sir Edwin (later Lord) Businessman; Ministry of Aircraft Production 1940–46 (Chief Executive 1945–46); Chief Planning Officer and Chairman, Economic Planning Board 1947–53; Chairman, Tube Investments 1963–76.

Quesnay, Pierre General Manager, Bank of France 1926–30; General Manager, BIS 1930–37.

Robbins, Lionel (later Lord) Member, EAC Committee of Economists 1930; Professor of Economics, London School of Economics 1929–61; Director, Economic Section of War Cabinet Offices 1941–45; President, Royal Economic Society 1954–55; Chairman, *Financial Times* 1961–70.

Robertson, Sir Dennis Economist; Fellow, Trinity College, Cambridge 1914–38 and 1944–63; member, Committee on Economic Information 1936–39; adviser to HM Treasury 1939–44; President, Royal Economic Society 1948–50.

Robinson, Sir Austin Economist; Joint editor of *Economic Journal* 1944–70; Economic Adviser and Head of Programmes Division, Ministry of Production 1942–45; Economic Adviser to Board of Trade 1945–46; member, Economic Planning Staff 1947–48; Director of Economics, Ministry of Power 1967–68.

Rosenstein-Rodan, Paul Economist; Professor of Political Economy, University College, London 1934–47; Economic Advisor to the World Bank 1947–52; Professor of Economics, M.I.T. 1952–68.

Rothermere, Lord Newspaper proprietor, *Daily Mail*; younger brother of Lord Northcliffe.

Rowan, Sir Leslie Assistant, later Principal Private Secretary, to Prime Minister 1941–47; Permanent Secretary, Office of Minister of Economic Affairs 1947; Second Secretary, HM Treasury 1947–49, 1951–58; Economic Minister to Washington 1949–51; Managing Director (1962–67) and Chairman (1967–71), Vickers, Ltd.

Snowden, Philip (later Lord) Chairman, Independent Labour Party 1903–6 and 1917–20; Chancellor of the Exchequer 1924 and 1929–31; Lord Privy Seal 1931–32.

Snyder, John W. American banker; Dirctor of Office of War Mobilisation and Reconversion 1945–46; Secretary of US Treasury 1946–53.

Van Lennep, Emile Treasurer-General, Ministry of Finance, Netherlands 1951–69; Chairman, Monetary Committee, EEC 1958; Chairman of Working Party no. 3, OECD 1962; Secretary-General, OECD 1969–.

Wilson, Sir Harold Labour MP since 1945; President, Board of Trade 1947–51; Leader of Labour Party 1963–76; Prime Minister 1964–70 and 1974–76

Wilson Smith, Sir Henry HM Treasury 1930–46; Permanent Secretary, Ministry of Defence 1947–48; Second Secretary, HM Treasury 1948–51; Director, Bank of England 1964–70.

Woods, Sir John Henry HM Treasury 1920–43; Principal Assistant Secretary, Ministry of Production 1943–45; Permanent Secretary, Board of Trade 1945–51.

Index

Abnormal Importations Act 18
Absorption approach to balance of payments 7–9, 136, 208–9, 227
Accompanying measures 3, 122, 132–3, 139, 141, 189, 191
Alexander, A.V., Minister of Defence, resists cuts in defence expenditure 138
Allen, Sir Thomas, member of Macmillan Committee, in favour of devaluation in 1931 61
American account sterling 24–5
American credits in 1931 65–6, 70–1; *see also* Central bank credits
Arab-Israeli War 187
Artus, J.R., on effects of 1967 devaluation 197–206
Attlee, C.R., Prime Minister, fears recurrence of 1931 119; in doubt over devaluation 120, 124, 133; is persuaded 126–8; supports cuts in public expenditure 136, 138
Australia, balance of payments difficulties in 1920s 48; reactions to devaluation in 1949 130, 132

Balance of payments, changes in 12–7, 35–7, 56–7 59, 73, 90, 93–4, 144–7, 157–8, 162–3, 175, 182–3; constraint 15, 54, 83–4, 116, 171; estimates for pre-war years 36, 74; factors governing 6–9, 74; model of 75–83; relation to Budget 100, 127; trend in 1949 and 1967 219
Baldwin, Stanley 55
Balogh, Thomas, initially against devaluation 166
Bank advances 101, 179; deposits 30, 41, 143–4; *see also* Credit restriction, Money supply
Bank failures 62, 73, 75
Bank of England 3, 4, 11, 22, 25, 28–30, 36–51, 58–9, 63–73, 78–83, 88–90, 100–3, 116, 121–2, 131–2, 139, 166–70, 184, 187, 210, 226, 229; *see also* Forward market operations, Intervention in exchange markets
Bank of France 29n., 44, 57, 58n., 65
Bank for International Settlements (BIS), estimates of sterling area deficit in 1928–9, 47–8; lends to United Kingdom 188; and gold points 58n., 59
Bank rate 3; after World War I 28; in 1920s 37–41, 44–51; in 1931 63, 82–3; in 1932 100–1; in 1964–7 120–1, 166, 169, 177, 180, 186–8; *modus operandi* 38–41, 50–1; Tribunal 156; and debt management 41–2
Bareau, Paul, expects devaluation 125
Beaverbrook, Lord, campaigns for Empire Free Trade 55
Bevan, Aneurin ('Nye'), Minister of Health, argues for early election 119n.; against more cuts 120; accepts prescription charge in principle 138
Bevin, Ernest, Foreign Secretary, advocates devaluation in 1931 54–5, 61n.; proposes a floating rate 60; opposes cuts in unemployment insurance 70; attitude to devaluation in 1949 117, 124, 128–32; wants lower extraction ratio

135; opposes cuts in defence 138; not decisive voice 142; persuades TUC to observe wage freeze 134, 228
Bilateralism 12
Black market for sterling 115
Board of Trade, efforts to explain increase in imports in 1968 202; estimates of balance of payments for 1931 56–7, 74n.; given power to impose import duties 18
Bolton, Sir George 117, 131
Borrowing, international, *see* Capital movements, Central bank credits, Foreign lending
Bradbury, Lord 54
Bretton Woods system of exchange rates 1–2, 213, 227
Bridges, Sir Edward, initiates inquiry into case for devaluation in 1949 116; role in persuading Ministers 118, 121–2, 126, 133–4
Brown, George, First Secretary of State, against devaluation in 1964 166–7; resists increase in Bank rate 169; champions incomes policy 174; is converted 177, 179, 180–1; moves to Foreign Office 181
Budget, in 1920s 42; of September 1931 71; of 1933 89; inter-war 43; of 1949 134; of April 1964 165; of November 1964 68–9; of 1965 176; of 1966 179; of 1967 186; of 1968 191, 195, 208; deficits 6, 113, 177; and exchange speculation 6, 56, 60, 64–5, 69–71
Building controls 178, 182
Bundesbank 170

Cairncross, Alec, suggests devaluation in December 1948 116n., 124; attitude to proposed devaluation in 1967 157n., 168n.; on position at end of 1968 211n.
Callaghan, James, Chancellor of the Exchequer, against devaluation in 1964 164, 166–7; introduces neutral budget 168–9; in exchange crises of July 1965 and July 1966 177–81; hopes to postpone decision until 1968 188–90; resigns 191
Cambridge Economic Policy Group (CEPG) 8n., 197
Canada, makes loan to Britain in 1946 114; complains of high export prices 122; rôle in Washington talks in September 1949 130, 153
Capital gains tax 135, 169
Capital issues 49, 96, 101
Capital movements 10–11, 21–3, 74, 96–7, 183, 218–9, 229; accommodating 87–8; short-term, in inter-war period 36–7, 44–6, 85, 87–8; in 1960s, 212; *see also* Controls, Exchange control, Foreign lending
Cassel, Gustav, on purchasing power parity 6; Central bank credits, in 1931 5, 65–9, 71; in 1967 5, 169, 171, 178, 184, 188–90, 193, 210–11, 215
Chamberlain-Bradbury Committee 39
Chamberlain, Neville 55
Cheap money 38, 84, 97, 100–1, 103
Cheap sterling 115
Churchill, Winston 41, 45
Citrine, Walter 70
Clarke, R.W.B., suggests devaluation in 1945 112; repeats suggestion 114–15
Cobbold, Cameron F., Governor of Bank of England, opposes devaluation in 1949 122–4; fears second devaluation 132
Cole, G.D.H., recommends devaluation in 1931 55
Commodity prices, in 1920s and 1930s 50, 93; in 1950–51 16
Commodity shunting 26, 115n.
Common Market, *see* European Economic Community
Commonwealth, conferences 26, 120, 123, 127, 150; debts to 4, 24; trade with 24; reactions in devaluation in 1949 132
Competitive power 32, 97–8, 113, 119, 156, 159–61, 174, 183, 214–15, 229
Confederation of British Industries (CBI) industrial enquiries 209; in favour of planning in 1961 161
Confidence in exchange rate 4, 5, 29–30, 58–9, 73, 179, 182, 187, 191, 212, 226; dependent on balanced budget 56, 66, 69, 71, 73; undermined by sterling liabilities 52

Consumer spending 182, 187, 194; spree in 1968 209–10; *see also* Hire purchase controls
Contingency plans in 1948 115; in 1960s 165, 168
Controls, over capital movements 3, 4, 11, 21–3, 39, 96–7, 100, 102, 214 (*see also* Exchange control, Foreign lending); on imports *see* Import restrictions; on investment 121, 143; on prices 13; war-time and post-war 114, 142–4
Conversion of War Loan in 1932 96, 100–1
Convertibility crisis of 1947 25–6, 114, 119, 227; as objective of policy 1, 23–4, 26, 118, 123, 132, 159
Corporation tax 169
Cost inflation 111; *see also* Inflation
Cousins, Frank, Minister of Technology, resigns 179
Couve de Murville, on French example in devaluation 188
Credit-Anstalt, failure of 62
Credit restriction 28, 40–1, 121, 134, 180, 214
Cripps, Sir Stafford, refuses to consider devaluation 116–9; proposals for action 120; opposes deflation 122; reactions to advice 123–4; discussions with Snyder 125; in Switzerland 126–8; agrees to devalue 129; fixes rate 130–2; on accompanying measures 133–8; rôle discussed 4, 139–43, 214, 228
Cromer, Earl of, Governor of Bank of England 169
Crosland, Anthony, President of the Board of Trade 179
Crossman, Richard, Lord President, on expenditure cuts 171, 182; in favour of floating 179
Crowding out 42
Cunliffe Committee Report 27, 31; minimum gold reserve 50, 57
Currency and Bank Notes Act of 1928 65

Dalton, Hugh, Chancellor of the Duchy of Lancaster, on discussions in Economic Policy Committee, June-July 1949 118–21, 133; October 1949 137; views on policy 139, 143, 228
Darmstadter Bank failure 62
Debt management 41–2; *see also* Fiscal policy, Monetary policy
Debts of United Kingdom 41, 61, 113, 210; *see also* Sterling area
Defence expenditure 102, 138, 176, 181, 214
Deflation 6, 59, 65, 122, 124, 134–5, 161, 166, 181–2, 195, 214; *see also* Packages of deflationary measures
Demand management 157, 174
Deutschmark, revaluation of 1968 197
Devaluation, as case-study in decision-taking 2–5; as a symbol 1, 4; measures to prevent 164; never contemplated by Labour Government in 1931 52; of dollar in 1933 86; of French franc in 1936 86; part of political process 214; secrecy in 214; speed of response 206; timing of 206, 216–17
Devaluation, effect on; balance of payments in 1949 151–5; in 1967 198 ff; economic expansion abroad 102–3; foreign debt 101–2; imports 201–4; investment 101–2; invisibles 205; manufacturing 191–2, 209; prices 98–9; wages 10, 98–9, 154, 206–8
Dillon Round 21
Discrimination in international trade 152–3
Disinflation 136–7
Dock strikes 192–3, 211
Dollar gap 113, 116, 122, 140, 144–6, 151–2, 218; pool 25; portfolio 211
Douglas, Lewis, US Ambassador, in consultations of July 1949 118
Dyestuffs Importation Act 18

Eady, Sir Wilfred, on devaluation in 1949 122n., 123
Eclipses of the moon and devaluation 218
Economic Advisory Council (EAC) 57–60, 73
Economic Commission for Europe (ECE), on overvaluation in 1949 117
Economic growth, in 1920s 33; in 1930s 84; in 1960s 171, 186
Economist, The, on gold losses in 1931 64; on American and French

credits 66; on conditions in exchange market on 19 September 1931 72
Economy Committee of Cabinet, 1931 69–70
Eden, Sir Anthony, on expenditure cuts in 1949 138
Edwards, L. John, Parliamentary Secretary to Board of Trade, in favour of devaluation in 1949 125
Einzig, Paul, on gold points 58n.
Elasticities approach to balance of payments 6, 126, 198
Elasticities of demand for exports and imports 6, 91, 124, 126, 198, 204–6
Election, of February 1950 119; of March 1966 178
Empire Free Trade 55
Employment in new industries 31
Euro-dollar rates 180, 197, 223
European Co-operation Administration (ECA) 17, 181
European Economic Community 12, 21; application to join 179, 187–8; and devaluation 188–9, 215, 217
European Free Trade Area (EFTA) 21, 168
European Payments Union (EPU) 20
European Recovery Programme (ERP) 130
Exchange control 12, 22–4, 114–15, 159, 164, 174–5, 178, 227
Exchange Control Act, 1947 22
Exchange Equalisation Account (EEA), introduced 11, 26; mechanism of intervention 88–90; reaction functions 108–9
Exchange rates: *see* Rate of exchange, Devaluation
Expenditure-switching 6, 60, 97–8, 205, 230
Export credits 175, 212
Export-led growth 102, 159
Export rebate 204
Exports of UK, growth in 19th century 10; commodity composition 14–15, 74, 90–1; regional distribution 13–14, 95; share of world market 161, 164, 192, 217, 219
Extraction ratio for bread 135

Federal Reserve Bank of New York 49, 57, 65, 67n., 70
Federal Reserve Board 38, 47–8
Federation of British Industries (FBI); *see* Confederation of British Industries
Fiduciary note issue 65
Financial innovation 7
Fiscal policy 28, 42, 121, 143, 168, 208; *see also* Budget, Public expenditure, Taxation
Fleming, J. Marcus, discusses appropriate rate of exchange in 1949 131n.
Floating rate: *see* Rate of exchange
Food subsidies 113, 120, 124
Foreign lending by United Kingdom 3, 10–11, 21–3, 93, 174; *see also* Capital movements, Controls
Forward exchange rates: *see* Rate of exchange
Forward market operations, in 1928 46; in 1931 58, 66, 72, in 1960s 171–3, 178, 184–5, 195–7, 210, 212, 215
Franks, Sir Oliver, UK Ambassador in Washington, reports on American views on devaluation in 1949 117
French bank credits 65–6, 70–1, 178
French franc, stabilization of in 1926 44–5; devalued 86, 188, 197

Gaitskell, Hugh, Minister of Fuel and Power, accepts case for devaluation 123n., 125–6; finds Treasury in agreement 118; perturbed by exchange losses 129; supports cuts 138; influence decisive 142
Gaulle, General de, vetoes British application to join EEC 21, 178, 187
General Agreement on Tariffs and Trade (GATT) 12, 135, 168
General settlement, as alternative to devaluation in 1949 125
General strike of 1926 33, 42, 44
Gold, bloc 86; drain in 1920s 37; embargo of 1919 28; embargo of 1933 in USA 86; points 38, 58, 59; pool 195; price 3, 130, 150, 156
Goldman, Sam, expecting larger dollar deficit in 1947 148
Gold standard 1, 7; managed by Bank of England before 1914 11;

return to in 1925 27–33; maintenance of endangered 44, 48–9; suspended 72, 88; effect of growth of Treasury Bill Issue 50–1
Great Depression 16, 52
Gregory, Sir Theodore, prefers devaluation to protection 71n.

Hague Reparations Conference 49
Hall, Sir Robert vii, 117n., 121n.; campaigns for devaluation in 1949 116, 122, 124, 126; visit to America in 1949 118, 142; advises on accompanying measures 127, 135–7, 227; and on rate of exchange 131
'Hand payments' of sterling 115n.
Hard and soft currencies 20, 114, 140, 219, 227
Harriman, W. Averill, visit to London in July 1949 118
Harrison, George L., warned by Montagu Norman 49; warns Norman 63
Harrod, Roy, on devaluation in 1949 111–12
Harvey, Sir Ernest, evidence to Macmillan Committee 41, 69, 71
Hatry scandal of 1929 49
Hawtrey, R.G., expresses 'Treasury view' 42; on devaluation in 1931 53; in 1949 111
Helmore, Sir James, undecided on devaluation 124
Henderson, Sir Hubert, argues for devaluation in 1931 29, 55; but not inevitable 69; contributes to Liberal programme 56
Higham, D.S., on effects of devaluation of 1967 193n., 198–9, 202n., 203, 205n., 209
Hire purchase controls 177–9, 182, 185, 187, 191, 195
Home, Sir Alec Douglas, suggests increase in Bank rate, October 1964 166
Hoover moratorium 62
Hopkins, Sir Richard, warns Chancellor of danger to the pound sterling 64
Housing boom of 1930s 101
Hume David, on the specie-flow mechanism 7

Imperial preference 19, 91
Import deposits 177, 195, 204
Import duties: *see* Tariffs
Import Duties Act of 1932 11
Import Duties Advisory Committee (IDAC) 19
Import restrictions, changes in 3, 12, 17–21, 113, 120, 143, 168; as alternative to devaluation 72, 111, 189, 213, 217
Import surcharge 168, 175, 177, 179, 182–3, 203–4, 214, 216
Imports into UK, commodity composition 13, 15, 90; geographical distribution 96
Income tax 169, 189
Incomes policy 122, 154, 164, 173–4, 179, 206–7, 214
Industrial production, fluctuations in 28, 34, 80, 165
Inflation, after World War I 28, 64; fear of in 1931 88–9, 100; after World War II 113, 121, 123, 127, 134, 137, 143, 154–5; in 1960s 206–8
Inflationary spiral 6
Interest rates 28, 30, 37, 40–1, 49, 53, 99, 102–3, 121, 139, 180–4; *see also* Bank rate, Euro-dollar rates
International liquidity 60, 62, 73, 156
International Monetary Fund (IMF) 5, 7n., 12, 142; Annual Meetings of 129, 156, 178; attitude to floating rates 131; campaigns for devaluation in 1949 117; endorses use of incomes policy 174; lends to UK in 1960s 161, 170–2, 184–5, 188, 190, 193, 211–12, 215, 224; notified of devaluation in 1949 132; see also Letter of Intent
Intervention in exchange markets 1, 39, 44, 64–8, 71, 87–90, 195, 211; *see also* Official financing of deficit
Invergordon mutiny 72
Investment, after devaluation of 1931 101–2; control of 121, 143; underestimated in 1940s 136–7; fixed — 97, 182; *see also* Foreign lending, Public investment
Investment currency market 23, 174–5
Invisible earnings 29, 37, 57, 60, 73, 91–4, 176, 200, 205

J-curve 198, 200
Jay, Douglas, for early election in

1949 119; against devaluation 121, 123; swings round 124–7; predisposed against cuts 133, 139; opposes surcharge in 1967 168n.
Jenkins, Roy, Chancellor of the Exchequer, in favour of devaluation in 1966 179; deflates in 1968 194–5
Johnston, Thomas, on devaluation of 1931 5n.

Kahn, Richard, expects devalution in 1949 125
Kaldor, Nicholas, presses devaluation on Gaitskell in 1949 126; favours floating in 1964–7, 161, 166
Kennedy Round 21, 204
Keynes, J.M., on purchasing power parity 6, 113; argues against pre-war parity 29, 37, 40; accepts new parity 44; against devaluation in 1931 53–6, 60–2; wants international reflation 59; regards devaluation in 1931 as inevitable 67, 69, 71; emphasises stability of prices after devaluation 99
Korean War 16, 112, 151–2, 154, 220

Labour Party and devaluation 4, 215–16
Leads and lags 150, 227
Leaning against the wind 89-90
Letter of Intent 190, 194–5
Lewis, Sir Alfred, on illiquidity in 1931 58
Liberalization of imports 12, 20
Life-cycle models 9
Liquidity, crises 62, 73–4; excess 143–4; in models 9
Loan Agreement of 1945 144
London and Cambridge Economic Service, on gold losses in 1931 64; index of industrial production 80
London Business School 197, 199–202
London money market, illiquid 51–2, 62, 73; *see also* Short-term debtor position of London

MacDonald, J. Ramsay, Prime Minister 58, 67, 69, 72
McDougall, Sir Donald, favours devaluation in 1964 166
McKenna, Reginald, Chancellor of the Exchequer, against return to gold 29; signs addendum to Macmillan Committee Report 61
McKenna Duties 17
Macmillan, Harold, on possibility of devaluation in 1962 156
Macmillan Committee of 1930–1 34, 36, 39–41, 51, 52–4, 60–2
Makins, Roger, favours devaluation in 1949 106, 124
Market power over exchange rate 5–6, 215, 226; *see also* Confidence in exchange rate
Marshall aid 114, 122, 128, 219, 222, 224
Martin, William McChesney, Chairman of Governors of Federal Reserve Board 118, 128, 177
Maudling, Reginald, Chancellor of the Exchequer, pursues expansionist policy in 1963–4, 161, 164–5; contingency plans 168–9
May Committee Report of 1931 58, 65, 67, 69–70
Military expenditure overseas: *see* Defence expenditure
Monetary approach to balance of payments 7–8, 206–7
Monetary policy 121, 123, 127, 134, 143, 195; conflicting objectives in 37–42, 100
Monetary situation at time of devaluation 222–3
Money supply, and balance of payments 7, 77–9; in 1920s 30; in 1930s 99–101; in 1949 120–3, 143–4, 168–9; in 1960s 7, 186
Moreau, Emile, Governor of the Bank of France, converts French sterling balances into gold in 1927 45–6
Morgan, J.P. and Co., approached for dollar loan, July 1931 64, 70, 224
Morrison, Herbert, Lord President, willing to consider devaluation 119, 124, 142; proposes cut in public expenditure 134, 136
Mortgages, local authority 178
Mosley, Sir Oswald, resigns in 1930 56
Multiplier, foreign trade 6

National Bureau of Economic Research, on turning-point in 1929 52

National Health Service, cuts in 135–8, 169
National Institute of Economic and Social Research, urges devaluation in 1961 160; on effects of devaluation 197–8, 203; forecasts for 1965 176; for 1969 195, 211
National Plan of 1965 177, 180, 185
National Treaty to adjust nominal incomes, 1931 54, 61
Neild, Robert, favours devaluation in 1964 166
New industries, rise of in 1920s and 1930s 31–2, 91
New York stock market boom of 1928–9 45–9, 81; collapses 49
Nicholson, E. Max, favours devaluation in 1949 124
Norman, Montagu, Governor of the Bank of England 37; views on domestic effects of a high Bank rate 39–40, 54; efforts to maintain the parity, 1927–9 45–50; warns Treasury of danger of a forced devaluation 59; visit to United States July 1931 63–4; falls ill 65; agrees on a 'clean' float after devaluation 88

Official financing of deficit 77, 87–88, 171–3, 183–4, 195–7, 211–12; *see also* Intervention in exchange markets Central bank credits
Oil embargo of 1967 187
Open market operations 3, 65, 100, 187
Organisation for European Economic Co-operation (OEEC/OECD) 21, 168, 190, 194; Four Year Plan of 1948–52 122; on incomes policy 174; on trend in British labour costs 164
Ottawa Conference of 1932 19, 96

Packages of deflationary measures 177–8, 180–1, 191
Pigou, A.C. 55
Plowden, Sir Edwin favours devaluation in 1949 116, 121, 126, 131
Poincaré, Raymond, Prime Minister of France 45n., 69
Portfolio shifts 8–9
Pressure of demand, changes in 135, 155, 164, 187, 215; excessive 3, 7, 160–1, 174, 209
Price, control 20n., 28; equations 109–10; fluctuations in 30–1; freeze 135, 181, 191; *see also* Inflation, Wages
Productivity, slow growth of in UK 156, 181; stability of trend 159; enhanced by undervaluation 161; as cure for balance of payments deficit 137
Profits tax 135, 138
Protection, *see* Tariffs
Public expenditure, cuts in 69–71, 121–3, 133–5, 136–9, 155, 195, 210, 222, 225, 227–8; increases in 64–7, 171, 180, 187; in inter-war period 42–3; *see also* Budget, Fiscal Policy
Public investment, cuts in 135, 138–9, 182
Public sector borrowing requirement (PSBR) 195, 222
Public works 53, 56
Purchasing power parity 6, 32–3, 86–7, 99, 107–8, 113, 226

Quesnay, Pierre, General Manager of BIS, on danger of a sterling crisis 55
Quotas, *see* Import restrictions

Rate of exchange, choice of in 1949 129–32, 141; effective 85–6, 91–2, 153, 201; floating 1, 4, 6, 9, 84, 100, 114, 115, 117, 121, 131, 159, 179, 213–14, 230–1; fluctuations in, in 1920s and 1930s 1, 30, 37, 84 ff; overshooting 85; overvaluation in 1925 32, 37; in 1967 164; undervaluation 161; in 1945 113; volatility 9; *see also* Forward market operations, Intervention in exchange markets
Rational expectations 8–9
Regulator 182, 195
Reserves, fall in, in 1931 63, 67–8, 71–2; boosted by EEA 88–90; in 1949 119–20, 127, 129, 147; in 1967 169–70, 180; hidden 51–2, 66; inadequate 88, 139, 148, 157, 210, 224; low level of 5, 45, 49–50, 59, 137 Model of reserve flows 74ff
Restructuring of industry 31–2, 44, 54, 167, 214
Robbins, Lionel 55, 112n.
Robertson, Dennis 23n., 46, 116n.

Robinson, Austin, on devaluation in 1949 116n.
Roosevelt, Franklin D., President of the United States, imposes gold embargo 86
Rosenstein-Rodan, Paul, converts Gaitskell 126
Rothermere, Lord, crusades for Empire Free Trade 55
Rowan, Leslie, favours devaluation in 1949 121
Rowe, J.W.F., favours devaluation in 1931 53

Safeguarding of Industries Act 18
Savings rates in 1967–8 209–10
Selective Employment Tax (SET) 179–80, 189, 191, 204
Shadow price of foreign exchange 175–6
Short term debtor position of London, before World War I 34, 36; in 1931 51–2, 58, 62, 73; in post-war years 113, 122–3, 215
Snowden, Philip, Chancellor of the Exchequer, rôle in 1931 devaluation 4, 49, 52, 56–8, 64–5, 70, 88
Snyder, John W., Secretary of US Treasury, favours devaluation in 1949 118, 125, 130
South African Loan Agreement
Special deposits 180
Speculation, in foreign exchange 6, 30, 45, 58, 71, 85, 88, 139–40, 150–1, 171, 195, 214; *see also* Market power over exchange rate
Steering Committee on Economic Policy (SEP) 189
Sterling, as an international currency 10–11, 111, 212–3, 225–6; *see also* Convertibility
Sterling area, development of 23–6; membership of 24, 26; origin of 11, 220; as a US market 13; controls over dollar imports 114, 144; deficits on current account 28–9, 47–8, 144–6; effects of devaluation on 4; not consulted over 1949 devaluation 132; trade with US 116, 119–20, 123, 136, 147–50, 152
Sterling War Book, 1948 114
Stockbuilding in UK 148, 160–1, 175, *214; in US 147, 150*
Stop-go 157, 159, 161
Suez Canal, closure of 187, 192–3
Swaps 170, 224
Swiss bank credits 170, 188

Tariffs 17–21, 84, 91, 96, 100; as alternative to devaluation 54, 59–62, 71; campaign for 55; *see also* Import restrictions Taxation, changes in 42, 69, 165, 195; *see also* Budget, Packages of deflationary measures
Tax rebates on exports 123, 135
Terms of trade, shifts in 3, 16–17, 32, 57, 113, 154, 157, 220–1; and real wages 207
Thorneycroft, Peter, Chancellor of the Exchequer, no intention of devaluing in 1957 156
Tourist expenditure 176, 182, 214
Trade Unions, and colour of bread 135; and wages 154; *see also* Incomes policy
Trades Union Congress (TUC) 134, 174
Transferable account sterling 25–6
'Treasury view' of fiscal policy 42

Unemployment insurance, cuts proposed 69–70; deficits 30–1, 56; rules relaxed in 1931 56
Unemployment rates, in inter-war period 3, 28, 31, 33, 52, 56, 83–4, 98; in 1949 3, 136; in 1960s 3, 157, 160, 165n., 171, 176, 178–9, 185, 187, 191, 209
United States, Loan of 1946 114; recessions in 3, 5, 111, 119, 150–1, 223; trade with 153–4
'Unmentionable', the 166
Unrequited exports 40, 140

Vacancies 187, 209
Van Lennep, E., on devaluation in 1967 189
Voluntary programme of control over foreign investment 22, 174, 179

Wages, changes in 30–2, 99, 154, 174, 191; drift 174; effect of devaluation on 6, 8, 98–9, 154, 206–8; equations 98, 109–10; freeze 134, 181, 191; rigidity 8, 31–2, 55; sliding scale agreements 31–2; structure 207;

real wage resistance 8, 229; *see also* Incomes policy
Washington talks, June and September 1949 118, 125, 128–30, 134
Wealth effects 8–9
Webb, Sidney, on devaluation in 1931 5n.
Whitehead, Edgar, Prime Minister of Rhodesia, on high export prices 123n.
Wilson, Harold, Prime Minister, ambiguous attitude to devaluation in 1949 116, 119–20, 124, 126–30, 142; against devaluation in 1964 164, 166–9; in crises of 1965 and 1966 171, 177–81; in 1967 187–93, 214–5
Wilson Smith, Henry, head of Overseas Finance Division in Treasury, role in 1949 devaluation 115, 118–9, 124, 131, 142
Woods, John Henry 116n.